WE SAW THE LIGHT

WE SAW THE LIGHT

CONVERSATIONS BETWEEN THE
NEW AMERICAN CINEMA
AND POETRY

·

DANIEL KANE

·

UNIVERSITY OF IOWA PRESS
IOWA CITY

University of Iowa Press, Iowa City 52242
Copyright © 2009 by the University of Iowa Press
www.uiowapress.org
Printed in the United States of America

Design by April Leidig-Higgins

The University of Iowa Press is a member of Green Press
Initiative and is committed to preserving natural resources.

Printed on acid-free paper

Library of Congress Cataloging-in-Publication Data
Kane, Daniel, 1968 –
We saw the light: conversations between the new American
cinema and poetry / by Daniel Kane.
p.   cm.
Includes bibliographical references and index.
ISBN-13: 978-1-58729-788-5 (cloth)
ISBN-10: 1-58729-788-4 (cloth)
1. Experimental films —United States —History and
criticism. 2. Experimental poetry, American —History and
criticism. 3. American poetry — 20th century — History
and criticism. 4. Motion pictures and literature. I. Title.
PN1995.9.E96K27 2009 2008041109
794.43'611 — dc22

To Jenny and Erica

CONTENTS

ACKNOWLEDGMENTS

I gratefully acknowledge the poets, filmmakers, and poetry/film savants who shared their knowledge and ideas with me over the past four years: Blaine Allan, John Ashbery, Emma Bell, Bill Berkson, Jed Birmingham, Marilyn Brakhage, Jacob Burckhardt, Fred Camper, Alvin Curran, Corin Depper, Thomas Evans, Rosalind Galt, Adrian Goycoolea, Tom Gunning, Ken Jacobs, Yvonne Jacquette, David E. James, Lisa Jarnot, David Kermani, Alfred Leslie, Joe Lizzi, Jenny Lund, Gerard Malanga, Laura Marcus, Scott MacKenzie, Susan McCabe, Taylor Mead, Jonas Mekas, Kristian Moen, Diane Negra, Matthew Noel-Tod, Ron Padgett, Simon Pettet, Brian Reed, Jennifer Reeves, Lytle Shaw, Joel Singer, P. Adams Sitney, Konrad Steiner, Christopher Wagstaff, Anne Waldman, and Ben Young. Extra thanks to those of you who gave me permission to quote from our correspondence and other archived materials. My apologies as well to anyone whose name I may have inadvertently omitted.

This work would not have been possible without the generous and enthusiastic help of the people in the following special collections libraries and film archives: Charles Silver of the Film Studies Center at the Museum of Modern Art, New York City; M. M. Serra of the Film-Maker's Cooperative, New York City; Andrew Lampert, Robert Haller, John Mhiripiri, Wendy Dorsett, and Jed Rapfogel of Anthology Film Archives, New York City; Polly Armstrong of the Stanford University Special Collections and University Archives, Stanford, California; Michael Basinski, curator, the Poetry Collection, State University of New York at Buffalo; Cara Gilgenbach of the Special Collections and Archives, Kent State University Libraries and Media Services, Kent, Ohio; and Marvin Taylor, director of the Fales Library and Special Collections at New York University, New York City.

To the faculty at the University of Sussex and the University of East Anglia, United Kingdom: your support will always be deeply appreciated.

I am indebted to the Arts and Humanities Research Council, United Kingdom (http://www.ahrc.ac.uk/), which awarded me a grant and research leave in 2006 that allowed me to complete research for and produce a working draft of this book.

My gratitude to series editors Alan Golding, Lynn Keller, and Adalaide Morris for taking this project on board in the first place, and to Joe Parsons, acquisitions editor, for being the sweetest, most efficient, and generous editor I have ever met. His enthusiasm for this project — even through the terrible Iowa floods of 2008 — was a tremendous comfort and inspiration. Finally, thanks to my outside readers for your support and excellent suggestions for revising earlier drafts of this manuscript; to Michael Levine for copyediting; and to the staff at the University of Iowa Press for your terrific mix of humor, professionalism, and passion for what you do.

Earlier versions of Chapter 2 appeared in *Texas Studies in Language and Literature* 50, no. 1 (Spring 2008): 34–57, and in *Talisman: A Journal of Contemporary Poetry and Poetics*, nos. 32–33 (Summer–Fall 2006): 18–26.

WE SAW THE LIGHT

introduction

Why Film and Poetry?

The postwar poetry and film cultures that emerged on the East and West Coasts of the United States presented audiences with some of the most compelling innovations of (and challenges to) formal, cultural, and political aspects of the developing American avant-garde. This book examines the relationships between verbal and visual arts cultures as they played out in the work of poets and filmmakers of the era. The guiding impulse behind my work is my belief that innovative American poetry affiliated generally with Donald Allen's seminal anthology, *The New American Poetry* (1960), has been informed by the practices of nonmainstream and formally experimental film of the 1950s and 1960s (which was variously and synonymously called "Underground," "avant-garde," "personal," "poetic," "independent," and "New American" Cinema)[1] to a greater extent than is currently recognized.

Why film and poetry? During the course of my general studies on the various poetic communities constituting the New York downtown world of the 1950s and 1960s, I became increasingly curious about the connections between poets affiliated with *The New American Poetry* (perhaps the book most responsible for introducing Allen Ginsberg, John Ashbery, Frank O'Hara, Robert Duncan, and so many other poets of the postwar avant-garde to a wider audience)[2] and New American filmmakers including Rudy Burckhardt, Kenneth Anger, Stan Brakhage, Robert Frank, and Alfred Leslie. It became clear to me that there was significant interplay between the filmmakers and poets associated with those scenes. Was it possible that there was a relatively unexplored site of influence between these two cultures?

I should also add that Tom Gunning's influential essay, "The Cinema of Attractions," which I read years back as part of an introductory film studies course, had a lot to do with sparking my current interest in the intersections between film and poetry. The final sentence, especially: "Now in a period of American avant-garde cinema in which the tradition of contemplative subjectivity has perhaps run its (often glorious) course, it is possible that this earlier carnival of the cinema, and the methods of popular entertainment, still provide an unexhausted resource — a Coney Island of the avant-garde, whose never dormant but always sensed current can be traced from Méliès through Keaton, through *Un Chien Andalou* (1928) and Jack Smith" (61). What, I wondered, was that period of American avant-garde cinema? What constituted the "tradition of contemplative subjectivity" Gunning spoke about in reference to spectacle and the avant-garde, and why had it run its course? Was Gunning implying a connection between film and poetry in his phrase "a Coney Island of the avant-garde," which was sure to evoke Lawrence Ferlinghetti's famous book of poems, *A Coney Island of the Mind*? Was there not an aura of belatedness associated with the subjective and, indeed, the visionary in a critical environment that continues to be practically dominated by the linguistic turn in the humanities?

I became curious about who these filmmakers were to which Gunning was referring. Could it be Stan Brakhage, whose film *Window Water Baby Moving* (1959) I remember seeing for the first time in, of all places, a sex education class during my stint at Tenafly High School in New Jersey? Might one of the filmmakers of which Gunning was thinking be Kenneth Anger, whose fantastically exotic and sensual *Fireworks* (1947) I first saw on a bootleg videotape in a college friend's dormitory room? That Gunning named Jack Smith in his pantheon of spectacle was perhaps one of the single most useful signposts I have ever followed. I remember going to Kim's Video Shop on Avenue A in New York's East Village, which was just around the corner from my apartment on East 6th Street, and renting a copy of Smith's *Flaming Creatures* (1963). The clerk behind the counter, normally po-faced, visibly brightened when he saw the box cover. "You're not going to steal it, are you?" he asked me, adding, "This always gets stolen." I was hooked. That poets I already knew and read avidly, including Diane di Prima and John Wieners, appeared in Smith's films only added to my desire to know more about this tantalizing and sumptuous film world that existed parallel to the poetic communities I was already committed to as a scholar and general reader.[3]

So began my autodidactic approach to learning about the New American Cinema, helped in great part by the presence of the still-extant Anthology Film Archives just four blocks away from my home. Anthology's *Essential Cinema* repertory series, featuring the work of so many of the filmmakers I have come to respect, remains one of the best schools for anyone unfamiliar but curious about the filmic avant-garde. That place, and the people who run it, taught me practically everything I know and continue to learn about formally innovative and daring film from Méliès on up to Barbara Rubin, Christopher Maclaine, Piero Heliczer, Ron Rice, Jack Smith, Marie Menken, and many others.

There is a proverbial bigger picture, however, that I want this book to address and that I will introduce now. Illustrating the fact that the material considered here illuminates a too-often ignored interdisciplinary community composed of filmmakers and poets is important, sure, but what does the work tell us beyond the fascinating cultural story? In a larger sense, analyzing the conversation between film and poetry has led me to wonder if the academy's dominant use of poststructuralist and postmodern theoretical/interpretive frameworks for innovative postwar art ends up freezing out, ignoring, or at times critiquing unfairly any number of productive sources — hermetic, heroic, mystically macho, religiously inspired — that were crucial to the creation of the various films and poems considered here. To use postmodern interpretative paradigms (particularly as they are linked up with feminist and queer studies to form a progressive triumvirate that more generally celebrates the decentered, denatured self as an ever-evolving site of freedom) results in the reader's missing out on much of what makes the poetry and film I discuss here so fascinating. (As P. Adams Sitney points out regarding the increasing influence of identity politics on film reception in the 1970s, Stan Brakhage for one was a casualty of the turn away from romanticism. "Fierce aesthetic battles over the prominence of minimal forms ['structural film'] and the status of video art were supplanted by even more acrimonious political disputes over sexism, imperialism, idealism, the importance of theory [especially French], and canon formation. Brakhage was the biggest and most battered target in these academic skirmishes" ["Tone Poems" 345]). That said, it would be naïve at best to ignore the fact that the line I draw from Kenneth Anger to Stan Brakhage to Alfred Leslie to Robert Frank to Andy Warhol through Rudy Burckhardt's work with John Ashbery in the late 1980s doesn't somehow parallel a growing awareness and enacting of the very concept of a centered self as contingent, arguable, veering dramatically away from a metaphysical rendering of selfhood. It is this movement from an intense, even mystical subjectivity to a gloriously powerful diffuseness and play that forms the basis for the story I tell here. I'll elaborate on these ideas throughout subsequent chapters.

Suffice it to say for now that I came to this juncture after a conversation with the poet Marjorie Welish some years ago. When I told Marjorie I was working on an essay studying the intergenre relationship between Kenneth

Anger and Robert Duncan, she immediately asked me (in an honestly in-quisitive as opposed to interrogatory way) why I was doing so, given that the mysticism in both artists' work was, well, kind of unfashionable. I re-sponded by saying something like, "I'm interested in stories that aren't being told anymore. I'm interested in what we miss out on when we're constantly looking in our experience of the avant-garde to be rewarded by instances of breaks between high and low, evidence of the decentered sign. What about sincere belief in God? Elves? Magic? Can't we appreciate that?" (As Stan Brakhage pointed out in an interview, "We have a lot of magicians in film. The most notable that I have known are Maya Deren, Kenneth Anger, and Harry Smith. . . . Why film attracts magicians in a certain way has intrin-sically to do with the light, because for me every mark that is put on film, which is particularly relevant when you're painting, is a diminishment of the light" [Johnson]). The memory of Marjorie's sympathetic and encouraging nods in response to my perhaps somewhat preciously plaintive comments has proved a consistent source of sustenance as I've worked my way through the chapters below.

Given that I believe, then, that the material considered here is telling us that much of what we consider to be first-generation postmodern art is grounded in a practically visionary tradition, I have arranged this book by beginning with the most obviously enchanted figures — Kenneth Anger and Stan Brakhage — highlighting how their self-consciously vatic work inter-sected with a poetry (Robert Duncan's *Passages* series and Robert Creeley's book-length *Pieces* [1969]) too often defined within the parameters of an aggressively secular interpretive approach. Questions I applied to my study include, "How did filmmaker Kenneth Anger and poet Robert Duncan think collaboratively about the functions of myth and magic in their work?"; "What is the relationship between the 'serial' poem and the avant-garde 'se-rial' movie series (i.e., Stan Brakhage's *15 Song Traits* [1964–1969] alongside Robert Creeley's *Pieces*), particularly given the use of the poetic fragment as a unit of composition?"

I then move forward to explore these and other questions in literary, social, and historical contexts, focusing after my analyses of Brakhage, Anger and others on filmmakers and poets who begin to interrogate more overtly that "tradition of contemplative subjectivity"— enter Frank O'Hara and Alfred Leslie; Allen Ginsberg and Robert Frank; Andy Warhol, Gerard Malanga, O'Hara, John Ashbery, and Ginsberg; and Ashbery and Rudy Burckhardt. I end on a simultaneously up-to-date and Romantic note (given the subjects' definition of their own work as practically organic extensions of their own lives) with an interview with contemporary filmmaker Jennifer Reeves and poet Lisa Jarnot.

In his otherwise fascinating account of the relationship between American film and poetry of the twentieth century, Lawrence Goldstein wrote "I do feel somewhat guilty for not attending to so-called underground film, but here I follow the lead of American poets, who have shown almost no interest in this worthy tradition of the avant-garde" (12). I expect that the wealth of evidence included herein will show Goldstein and many others not just the profound interest American poets had in Underground film, but how that interest illustrates the ways in which poets and filmmakers discussed below were making profound philosophical investigations into the role of technology, the relationship of formal innovation to conceptions of visionary experience, the function of realist narratives in a world marked by imperialist wars abroad and racism at home, and the possibilities for an interdisciplinary art form to create new and progressive forms of consciousness.

No monograph of which I am aware currently exists that analyzes the significance of the influences that innovative cinema cast over postwar American poetry. However, some published work explores the influence of twentieth century American poetry on postwar American film. R. Bruce Elder's *The Films of Stan Brakhage in the American Tradition of Ezra Pound, Gertrude Stein and Charles Olson* (1998) considers Brakhage's output in the context of modernist literary predecessors. Reva Wolf's book *Andy Warhol, Poetry, and Gossip in the 1960s* (1997) is, like Elder's work, concerned mainly with a single artist's oeuvre in terms of how that work has points of aesthetic intersection with American poetry. Wolf provides the reader with a cultural history of Warhol's exchanges with New York–based poets, and uses that history in the service of offering new readings of Warhol's visual art.

While influenced and informed by these books, my aim is quite different. I try here to provide readers with fresh, historically informed re-readings of major work affiliated with the New American Poetry scene; I address a wider range of poets and filmmakers; and I pay more attention to the influences of film on poetry rather than the other way around. Additionally, as I've stated, I hope I do more than simply reframe the way we talk about influence in terms of how film affected poetics. This book will, I hope, help us reassess how radically disjunctive forms have been used for effects antithetical to what we loosely call postmodernism. At the same time my concentration on poets, including John Ashbery and Frank O'Hara, long associated with a more ludic and surface-oriented aesthetic, will provide readers with a set of competing approaches among the poets considered here that interestingly are defined by shared textual practices: seriality, pastiche, pronominal shifts, textual collage and montage, and the like. I say this particularly because I have become convinced that even Ashbery and O'Hara, when studied in light of their collaborative work with filmmakers, are not as far removed from the more spiritual and political aspects of the New American Poetry phenomenon as many critics would have us believe.

Perhaps one of the most reasonable complaints readers might have is, "Why these poets and filmmakers; what about everyone else?" Figuring out on whom to focus for a book destined to end at three hundred double-spaced typed pages has, unsurprisingly, been my hardest task. After all, I could have discussed any number of films and poems — analyzing, for example, how Bruce Baillie's *Castro Street* (1966) seems to indirectly represent Ginsberg's poem "Sunflower Sutra" in its effort to "simultaneously retrieve the earlier, romantic pleasure in the industrial landscape . . . and model the retrieval of nature, as an idea and as a reality, from the ravages of modern industrialization" (MacDonald, *The Garden* 193). (Indeed, I might very well have written a tome focused entirely on Allen Ginsberg's relationship to film and filmmakers as various as Harry Smith, Barbara Rubin, Stan Brakhage, and so forth.) I might have discussed how the poet Lew Welch's appearance as a cop walking through a number of surrealistic landscapes in Robert Nelson's film *The Great Blondino* (1967) invites us to consider the surrealistic, allusively cinematic nature of Welch's own writing, particularly his serial compositions including "Taxi Suite" and "Supermarket Song." I could have expanded the field of reference by moving forward into the late 1960s and 1970s and studying so-called structural film. Certainly, given the focus of this book, much could have been made of the work of filmmaker/poet Abigail Child, who began her more experimental work in the mid-1970s and published books of poetry beginning in the early 1980s.[4]

However, there must be limits, and so I set myself some beyond the chronological considerations that I've already noted. I was determined to read deeply into individual films and poems, as opposed to providing readers with abbreviated descriptions and hurried analyses of film/poem exchanges. I determined that comparing work affiliated with the New American Cinema to parallel developments in the French *nouvelle vague* and innovative American documentary filmmaking (the Maysles brothers, D. A. Pennebaker, Emile De Antonio et al.) would, while certainly feasible and interesting, detract from the focus on an essentially non-narrative film/poetry culture. I was also moved to cover films that have not been extensively discussed and analyzed to this day. This effort on my part caused me to avoid dealing with such relatively well-known films as Shirley Clarke's *The Connection* (1961), Stan Brakhage's *Dog Star Man* (1961–1964), Alfred Leslie's and Robert Frank's *Pull My Daisy* (1959), John Cassavetes's *Shadows* (1959), Jack Smith's *Flaming Creatures* (1963), and so on. (That said, you will find me referring to some extent to these and similarly well-known works below. You will also find me discussing Kenneth Anger's celebrated *Fireworks*, albeit in a heretofore unprecedented way in relationship to Robert Duncan's poetry.) I was also committed to focusing on poets who not only were demonstrably influenced by film, but who had to some extent collaborated with a filmmaker in the production of a film or connected deeply through their poetry with a specific film. Thus, my concentration on the work of Robert Duncan, Robert Creeley, John Ashbery, Frank O'Hara, and Allen Ginsberg, all of whom variously represented (in some cases interchangeably) the highly permeable, often problematically defined groupings Donald Allen named as the Black Mountain, San Francisco Renaissance, Beat, and New York schools of poetry.

As you will find, Robert Duncan, whose book *Bending the Bow* (1968) contains poems dedicated to filmmaker Kenneth Anger, was engaged with the New American Cinema and appeared in and/or supported the work of his filmmaker peers, including Anger, Stan Brakhage, and James Broughton. I believe that in reading Duncan's serial form in light of his repeated reference to film in his poetry and his deep friendships with filmmakers, we will discover how Duncan's poetics are informed in part by filmic techniques including seriality and disjunction, rhythmic sequencing, and collage. As poet Michael McClure put it, "The long serial poem Robert wrote called 'Passages' shifts over and becomes another poem and then returns to the streambed of its poemness, and then disappears while he's writing other poems, and then these other poems connect with other poems. . . . It's a tangled, big, unseen, vital presence going on underneath the creativity, which we then see as the flowers of individual *series* or *circuits* of films or as *films themselves*" ("Realm Buster" 173). In particular, Kenneth Anger's baroque, queer aesthetic — embracing a visual palette of gargoyles, gardens, and people in fancy dress, in combination with a mystical and deeply transgressive sexuality — was to figure in Duncan's work. Considering the influence that Anger had on Duncan, I have set out to illustrate how certain aspects of Duncan's work are informed by the New American Cinema generally and Anger's work particularly. I focus especially on Kenneth Anger's *Fireworks*, illustrating how its form and content appear evocatively throughout several poems in Duncan's serial *Passages* sequence in *Bending the Bow*.

Continuing on to Creeley and Brakhage (who described his own works as "film poems" and began his career as houseboy for Robert Duncan and the visual artist Jess), I note that the two engaged in a decades-long correspondence and friendship. Complementary to Brakhage's insistence that his films were poems, Creeley produced a poetics — especially in evidence in his book *Pieces* — informed to a degree by Brakhage's filmic techniques. I show how the work of these two artists was in part determined by a radically interdisciplinary approach to form, one that blurred the very boundaries between film and poetry. I read Brakhage's *Two: Creeley/McClure* (1965) and — relying in part on historical anecdotes and personal correspondence between the two artists around the time the film was produced — play Brakhage's film against Creeley's poems in *Pieces* in an effort to foreground the connections between two ostensibly distinct forms.

Things then shift quite a bit when it comes to reading through Frank O'Hara and Alfred Leslie. O'Hara has often been associated with visual art to the occlusion of his direct participation in the avant-garde film scene. And yet O'Hara *was* engaged as audience and participant in the New American Cinema. O'Hara's friendship with and interest in poet and filmmaker James Broughton and his circle, for example, is a little discussed fact of literary history. In a letter to Broughton (July 15, 1957), for example, O'Hara writes: "I think you should apply to the Poet's Theatre, which would involve working with the theatre as well as having the leisure to write, and undoubtedly be rewarding either from the inspiration or irritation standpoint. . . . I strongly recommend one of the most talented young poets in existence, John Wieners, for a friend if you go or visit. He is an enchanting person. . . . Hope you are having a pleasant summer and look forward to seeing you here in the Fall. Making any new movies?" O'Hara was also friendly with filmmaker and poet Willard Maas, who, as Gerard Malanga's friend and teacher at Wagner College, was a link to the Warhol scene — a scene O'Hara would ultimately participate in (if marginally) and acknowledge was significant. O'Hara collaborated with Rudy Burckhardt, wrote the hilarious and compelling subtitles for Alfred Leslie's *The Last Clean Shirt* (1964), produced "screenplays" for Leslie's *The Birth of a Nation* (a film that was tragically lost in a fire) and a never-to-be produced Andy Warhol film, and lauded the work of film stylists including Warhol and Jack Smith. And yet the work that does cover O'Hara's relationship to film focuses almost entirely on his many references to Hollywood movies of the 30s and 40s and his demotic approach to popular culture generally, despite O'Hara's very real historical connections with a non-narrative, experimental cinema. It is in this gap that I insert my analysis of O'Hara's conversation with innovative cinema, paying particularly close attention to his participation in Leslie's *The Last Clean Shirt*.

As I stated above, an entire book might be written about Ginsberg's relationship to filmmakers. In an effort to control the overall direction of this book, I start by framing Ginsberg's poetics initially in relationship to his beloved Charlie Chaplin. I then move on by choosing a film work that was not as well-known as Robert Frank's and Alfred Leslie's *Pull My Daisy*, but which nevertheless included Ginsberg as a major figure and, more importantly, illustrated how some of Ginsberg's important work from the 60s, including "Kaddish" and "Wichita Vortex Sutra," can be revealed as embodying and extending a filmic poetics. Thus, I focus on the conversation between Frank and Ginsberg. I begin with Frank's foiled attempts to turn Ginsberg's poem "Kaddish" into a movie and concentrate on a sustained reading of Frank's tremendous and sad film *Me and My Brother* (1969), a kind of impressionistic documentary of Ginsberg's and Peter Orlovsky's travels through Kansas and other states accompanied by Orlovsky's mentally ill brother Julius.

Of the poets mentioned so far, Ginsberg, Ashbery, and O'Hara all had relationships of one kind or another with Andy Warhol. Beginning around 1964, Warhol would — after taking the art world by storm, as they say — go on to take the Underground film world by storm. Warhol produced a group of films prior to his more commercially viable work with Paul Morrissey, including *Couch* (1964), *Blow Job* (1964), *Sleep* (1963), *Empire* (1964), and the *Screen Tests* series (1964–1966). As Reva Wolf has already shown, Warhol's expanded work in film coincided with his increasing participation in the Lower East Side poetry community. Poets played a "starring role," as it were, in his early films, and it is here where I introduce the conversations between poets and Warhol as they took place primarily in and among the making of the *Screen Tests* series. Working his way out of a discourse around art disseminated in the 1950s by critics like Harold Rosenberg — one that was characterized by a romantic valorization of intense subjectivity associated with the grandmasters of abstract expressionism — Warhol perhaps more than any other Pop artist helped redefine the terms towards a variously fun, coolly clinical, impersonal aesthetic that resisted the authentic, the original, the symbolic. To put it simply, Warhol radically usurped the notion of art as self-expression. My chapter on Warhol's work with the poets explores the ramifications of such a stance as it affects our reading of innovative American writing, even as I (as Reva Wolf and others have done previously) complicate the stability of the postmodern aura that surrounds Warhol by examining the ways lyric practice interacts with his films.

I end the main section of this book by leaping two decades into the future in an effort to see whether John Ashbery's more recent collaboration with the filmmaker Rudy Burckhardt in Burckhardt's film *Ostensibly* (1989) continues to extend the kinds of aesthetic and philosophical concerns evinced during the heyday of the New American film/poetry phenomenon. Often aligned with visual art due to his decades-long work as an art critic and his friendships with artists including Jane Freilicher, Fairfield Porter, Larry Rivers, and Trevor Winkfield, John Ashbery nevertheless was significantly influenced by film and also had important working relationships with some of the filmmakers associated with the New American Cinema from the early 1950s through the 1980s, including Burckhardt and Andy Warhol. In terms of Burckhardt's work, Ashbery was a participant early on, starring in Burckhardt's *Mounting Tension* (1950). Burckhardt recalled that he and Larry Rivers "made a movie — *Mounting Tension* — about Larry being a genius painter and Jane [Freilicher] his psychiatrist. We sort of made it up as we went along. It made fun of modern art and psychoanalysis, two pretty sacred subjects at that time. And I remember Jane said, 'Oh, I have this friend, maybe he could be in the movie too?' So she brought him along and that was John Ashbery, and he played the part of a young man with a baseball bat who hates modern art but gets dragged to the Modern Museum and ends up an abstract painter himself" (*Talking Pictures* 142). As Ashbery acknowledged, "I ended up writing about art by chance, really. If I'd decided that I was going to write criticism I probably would have written film criticism. If I had known that I was going to be writing criticism for a living, I would have felt well, probably, I know more about films and I'm more interested in them than I am in the art world or the history of art. It was only because somebody offered me . . . Thomas Hess hired me at a point where I needed the extra money . . . then I started writing art criticism and was unable to stop" (personal interview; ellipses in original).

Ashbery, included in Allen's *The New American Poetry* and consistently exhibiting an (if historically occluded) engagement with film and more overtly "spiritual" poets including Robert Duncan, is an especially interesting figure to consider here. His work continues to be a kind of litmus test for competing groups of scholars and poets. It is championed by critics like Harold Bloom and Helen Vendler, who tend to highlight Ashbery's work in relationship to a recognizable tradition grounded in romanticism and American transcendentalism. On the proverbial other hand, academics and poets affiliated with language writing (Charles Bernstein, Andrew Ross, Ron Silliman, Bruce Andrews, and others) emphasize moments of practically aggressive polysemy found in some of Ashbery's work while ignoring or pooh-poohing the more recognizably narrative or emotive strands of his output. That said, Ashbery's poems in books from *Some Trees* through the break-through *The Tennis Court Oath* and beyond provide the dedicated reader with a complex blend of discourses that embrace the narrative, the personal, the metaphysical, and even the mystical.

Finally, I end this book with an actual conversation — one between myself and two of my own contemporaries, the filmmaker Jennifer Reeves and the poet Lisa Jarnot, both of whom became friends with Stan Brakhage, collabo-rated with each other, and continue to some extent to look to underground cinema of the 1960s as an inspiration for their own work. (I would add that Reeves's material practice is practically anachronistic in what has become an increasingly digitized medium. She works predominantly with 16mm as opposed to digital video, using her viewer and splicer and tape splices for the assembly cut, and sometimes even for the rough cut, before putting the ma-terial onto her computer for further editing and sound design. What is pretty much unique about Reeves's filmmaking is that she assembles the final edit on 16mm and exhibits almost always on 16mm, even though film venues and galleries as they move away from 16mm exhibition continually request Reeves's films on video. Indeed, two of her films — *Light Work Mood Dis-order* (2006–2007) and *He Walked Away* (2003–2006) — were edited solely on 16mm).[5] It is here where we take an opportunity to discuss and extend several important issues covered throughout this book.

I am sure by now that several readers have already complained about this book being a boy's book, particularly given the preeminent role filmmakers, including Maya Deren, played in New York and San Francisco just prior to the advent of the New American Cinema phenomenon, and, more retrospec-tively, the crucial role poets and artists like H.D., Gertrude Stein, and Bryher served in linking the two genres. In this final conversation, Jennifer, Lisa, and I take the opportunity to discuss the lack of representation of women filmmakers and poets in the annals of the postwar American avant-gardes prior to the advent of structural filmmaking in the late 1960s and 1970s, what the relationship between contemporary filmmakers and poets is now at the turn of the twentieth century, the link between disruptive form and dissi-dent politics, and so on. Most importantly, we spend some time unpacking the processes and ideas behind one of Reeve's best-known films, *The Time We Killed* (2004), a film that features Jarnot herself and incorporates Jarnot's poetry. I end here, with a conversation between two artists who trace part of their lineage to the poets and filmmakers mentioned throughout this book, in an effort to show how film and poetry continue to talk to each other, inform each other, and cross each other's aesthetic and generic boundaries in an ever-developing and consistently intriguing way.

Finally, I would like to end this introduction by pointing to a yawning chasm in the conceptual and historical trajectory of this book. Collaborations between poets and filmmakers did not suddenly erupt out of New York, San Francisco, and Los Angeles in the 1950s and 1960s. Rather, we should at least point to an early modernist dialogue between film and poetry, particularly given the fact that so many of the poets and filmmakers in the New American Cinema communities looked to Stein, H.D., and the poets and artists of the French and Russian avant-gardes as crucial predecessors. Much work has already been done in this area, and I would urge readers to consult the fascinating historical and critical analyses of modernist film and poetry provided us by Laura Marcus,[6] Lawrence Goldstein,[7] Richard Abel,[8] Susan McCabe,[9] David Kadlec,[10] Michael North,[11] Marjorie Perloff,[12] and Bruce Fleming,[13] to name just a few. These critics have explored the work of writers including John Dos Passos, William Carlos Williams, Ezra Pound, H.D., Gertrude Stein, Vachel Lindsay, and the European avant-gardes more generally in terms of their exchanges with both non-narrative experimental film and more mainstream vehicles associated with popular early cinema. Taken as a whole, their work provides us with an excellent survey of the connections between film and poetry in pre–World War II America and Europe, a survey that will do much to contextualize more fully the work that follows in this book.

one

Some Early Conversations

HERE WE GO UP AND DOWN AGAIN:
MAYA DEREN DESPITE THE FACTS

Let us travel back to 1953, New York City, and revisit what must surely have been a remarkable event sponsored by Amos Vogel's Cinema 16 film club.[1] Titled "Poetry and Film: A Symposium," this event was one of the most official signs yet that there was a postwar dialogue between two ostensibly different genres. The panel participants were composed of heavyweight poets, dramatists, and filmmakers Maya Deren, Parker Tyler, Willard Maas, Dylan Thomas, and Arthur Miller. Like the heavyweights they surely were, they spent their time engaged in rhetorical battle as they somewhat torturously tried to theorize relationships between lyric text and projected light. When we ask ourselves why talented women filmmakers including Marie Menken, Storm De Hirsch, Shirley Clarke, and Barbara Rubin received relatively short shrift in existing accounts of the avant-garde film cultures of the 50s and 60s, we can turn to the utterly contemptuous comments made, especially by Miller and Thomas (and to a somewhat lesser extent by Tyler and Maas), at this event to illustrate the prevailing attitudes that male intellectuals and artists had towards their female counterparts.

Deren worked vigorously to link her work with poetry generally, even as she faced resistance not just from mainstream artists and writers but from her avant-garde bedfellows as well.[2] After Deren discussed her conceptions of "vertical" and "horizontal" aesthetics, Miller interpolated, "To hell with that 'vertical' and 'horizontal': it doesn't mean anything. . . . So that it is simply a question of, here again, an image, which is, in one case, when you speak of 'vertical' and 'horizontal,' rather mechanical. And I'm sure the lady didn't mean it that way, and that's why it was taken so absurdly" (Deren 62). The "lady" in question responded, "I'm a little bit flabbergasted at the fact that people who have handled words with such dexterity as Mr. Thomas and Mr. Miller, and Mr. Tyler, should have difficulty with such a simple idea as the 'vertical' and the 'horizontal.'" To this, Dylan Thomas remarked jocularly, "Here we go up and down again." In her own defense, Deren chose to take Thomas's words seriously and suggested that the rhythms of fucking resonated with her cinematic practice: "These seem to me the most elementary movements in the world and really quite fundamental." Willard Maas — who had so far refused to come to Deren's defense or chastise Thomas for his untoward comments — chose this particular moment to chastise *Deren* for her sexually suggestive language: "I don't think you ought to get vulgar." That Maas would join the boy's group in Deren-bashing seems especially sad considering Maas's own place in New York's poetry community and his film works, including *Geography of the Body* (1943), described by Parker Tyler as "a true poem of the nude" ("Willard Maas" 53). Basically a visual meditation (with a voice-over of British poet George Barker providing a kind of poem/ commentary) on the human form composed of extreme close-ups on ears, legs, breasts, a mouth parting suggestively, a tongue, and so forth, *Geography of the Body* certainly anticipates the kind of candor and Romantic exaltation of erotic sensation we associate with Beat-affiliated poetry.[3]

So, despite what is now commonly acknowledged as Maya Deren's preeminent role in the nascent Underground, it is clear from anecdotes such as these that she was not entirely welcome or understood in her own contemporary moment, even by her supposed colleagues. Nevertheless, certain comments from panel members, including Parker Tyler, are worth revisiting. Tyler helpfully linked Deren's work (along with Kenneth Anger's, Curtis Harrington's, and James Broughton's) to a kind of tradition of non-narrative film:

> Now, poetical expression falls rather automatically into two groups: that is, poetry as a visual medium and poetry as a verbal medium, or in a larger sense as auditory, and that would, of course, include music. We might well begin with some of the shorter films which concentrate on poetry as a visual medium, and this, of course, leads right to Cocteau's "Blood of a Poet," and to Buñuel-Dali's "Andalusian Dog," and to Watson's "Lot in Sodom." All these are classics now and they emphasized a surrealist poetry of the image, and gave rise to schools and styles of avant-garde all over the world. Cinema 16 patrons are familiar with some of these outstanding works — those of Maya Deren, of James Broughton, of Kenneth Anger, of Curtis Harrington. All these film-

makers concentrated on what might be called pure cinema — entirely without
words as a rule, although sometimes with music. (ibid. 55)

Deren went on to qualify Tyler's point about film as poetry, emphasizing not
her film's use of poetic rhythm as a sequencing model but poetry's freedom
from narrative structure. "Now poetry, to my mind, consists not of asso-
nance; or rhythm, or rhyme, or any of these other qualities which we associate as being characteristic of poetry. Poetry, to my mind, is an approach to
experience. . . . The distinction of poetry is its construction (what I mean by
'a poetic structure'), and the poetic construct arises from the fact, if you will,
that it is a 'vertical' investigation of a situation, in that it probes the ramifications of the moment, and is concerned with its qualities and its depth, so that
you have poetry concerned in a sense not with what is occurring, but with
what it feels like or what it means" (ibid. 56). Deren continued by clarify-
ing what she meant by the term "vertical," setting it up in opposition to the
narrativity inherent in what she defined as a "horizontal" approach to composition. "This may be a little bit clearer if you will contrast [the 'vertical']
to what I would call the 'horizontal' attack of a drama, which is concerned
with the development, let's say, within a very small situation from feeling
to feeling. . . . You know, if it's establishing New York, you get a montage of
images, that is, a poetic construct, after which what follows is a dramatic
construct which is essentially 'horizontal' in its development. . . . Now, the
short films, to my mind (and they are short because it is difficult to maintain
such intensity for a long period of time), are comparable to lyric poems, and
they are completely a 'vertical,' or what I would call a poetic construct, and
they are complete as such." Poetry as a genre informing Deren's practice
was valuable precisely for its ability to create sensations through what Deren
tacitly suggests is a kind of textual montage, one in which juxtaposition leads
to impressionistically attained insight free from the linear strictures inherent in dramatic form. As Deren suggested later, "film, I believe, lends itself
particularly to the poetic statement, because it is essentially a montage and,
therefore, seems by its very nature to be a poetic medium" (ibid. 59).

This is not so far away from Ezra Pound's earlier poetics of imagism, a
fact that was not lost on the panel's moderator, Willard Maas.[4] Responding
to a particularly cranky and uninformed assertion by Arthur Miller that
revealed his total lack of understanding not just of the panel's purpose, but of
Deren's distinctions between "horizontal" and "vertical" approaches,[5] Maas
clarified the subtleties between narrative and the lyric: "Well, surely Mr.
Miller, you must see the difference between presenting something by words

or dialogue, as you do and Mr. Thomas does, and presenting something by the visual image. Now Ezra Pound said in a definition of the image that it is an emotional and intellectual complex caught in an instant of time. It's a very direct and quick way of saying things, a lyric way of saying things, while the way a dramatist says things is by putting the characters that speak back and forth in conflict" (ibid. 62). That Maas would attack Miller by referring back to an innovative poetic predecessor speaks volumes about the links between experimental cinema and radical poetic practice of the twentieth century generally. Poetry and film were being fused as a counter to prevailing narrative modes, of which Arthur Miller and Dylan Thomas were, at least through the 1950s, the United States' most renowned representatives. Rippling out of Maas's comments lies a whole set of tensions — between narrative and lyric, spiritually-tinged avant-garde practice and normative prose, mainstream and outsider art, male centrality and female marginalization — that would inform and complicate the emerging and interlocking poetry and film communities of the 1960s.

A SKETCH ON POETRY AND FILM IN THE 1950S AND 1960S

Let us just dip back a little further into the 1940s to expand on the context of the developing film/poetry scenes of the 50s and 60s. In San Francisco following the end of World War II, Sidney Peterson's cinema workshops at the California School of Fine Arts were some of the earliest postwar models of an adamantly experimental "poetic" cinema situating itself outside the Hollywood industry. Peterson was a significant figure in the Bay Area movement whose films, including *The Potted Psalm* (1946) (made with poet and filmmaker James Broughton), *The Cage* (1947), and *Lead Shoes* (1949), influenced succeeding generations of innovative filmmakers. Given Peterson's collaboration with Broughton in *The Potted Psalm*, it is not out of the realm of possibilities that the opening scene of that particular film — a pan over a field of grass that soon reveals itself as a hill in San Francisco — is designed to remind viewers of Whitman's leaves of grass, particularly as that grass resonates with a practically morbid polymorphous eroticism latent in many of the scenes that follow. (Shots of tombstones and figures wandering about the graves feature prominently as they are balanced against scenes of women lying in bed, feet twirling round coquettishly, lacing up of boots, feet stroking against each other, lips pressed directly against the camera, a shot of a young man standing next to a statue of a naked man, and so on).[6]
While Peterson was very much of San Francisco, experimental cinema

bubbled in the interstices of the city that Warner Brothers and Paramount called home. Most famously, Maya Deren and Alexander Hammid's *Meshes of the Afternoon* (1943) was dreamed up and produced in Los Angeles, and Deren would go on to inspire filmmakers including Curtis Harrington. (Harrington recalled, "Whenever [Deren would] come to Los Angeles, I'd throw a little party for her and provide bongo drums so that she could dance. Maya loved to dance" [ibid. 43].) "It was there in the City of Angels that Harrington and his friends Kenneth Anger and Gregory Markopoulos began to create their own stylised, personal 16mm works that were central to the experimental film renaissance" (ibid. 43). An experimental film community, instigated in great part by Deren, expanded.

So, thanks to Deren, multimedia artist Wallace Berman, and others, Los Angeles by the 1950s could claim to be a satellite of the New American Poetry and Cinema scenes. As Robert Pike described it in 1957, "In Los Angeles, Wallace Berman has begun a series of poetry readings by the rising poets of that city. The first evening was attended by Curtis Harrington, Cameron Parsons, Samson De Brier, and many others both interested and active in art and poetry. Berman is also starting work on his first experimental film" (9). A letter from Willard Maas in New York to James Broughton in San Francisco (May 27, 1956) suggests the relationship between poets and filmmakers was not just fluid between genres but fluid between coasts and cities as well. We learn how Broughton's film, *The Pleasure Garden* (1953), was shown in New York, though attendance was sparse due to Amos Vogel's decision to show the film in another venue on the same night and, interestingly, because there was a Frank O'Hara reading going on as well. In the same letter Maas wrote, "I don't know how really the showing was a success, for everyone who regularly comes to films of this sort (hardly a person there from OUR crowd because Frank O'Hara was Uptown reading his poems and Amos, the SAME night, was showing PLEASURE GARDEN at the New School." Poetry and film are positioned here as visual coterie events — a "showing," to use Maas's word, of either the poet projecting his voice to the crowd or the projector itself beaming light onto the screen for the benefit of an audience.

Maas and his partner Marie Menken were, early on in the game, instigators of and grande dames of the film/poetry community, holding court at countless parties in their home in Brooklyn Heights. As I mentioned earlier, Maas was friendly with Frank O'Hara. In a letter to James Broughton (January 20, 1957) Maas wrote, "Called Frankie — not home, but spoke to his room-mate who is one of my closest friends, Joe-Joy Le Suerer [sic], who reported F had gotten the most charming letter from you, LIKES your book and you and gathers he is asking for it somewhere. So you see! He is having a book from Grove about the same time."[7] Maas and Menken were also close to Gerard Malanga, and both would become intimate participants in Andy Warhol's Factory and the poetry scene swirling around that particular artist. (Maas is reputed to have played a part offscreen as a fellator in Warhol's film *Blow Job* [1964]. Marie Menken went on to create the impressionistic film "document" *Andy Warhol* [1965], showing the artist in the process of producing his Brillo Box series with Malanga's assistance.[8] She also played the part of Malanga's mother in Warhol's *Chelsea Girls* [1966].)

Mass and Menken's home was, of course, not the only social center in town. Maya Deren herself seemed to draw people toward her wherever she went — by the end of the decade Deren was increasingly celebrated in New York's arts community, one which found her rubbing shoulders with poets, playwrights, musicians, and other assorted artists. In February of 1959, independent cinema filmmaker and champion Jonas Mekas "described the scene at another Deren show: the Living Theater was 'bursting with people, sitting everywhere, on the floor, standing by the walls, on the stairway.' . . . The spring's other public manifestations of the film scene included Mekas's column in praise of Village resident Len Lye; Rudy Burckhardt's show at the Provincetown Playhouse; and the 'Gryphon group' screening organized by Willard Maas at the Living Theater" (Hoberman, "The Forest" 104).[9] Stan Brakhage made both Deren's influence and what he called the "convergence" of film with poetry literal in a letter to Jonas Mekas. "I begin to see (as I see *thru* the works of other, *by way of* my own films) an inter-related convergence. . . . All of the promise (as I foresaw it at the time) in the fact that both Maya Deren and I independently, separated by nearly 2000 miles and 2 years of non-communication, formulated specific filmic ideology directly related to Haiku poetry" ("Letters" 76).

By the late 1950s, then, the connections between film and poetry were becoming increasingly clear to a bicoastal avant-garde. Alfred Leslie's and Robert Frank's seminal *Pull My Daisy* (1959), set in New York and starring Beat and New York School icons Larry Rivers, Alice Neel, Allen Ginsberg, Peter Orlovsky, Gregory Corso, Jack Kerouac (providing voiceover), and others, and Ron Rice's important film *The Flower Thief* (1960), set in San Francisco and featuring the irrepressible poet and underground film star Taylor Mead, went far in establishing an interdisciplinary relationship between screen and page. Both films suggested that poets were as engaged with film (on aesthetic, social, and collaborative grounds) as filmmakers were with poetry.

Pull My Daisy was based on a play by Jack Kerouac titled *The Beat Generation* (2006; written in 1957), which Alfred Leslie then adapted for his and Frank's film. As Leslie recalls it:

> One day, I went out with Robert [Frank] to where Jack was living with his mother some place in Long Island, Red Neck, Great Neck, one of those places like that, we brought out Dodie Muller who he was in love with at the time, they were supposedly engaged. When the three of us got there Jack and Dodie immediately went to a motel for a conjugal visit . . . the one thing that he had given me was this play he had written called "The Beat Generation: The Bishop of the New Aramanian Church." He had given me the play and I thought, well, the play didn't do anything for me, none of the things did, except as literature. I could *read* them but to take that next step and find the concept for the work, the overriding concept for the film, I didn't get it clearly. When he left, he left a note beside his tape recorder, and he had made a tape-recording of his reading out loud, he said "Maybe this'll give you a different perspective of the play" or something like that. Now, when he was reading it on the tape, he was listening to Symphony Sid.[10] So he's reading this play, and probably high, and in the background is Symphony Sid —"Oh hey there, man, this is Sid, now we're gonna hear Illinois Jacquet . . ."—and this music comes on, so at that point I realized all of the characters in Jack's novels were Jack Kerouac. There were no characters. There were no separate people. It was just one long prose poem, as it were, from beginning to end, and that he was impersonating, when I heard his voice, I said this is the way the film has to be done. So that's the way I found the concept through the language of his connecting to the sound. (personal interview)

Note the way Leslie describes his own moment of illumination — the play becomes a potential film once Leslie understands the serial nature of the text ("one long prose poem") and the simultaneity of sense perceptions (sight, sound, music, speech) afforded him by the recording and latent most powerfully in the medium of film. *The Beat Generation* was, in a sense, already a potential film, and it was up to Leslie and Frank to manifest that possibility.

Pull My Daisy itself "took place in Al Leslie's Lower East Side loft and, by all indications, it was a miracle that a finished movie was ever produced. Frank and Leslie were not interested in, nor could they afford, professional players for each of the roles, so they decided that for verisimilitude it would be best if Beat figures played the characters. Allen and Peter played themselves, while Gregory Corso took the Kerouac role. Larry Rivers played Neal

[Cassady] (renamed Milo in the film), and musician David Amram played a hipster friend. Richard Bellamy portrayed the bishop. The sole professional in the cast was Delphine Seyrig, who took the Carolyn Cassady part"[11] (Schumacher 304). In discussing his vision for *Pull My Daisy*, Leslie suggests Kerouac was already engaged with film as a kind of aesthetic influence and helps us understand how Kerouac might have seen the mythic scroll on which he wrote *On The Road* as materially analogous to the film reel: "*Pull My Daisy* was made in response to Jack's language. Jack used the typewriter as an instrument. He would sit down, he would get into his state, whether he was high or not, the idea was to get himself free enough to unleash all of those ideas and thoughts, but since he was a speed typist, he was able to put that stuff out as fast as he could get it all down, and then by having his so-called roll of paper he was able to do it without any interruption, the way Coltrane would" (personal interview). As Leslie phrases it, serial improvisation is an act that transcends the material limitations of any given art form.[12] Phrases like "unleash" and "put that stuff out as fast as he could get it all down," particularly as they resonate with the "roll of paper" (unwinding, we might imagine, like the roll of film), suggest a blurring of the boundaries between the various mechanisms of typewriter, film projector, and saxophone. Jack Sargeant makes a good point regarding the intergenre nature of *Pull My Daisy*: "[It] is this very affirmation of playing with language, of spontaneous poetry, which Kerouac's narration both excels in, and reveals. *Pull My Daisy* thus demands to be understood as Kerouac's singular cinematic prosey [sic], as the only film to be produced by/with the 'central' Beat writers during the time at which their work was first being recognized, yet was still largely a product of the underground" (*Naked Lens* 23). A "prosey" that is already "cinematic" thus becomes, in the hands of Alfred Leslie and Robert Frank, fully realized once it is inscribed on celluloid.[13]

The Flower Thief was, in a way, San Francisco's answer and homage to *Pull My Daisy*. Ron Rice's film "may . . . be viewed as a direct reference to Leslie's and Frank's *Pull My Daisy,* which greatly influenced both Ron Rice and Taylor Mead" (Sargeant, *Naked Lens* 71). Mead was a nomadic, Chaplinesque actor and poet who made his home in both New York and San Francisco and who influenced a number of Lower East Side–based poets with his outrageous amalgam of complete candor alongside a faux-naif writing style that suggests Jean Genet crossed with Rod McKuen. Jack Sargeant states, "Visually *The Flower Thief* embraces a spontaneous filmmaking style, with wildly varied lighting, and occasional chaotic camera work, which is manifested via styles such as faked slow-motion, montage sequences, speeded up footage, and double-exposures. This draws attention to the belief in film as Beat poetry, as a way in which to get things down with as much immediacy as possible" (ibid. 74). To this we might add that Mead's own spontaneous antics on the underground screens informed younger poets such as Ed Sanders, who — in his journal *Fuck You / a magazine of the arts* — celebrated Mead consistently and whose outrageous and playful poems (including such standouts as "Sheep Fuck Poem"), alongside his consistently celebratory take on what he called "multilateral indiscriminate apertural conjugation," points to crosscurrents of influence.

The scenes in San Francisco, New York, and Los Angeles resulted in what was practically a renaissance of film and poetry that was to unfold throughout the 1960s — we can refer certainly to Canyon Cinema in San Francisco,[14] as well as New York–based if ultimately internationally influential institutions, including the Film-Makers' Cooperative and Anthology Film Archives;[15] the Gate Theater;[16] the Millennium Film Workshop led initially by filmmaker Ken Jacobs (formed in 1966 and based at St. Mark's Church in New York out of the same federal grants scheme that funded the still-extant Poetry Project);[17] The Filmmakers Cinematheque, Jerome Hill, Peter Kubelka, and The Invisible Cinema;[18] and others, particularly as they engaged with poetry institutions including Le Metro and the Poetry Project at St. Mark's Church (both in New York City) and the various reading scenes in San Francisco.[19]

Stan Brakhage, perhaps the figure most strongly associated with the avantgarde film scene of the 60s, consistently framed his and his colleagues' work in film within the context of the lyric. Responding to Marie Menken's films, Brakhage wrote, "Marie was also a cinematic poet in the sense that she made a translation of poetic possibilities into the language of cinema. . . . Thus, when I say that she translated poetry into cinema, I mean that she had to invent a cinematic corollary, and one which would not diminish the art of language with some cheap pictorialization of verbal meanings. Her tactic was to take notice of what the two media, poetry and film, share — that they are continuity arts very dependent on rhythm — and work with that" (*Film at Wit's End* 42). Filmmakers including Jonas Mekas and Gregory Markopoulos published books of poetry; in his introduction to Markopolous's *Poems* (1964), poet and filmmaker Gerard Malanga wrote, "A film-maker, indeed an artist, his poetry is an assertion for the revival of the Romantic temperament which moved Chopin and Byron. The poet esoterically investigates *his* own human experience relative to all human experience. . . . Through contemplation and observation Mr. Markopoulos has attempted to recreate, out of what little we know of the past, the events, legends, and myths that add meaning to the tenor of present-day experience. It is through this method that the nineteenth century has become *more* relevant to his intellectual and spiritual outlook, in tone and in method, than has the twentieth century. The style of Mr. Markopoulos's poetry, as well as the style of his films, has been to re-create an event out of classical Greece" (n.p.). Malanga might have added that Markopoulos's poetry owed as much to Allen Ginsberg's homoerotic candor and exclamation-mark heavy urgency as it did to nineteenth-century romanticism. Markopoulos's attempts at writing lyric helps us understand the increasingly blurred boundaries demarcating poetry from film:

> Anus Anios!
> Waist to lips.
> Adrift! Adrift!
> Cinema's cosmic pulse.
> Scoop, silver ladle, scoop!
> Never the one alone. (ibid. 12)

Markopoulos's sacralizing gestures, as they are aligned both to cinema and heavy-handed hints of homosexual fellatio and buggery, echo Ginsberg's own grandiose mythologizing of his poetic company. We might argue that Markopoulos further extends Ginsberg's aesthetic into an intergenre space characterized and projected both by textual meter and "cinema's cosmic pulse," in which the word "pulse" is designed to point back to the line's own rhythm. Cinema and poetry are at least conceptually synthesized here, all in the name of foregrounding homosexuality as a form of transcendent Eros through which the "one" is never "alone."

As we find in Markopoulos's poem, there is a sense of unorthodox community spread in part through the association of experimental film and poetry. Further, the presence of poets including Ginsberg and Orlovsky in Markopoulos's film *Galaxie* (1966) points once again to the ways in which poets played very real social and aesthetic roles in positioning experimental cinema with the counterculture overall.[20] A contemporary review of *Galaxie* makes much out of the dissident sociability engendered by the pairing of filmmaker and poet:

> [*Galaxie*] is an hour and a half long and involves one reel change. There is no sound, except for the metered chiming of Hindu bells, and the whole film consists of 30 three-minute portraits of semiknown and unknown people. Jasper Johns, Eric Hawkins, Ben Weber, Parker Tyler, Susan Sontag, Shirley Clarke, Jonas Mekas, the Kuchar twins, Storm de Hirsch, Allen Ginsberg and Peter

Orlovsky, Gian Carlo Menotti, Charles Boultenhouse, Ed Emshwiller, Ethel and Robert Scull and 16 others. They decorate their frames like living objects . . . in which other objects that relate to their lives are juxtaposed — musical scores, stuffed animals, pop art, transvestite paraphernalia, assorted junk.

The major exodus from the Playboy Theater, where the festival was held, came after the Ginsberg-Orlovsky episode. The two beat poets had spent two and half of their three minutes lethargically reading comic books and eating ying or yang, when nonchalantly they turned to each other and laughingly kissed — on the mouth. One matron, as she pedalled up the aisle, hissed at another seated woman who was laughing delightedly, "It's disgusting and degrading and I can't see what's the least bit funny," to which the acerbic reply caromed into the darkness, "It's just people, Baby, and what's funnier than people?" (Williams 42)

The casual homoeroticism that Markopoulos recorded found its echo in Ginsberg's own poetry. That poets appeared in the film, that the filmmaker wrote poems, and that the film itself — with its insistent and allusively imagistic superimpositions, visual rhymes and repetitions, and its rejection of a narrative framework — so clearly owed a great deal of its mechanisms to the innovative lyric model further illustrates how the two genres were very much engaged in fruitful conversation.

A WORLD OF FLOWERS OF EVIL

In 1963 Jonas Mekas, perhaps the most influential promoter of the New American Cinema, announced, "Ron Rice's 'The Queen of Sheba Meets the Atom Man': Jack Smith's 'The [sic] Flaming Creatures'; Ken Jacobs's 'Little Stabs at Happiness'; Bob Fleischner's [sic] 'Blonde Cobra'[21] — four works that make up the real revolution in cinema today. These movies are illuminating and opening up sensibilities and experiences never before recorded in the American arts, a content which Baudelaire, the Marquis de Sade, and Rimbaud gave to world literature a century ago and which Burroughs[22] gave to American literature three years ago. It is a world of flowers of evil, of illuminations, of torn and tortured flesh; a poetry which is at once beautiful and terrible, good and evil, delicate and dirty" ("Movie Journal" 86). Linking the utopian gestures typical of Beat-affiliated poetry with his favored filmmakers, Mekas wrote poems which make explicit the major themes discussed here. Note, for example, his poem titled "Press Release" (here excerpted):

Breer, Menken, Brakhage, Vanderbeek, Boultenhouse, Rice, Markopoulos, Preston, Wisniewski, Jacobs, Joffen, Anger, Maas, Zimmerman, Smith, Baillie, MacLaine [sic] are the film poets of America today.

II.

There are poets singing in movies today with such beauty that
it makes Ugliness weep

but Everyman is deaf to poetry
Everyman and the critics have become pompous
they approach poetry like pigs

there should be fasting and meditating before seeing a
Menken, a Brakhage, a Breer, a Kenneth Anger, a Carmen
D'avino; . . .

The poets &
The Old Masters Know What I Am Talking About

only *very* new cinema can be art
only *very* new cinema can be moral
only *very* new cinema has no image of itself
only *very* new cinema can be beautiful & good
only *very* new cinema is FREE OF ANY RATIONAL RESTRICTIVENESS
is humble is for its own sake ("Press Release" 7)

Throughout the 1960s articles in *Film Culture* and related journals would regularly define work as "film poetry." (Ken Kelman directly titled one of his essays "Film as Poetry.") Poets seemed particularly delighted to be in the company of Stan Brakhage, who filmed and collaborated with writers including Creeley, William Burroughs, Ed Dorn, Ginsberg, and many others. A letter from Brakhage to Robert Kelly (March 12, 1967) illustrates the casual exchanges between poets and filmmakers in the later part of the decade: "I'll enclose this [letter] off with some pictures of the children, and some from Allen Ginsberg's visit here (which was a pleasure, along with many other visits we've been graced with this year: Peter Kubelka's, Michael McClure's, Jonas Mekas', Diane di Prima's, along with Alan Marlowe, their lovely children, friend Zen — it was also good to see Peter Orlovsky again, meet his brother Julius and Maretta Greer)." What a scene!

Not surprisingly, such a scene had as its backdrop a roiling political landscape characterized by the Vietnam War abroad and the counterculture at home — a counterculture that borrowed heavily from the cultural output of its artistic avant-gardes. A flyer published by the Film-Makers' Cooperative in New York paints a picture of a film and poetry community under assault by censorious city governments anxious to push their undergrounds literally out of sight:

TO THE FRIENDS OF CINEMA,

These are the facts:

February 17, 1964: Film-Makers' Showcase at the Gramercy Arts Theatre closed. Summons issued by the City Department of Licenses for Ron Rice Show of December 9, 1963.

Pocket Film Society screenings at the Pocket Theatre closed. Summons issued by the City Department of Licenses for Sidney Peterson Show of December 9, 1963.

March 3, 1964: Jack Smith's film FLAMING CREATURES seized at the New Bowery Theatre by detectives from the District Attorney's office. Kenneth Jacobs, Jerry Sims, Florence Karpe, and Jonas Mekas arrested.

March 7, 1964: Kenneth Anger's film SCORPIO RISING seized by the Los Angeles Vice Squad at the Cinema Theatre.

March 13, 1964: Jean Genet's film UN CHANT D'AMOUR seized by the New York police at the Writers' Stage Theatre. Pierre Cottrell and Jonas Mekas arrested.

March 16, 1964: The Gate Film Club, at the Gate Theatre, closed under pressure from the City Department of Licenses.

March 17, 1964: Kenneth Anger and Stan Brakhage Show cancelled at the New Bowery Theatre. Screening harassed by the New York police, fire and City License departments, detectives, and the State Division of Motion Pictures. Summons issued by the City Department of Licenses for "violation of the Administrative Code."

March 18, 1964: Kuchar Bros. program cancelled at the New Bowery Theatre under pressure. Substitute program of "Film-makers Without Films" locked out of the theatre by the New York police under order secured by the theatre owner. Summons issued by Louis Pesce, director of the State Division of Motion Pictures, to the Film-Makers' Cooperative and to the American Theatre for Poets "for exhibition of an unlicensed motion picture in public place of amusement for pay."

Despite the lively nature of the language excerpted above, this was no Keystone Cops scenario wherein the good avant-garde poets and filmmakers all scamper away from the fumbling hands of the Law. A letter in 1964 from Brakhage to Creeley dated, as Brakhage put it, "March (?) — God Knows . . . somewhere late in it," underscores the seriousness of the threat to the film and poetry communities: "We're IN New York, arrived several days ago care/of Film-Maker's Co-Op . . . and finding ourselves having to care more for *them*, for the time being, because Jonas Mekas has been twice arrested for showing (1) Flaming Creatures and (2) Genet's 1950 film 'Un Chant D'Amour,' now faces minimum year jail sentence (which would, of course, end Film Culture, end Film Co-Op, etc.) and all monies, which amount to very little, having to go to court expenses, all Co Op equipment seized by police, all N.Y. theatres scared to show anything, closing doors to us, thus." This was a matter of concern for the poets as well. They appeared in films associated with the New American Cinema, and John Ashbery, Allen Ginsberg, and Robert Creeley wrote about New American filmmakers in their poems and in affiliated journals, including *Film Culture* (discussed below). Also, writers associated with the Lower East Side scenes were busy defending poetry readings and avant-garde theater productions from similar assaults by city authorities. As a newspaper article at the time explained rather breathlessly:

> The most intriguing sign in town appeared today outside the New Bowery Theater, 4 St. Mark's Pl. It said:
> NO SHOW TONIGHT.
> FLAMING CREATURES SEIZED BY POLICE.
> It replaced a sign reading "TONIGHT FLAMING SURPRISE PROGRAM," which in itself was intriguing enough to attract the attention of police.
> Among the 90 persons who paid $1.25 each to watch last night's screening of "Flaming Creatures," the theater's controversial main attraction, were Detectives Michael O'Toole and Arthur Walsh.
> They sat through the first half of the hour-long movie. Then they stopped the show, claiming it was obscene.
> "It was hot enough to burn up the screen," one of the officers observed. They proceeded to remove the fire hazards, confiscating the film, the projector, the sound track, the screen — everything but the seats, which were bolted down.
> They arrested the ticket seller, the ticket taker, the projectionist and Jonas Mekas, 41, an independent movie producer who is a leader of the avant-garde film wave known as "Underground Cinema." (Meskil)

In her own article on the fracas, Stephanie Bevis Harrington added, "Diane di Prima, an officer of the American Theatre for Poets, Inc., which has a temporary lease on the New Bowery and is presenting New American Cinema films as part of its program, also asked to be arrested. She says, however, that the police told her they already had four people. The audience was dispersed, and the four were taken to the Ninth Precinct house on East 5th Street. . . . They were arraigned shortly before noon the following day on a charge of showing an 'indecent, lewd, and obscene' film and released without bail on the recognizance of their lawyer" (13).

I detail these stories not merely to show how poets and filmmakers hung out with each other, supported each other's work, collaborated, and were even willing to go to jail for each other, but to provide a basis for an assertion that underlies much of the remainder of this book: that, to a surprising extent, film informed the content and form of much of the postwar American poetic avant-garde. Smith's *Flaming Creatures* (1963) and *Normal Love* (1963), for example — with their visual lavishness, cut-and-paste aesthetic, and overtly pansexual ethos — were models for poets, including Ginsberg, of a truly liberated subjectivity free from the strictures of both narrativity and an attendant subordinate position to discourses of power. While it is certainly true that Ginsberg was unabashedly homoerotic in his work well before the advent of the New American Cinema, I would suggest, however tentatively, that the festive aspects of Ginsberg's homoeroticism were consistently compromised by the practically jeremiad-like tones attendant to his Old Testament persona in poems including "Howl" and "Kaddish." Add to this the fact that the core group of Beat poets (Corso, Kerouac, Neal Cassady, Burroughs), no matter what its members' often-fluid sexuality predisposed them to, fulfilled any number of macho stereotypes. As Michael Davidson puts it, "Although Kerouac's milieu contained numerous homosexual males, its social semiotic was based on a heterosexual model of heavy drinking, hard living, fast cars, sports, and sexual excess. The 'boy gang' of which Ginsberg dreamed . . . was distinctly *not* 'society's perfum'd marriage,' yet it was by no means a post-Stonewall sexual revolution either" (*Guys Like Us* 16). Might we look, however carefully, to Jack Smith and his films as *one* of the models for an increasingly sissified and celebratory Ginsberg, a model that in part helped point the way forward for a Ginsberg who finally embraced, as he put it, "The screaming young queen — there's something very ancient and charming about that; great company, total individuality and expressiveness" (Young 321)?

Let us turn, then, to a detailed consideration of some of the major poets and filmmakers associated with the New American communities. Revisiting their body of work will help us reassess and reimagine the sources and motivations behind some of the major texts of the postwar era, as it will illustrate how poets and filmmakers used interdisciplinary collaborations and conversations as a basis for inspiration, philosophical investigations, innovation, and delight.

Obviously, the anecdotes provided so far do not constitute a comprehensive history of the Underground in film and poetry. Indeed, I feel compelled to remind myself that this first chapter is more about providing readers with a *sense* of the exchanges between filmmakers and poets in the 50s and 60s as opposed to a detailed chronicle of the era. I hope this chapter serves as a goad to any cultural historian able to sift through the wealth of materials associated with the many institutions and individuals associated with the New American Cinema scene in particular. The focus of *this* book, however, is to move deeply into readings of specific — and still undervalued and barely analyzed — poems, films, and poem/film collaborations in an effort to recuperate what was once a profoundly significant conversation between film and poetry.

two

The Conversation between Kenneth Anger and Robert Duncan

ROBERT DUNCAN'S MODERNIST SHAME

In sifting through the correspondence between filmmaker Kenneth Anger and poet Robert Duncan, and in reading sections of Duncan's unpublished "Notebooks," we find Duncan referring in various ways to the influence that Anger had on his developing poetics and "spirit." In a notebook entry (April 14, 1954), Duncan wrote:

> The violations of art are ruthless, and Kenneth Anger's film in reaching out to disturb the centers of life has corrupted his actors until thru the decompositions of their individual being enigmatic avatars appear; he has corrupted the motion of the film, ripening it and pushing it on to the inertias of human pleasure. . . . O felix culpa, Augustine cries — And this cry I heard repeated as I lay awake after this film. These images of pleasure having forced themselves thru Anger's art to address my spirit that recoils at pleasure. For all spirit as it has dedicated itself to joy has sought, as it is weak, escape from pleasure and, as it is strong, defeat of pleasure. . . .
>
> Whatever the war of our existence — in living we are at every moment upon a partisan front — of this world or the other, the artist is dedicated finally not to life or to death, not to creation or destruction but to truth. And this is the final authenticity of Anger's art: it has not shied from the true thing which its process reveald [sic].

Here, Duncan grants Anger credit for challenging his resistance to heightened sensuality: "These images of pleasure having forced themselves thru Anger's art to address my spirit that recoils at pleasure." Duncan appears to look to Anger in part for permission to go back to what at this point in time seems like a practically corny, Romantic conceit — the pursuit and enactment of "truth." As Keats, Coleridge, and Blake understood before him, Duncan sees inherent in the moving visual image (be it the magic of absinthe-induced hallucination, a vision, or the process that finds light projected onto the cinema screen) a point of entry into a state of consciousness free from binaries. Interestingly, words including "decompositions" and "corrupted" are used here to describe Anger's actual effect not only on the actors, but also on the material of the film itself. A filmic process that tends to "disturb the centers of life," to corrupt, to violate, all in the name of articulating a nonbinary truth suggests that Duncan saw in Kenneth Anger's work a Keatsian ability to flourish in doubt and decay.

Duncan appears ready here to at least consider a derangement of the senses, one that will lead him in no uncertain terms to the promised land of visionary certainty. It is significant that this entry was written in 1954, a time that found Duncan becoming more involved personally with filmmakers including Anger and Stan Brakhage as he reacted against certain aesthetic practices associated with modernism in favor of a nineteenth-century in-flected romanticism.[1] In his *Stein Imitations* (1953–1955), for example, we find Duncan beginning to link the material practices of film with his use of serial composition in poetry:

> A little movement when I was listening
> begins in the sequence, a stir
>   across words in a sentence
> I am listening to faster than a little
>   movies of still words in sequence
> makes move move I meant in listening (*Writing Writing* 80)

The "sequence"— that is, the part of the poem which is in essence a cellular part of the larger *Stein Imitations* book — is composed here of words that are impelled into presence and movement through the metaphor of the movies. This is no nostalgic look back to the golden era of the silent movie, however. Duncan is "listening" to as well as watching the "movies of still words" move. Here, the archaic orality attendant to traditional understandings of the poem in community are yoked to the wholly contemporary possibilities Duncan finds in film, possibilities that are latent in part in the sequential nature of the filmstrip.

I want to emphasize this word "latent," particularly as Duncan was so committed to an essentially mystical ethos that, as in Kenneth Anger's work, was leavened consistently by an engagement with popular culture. Film in Duncan's eyes was magic, but embedded in that magic were elements of a kind of numinous fun. Note this excerpt from Duncan's "Light Song," in his book *Letters: Poems 1953–1956*:

> The Divine Garbo has appeard in her guise;
> Chaplin Lawrence said was beauty in a man
> > in 'City Lights'
> the silent moving picture speech or
> indistinguishable metropolis murmuring a loud
> > we do not hear
> > > > suggests
> > > the language we long for,
> > > > Hidden. (108)

The word "divine" is packed with referential possibilities. Garbo is divine in the sense of her being a god-like creature appearing magically through light on a screen; she is divine in the 1928 silent film *The Divine Woman*; and, as a gay icon, she is simply divine as that word might be uttered exaggerat-edly, flamboyantly. And, as every sensuous Queen must have her King, so Chaplin appears too, his carnality emphasized through his association with D. H. Lawrence. Note here how even the silent film has within it a practically mystical "speech" ready to be decoded, a speech which an undifferentiated audience or "metropolis" longs for. As Duncan conceived of words as a kind of hieroglyphics (in evidence especially in his extensive use of puns), so film too contains within it a hidden language that can potentially be unlocked by the enchanted poet.

So, while summoning modernity through the figures of Garbo and Chap-lin, Duncan imbues the modern with suggestively spiritual undertones, act-ing in a practically reactionary way to add mystical depth to what he sees on the surface of the screen. Might this be because, parallel to Duncan's increasing interest in cinema in the early to mid-1950s, his readings of Blake informed his developing self-positioning as romantic poet? "Sometime in 1953, the poetess Helen Adam brought Blake's introductory song from *Songs of Experience* as an example of great poetry to a workshop and read it in a sublime and visionary manner, as if what was important was not the ac-complishment of the poem but the wonder of the world of the poem itself, breaking the husk of my modernist pride and shame, my conviction that what mattered was the literary or artistic achievement" (*Fictive Certainties* 30). After discussing Blake in some detail, Duncan added, "I was already a convert to the Romantic spirit, and myth in that spirit is not only a story that expresses the soul but a story that awakens the soul to the real persons of its romance, in which the actual and the spiritual are revealed, one in the other" (ibid. 31). The great conversion narrative described above, unfolding within a year of Duncan's acknowledgment of the effects of Anger's cinema on his writing, is startling in the way in which Duncan almost aggressively works against contingency in favor of highlighting the Romantic vatic role as it elicits actual community, the "story that awakens the soul to the *real persons* of its romance." Getting over his "modernist shame," Duncan begins in the 1950s to write the great poems of what we might call his early Romantic period.

Duncan's friendship with other filmmakers, including James Broughton and Brakhage, suggests that the sexually transgressive and celebratory aspects of New American Cinema—from Willard Maas's *Geography of the Body* to Broughton's *The Pleasure Garden* to Stan Brakhage's *Flesh of Morning* to Jack Smith's *Flaming Creatures*—offered Duncan representations of liberated sexuality which informed his increasingly candid writing. In a 1965 letter to Broughton, Duncan tells Broughton how the "poetic world" of Broughton's films helped Duncan defeat his own "hypercritical censor," a comment that resonates with Duncan's earlier crediting Adam for helping him get over his "modernist shame." As Duncan put it to Broughton, "Your pleasure in my work still means much to me I find. Certainly in writing *Adam's Way* I was often thinking that you wld [sic] enjoy my numerous defeats of my own hypercritical censor, or maybe better than 'defeats' bewilderments. And certain poetic moods and modes of mine must always owe part of their inspiration to your poetic world that was for so long an environment I relisht [sic] in." Duncan's Romantic and erotic modes appear to be based partly on an understanding of film as a potential model. I stress "partly" here, as Duncan of course was open about the vast range of influences that informed his work, and insisted on framing himself as "a derivative poet." The point here is to reveal that film was one—not *the* one—significant part of the field of derivation on which he played.

In his work, Duncan emphasizes the connection between movement and sight as a kind of metaphor for the dance of his own imagination: "The act was dancing, the product of the act was the dance, poetry. In one kind of dancing the hand and the eye danced together. Thus the hand 'saw' the stones and sticks, and the eye 'felt' them" (*Fictive Certainties* 61). The synaesthetic dance is an analogue for the serial nature of much of Duncan's work, culminating in the "Passages" sequence. Duncan considered seriality as linked conceptually to the cinema, particularly in terms of how cinema was materially able to, in Duncan's words, go "on and on." In a letter to James Broughton (fall 1952), Duncan explained, "Before I was always trying to write some great Design instead of going on and on. And what I really love in movies or the stage, my modern sense of it, is just the going on and on. Why we recently have seen over and over Renoir's THE RIVER and Kelly-Donan's SING-ING [sic] IN THE RAIN. Amazing compositions of just anything. Well, THE ADVENTURES OF JIMMY and LOONEY TOM were just that. . . . Because, that is, they suggested 'doing things' to my episodic mind."

The "episodic mind" visible in films as diverse as Broughton's *Loony Tom, the Happy Lover* (1951) and Gene Kelly's *Singin' in the Rain* (1952) offers Duncan a way out of the stasis he believed results from a monumentalizing or totalizing poetics, one in which "a great Design"— that is, a discrete, closed-off entity — freezes out contingency, openness, and a material movement predicated on serial form. Duncan's colleague Jack Spicer appeared to suggest as much when he insisted that "Duncan, [Robin Blaser], and I had a kind of similarity, and what was it? And it occurred to me that it was a serial poem" (which, as Spicer added later), "has to be chronological" (Gizzi 52–53). As Robert Bertholf adds, "For Spicer, [Duncan's] *Medieval Scenes* was the initial spectacle of the dictated poem and of the serial poem — by which he meant nothing as recondite as serial composition in music might lead one to believe, but the episodic appearance of a movies serial" (n.p.). For both Spicer and Duncan, film was one of the crucial models for the "open" poem, one that necessarily presented the text consistently in relation to other texts, always moving forward.

Duncan attests retrospectively that movement, as opposed to the objective, unadorned presentation of a fixed image, determined the development of his poetic: "When I try to remember, before learning to read for myself, first hearing of poetry, what comes immediately to illustrate — it must be set in the pattern of things it comes so readily — is my sitting with my sister, my mother between us, looking at the pictures in a book as my mother reads aloud. . . . There is a poem that goes with that picture on the page. But this is not the poem that comes to mind even as I see the picture. For as I remember that moment, there is another scene superimposed, a double exposure, in which the very plash of a frog jumping into an old pond appears as if from actual life itself" (*Fictive Certainties* 10). Using the language of the experimental cinema —"superimposed," "double exposure"— Duncan defines his initial encounter with poetry as a primarily visual experience, one, however, that is in motion as opposed to fixed in time. "There is a poem that goes with that picture on the page" underscores the way in which Duncan's musings shift into present tense. Memory ("For as I remember") serves as an impetus for action as we find Basho's frog haiku entering the narrative "as if from actual life itself." Movement for Duncan results in a sense of the real that could not be achieved via a static image. Importantly, in Duncan's case such a series of moving visual pictures is evoked more by recollecting writing ("poetry") than by reference to a visual artist's production of discrete images. Duncan appeared to conceive of the link between writing and visual, serial movement as early as 1940. In a letter that year to friend and soon to be renowned film critic Pauline Kael, Duncan insisted, "Painting is as limited in meaning as a single scene in a dream is, but in writing we can give a sense of the movement of images, their constant fluctuations of meaning, and in motion pictures . . . the very birth seed of surrealism seems to grow from the potentialities of the film" (Faas 71).

EXPERIENCING INTEGRALITY: ANGER'S *FIREWORKS*, DUNCAN'S "THE TORSO," AND THE ENACTMENT OF RITUAL

Perhaps the one book that most clearly shows the effects that cinema generally and the New American Cinema specifically had on Duncan's developing Romantic aesthetic is *Bending the Bow*.[2] Indeed, Duncan reenacts and extends the specifically ritual aspects of Anger's film *Fireworks*, creating a kind of cross-genre dialogue between poetry and film predicated on Anger's attempts to achieve what he called "integrality," a state in which binaries are reconciled and ultimately synthesized via a practically ceremonial serial composition. Kenneth Anger insisted, "With my researches in cinema, I am trying to restore the dream to its primal state of reverence. *Fireworks* remains for me a key to existence: it re-presents research toward experiencing integrality" (Hutchison 39). Crucially for Duncan, this "integrality" was represented in Anger's film as a specifically queer cosmos attainable via the yoking of dream time with real time.[3]

The vulnerable homosexual dreamer in *Fireworks* manages, through the magical process of the film narrative, to ritually evoke, benefit from, and transcend his demons, and he ends with a gloriously affirmative vision of homosexual lust and love. Anna Powell reads this ritualistic pattern in the context of Anger's own well-known adherence to the tenets of occultist Aleister Crowley: "On the mundane level, we witness a sado-masochistic, homophobic attack in the Gents lavatory. The underlying theme, however, is Crowleyan in inspiration: an initiate's symbolic death, rebirth and self-realisation. It has been linked by Robert Haller to the ritual of The Building of the Pyramid (*Liber Pyramidos*) in which the candidate undergoes a rigorous self-initiation. The Dreamer (played by Anger himself) seeks Lucifer as well as a light for his cigarette" (Powell 62).

Fireworks, alluded to in Duncan's "The Torso, *Passages* 18" and cited in his "The Earth, *Passages* 19" and "An Illustration, *Passages* 20 (Structures of Rime XXVI)," partly informed Duncan's own overtly ritualistic use of serial movement, queer themes, and symbolism. Interestingly, in January 1954 Duncan admits in his diaries to having some desire for Anger. Detailing his attempt to lure Anger back to his home on Baker Street after a visit to Philip Lamantia's house, Duncan wrote: "There had been, cavalierly, some machination on my part toward Kenneth's coming back to Baker Street and so some wanting, a rift of desire in the excitement — and I knew an over-reaching betrayd [sic]" ("Notebooks"). The combustible mixture of Duncan's early attraction to Anger, alongside Anger's role as a pioneer in depicting homosexual desire through a ceremonial form, appears to have partly influenced Duncan's growing interest in the mechanisms of cinema generally and Anger's film specifically.

I would like to focus on several moments in *Fireworks* to suggest that we can fruitfully read "The Torso, *Passages* 18," perhaps Duncan's most famous overtly homosexual poem, as extending some of the basic themes in Anger's film. The poem precedes Passages 19 and 20, both of which refer directly to *Fireworks*, and given the serial nature of the "Passages" poems, the chronology of "The Torso" invites the reader to detect thematic links between allied texts. Indeed, "The Torso" practically asks to be read in the context of Anger's film. Consider that *Passages* 20, dedicated "for Kenneth Anger," contains the line "From the moaning body of the boy the man he is breaks like a wrathful husband his fiery torso" (*Bending the Bow* 68). The repetition of the word "torso" creates a dialogue with "The Torso, *Passages* 18," encouraging the reader to make the connection between what is overtly ceded "for Kenneth Anger" in Passages 20 and what is less obviously evoked in "The Torso." I would also add that the poem preceding "The Torso" is titled "Moving the Moving Image, *Passages* 17." The title's overt nod to film, coupled with that poem's use of themes and images that resonate with Anger's *Fireworks* (its combining the daemonic with the Christian in the phrase "Kore and Christmas," for example, and its celebration of the Sun — associated strongly as it is in Anger's cosmology with Lucifer), suggests that *Fireworks* informs "The Torso" to no small degree.

One of the final and most memorable images in *Fireworks* features the dreamer balancing a Christmas tree on his head. A burning candle is attached to the tip of the tree. The tree/candle is then pointed into a fireplace and used to set photographs of the protagonist in a sailor's arms aflame. The film concludes with a shot of the pictures burning in the fireplace and a pan to the bed, where the protagonist is lying next to his male lover, whose face appears to be ablaze due to Anger's having scratched lines onto the surface of the film. "Scratches over the filmed images hide [the lover's] face from us. The pan continues to the plaster hand, now repaired so that all its fingers are whole. The hand falls into the water, where the torch had been quenched in the first shot. 'The End' appears in superimposition over the water" (Sitney, *Visionary Film* 87). The plaster hand, which at the beginning of the film was shown to have broken fingers, is now restored. The ritual is complete "as the initiate's virile power is restored" (Powell 64).

Anger's use of a Christmas tree is symbolically rich, given the events depicted in the film. Christmas is generally understood to be a Christianization of pagan ritual, one that specifically uses an evergreen to symbolize fertility. According to Phillip V. Snyder, "Prehistoric man would regularly take in green boughs or full evergreen trees at the winter solstice for use in magical rites intended to insure the protection of his home and the return of vegetation to the otherwise brown and dead forest. As Christianity supplanted older, pagan religions, the decorating of evergreens continued in various parts of northern Europe on many special occasions, including Easter and Midsummer's Day. The Maypole is known to have begun as an evergreen tree and originally bore many of the same decorations that were used on the first Christmas trees" (12). In light of the practically unprecedented filmic evocation of homosexuality in *Fireworks*, Anger uses the pagan elements inherent in the Christmas tree to refer ironically to fertility (the restoration of "virile power").

Anger himself put it rather archly in 1966, "This flick is all I have to say about being seventeen, the United States Navy, American Christmas, and the Fourth of July" ("Program Notes"). Beyond Anger's use of the Christmas tree to associate homosexuality with fertility and power, it is important to recognize that Anger is humorously critiquing "American Christmas" itself by self-consciously realigning the holiday to its pagan origins. As Sir James Frazer shows in *The Golden Bough* (1922) (a book that Anger and Duncan read dutifully),[4] the origin of Christmas can be traced back to Christian ecclesiastical authorities' attempts to ban the "Nativity of the Sun" festival celebrated by the pre-Christian Mithraic cult: "It was a custom of the heathen to celebrate on the same twenty-fifth of December the birthday of the

Sun, at which they kindled lights in token of festivity. . . . Thus it appears that the Christian Church chose to celebrate the birthday of its Founder on the twenty-fifth of December in order to transfer the devotion of the heathen from the Sun to him who was called the Son of Righteousness" (416–17). Considering that *Fireworks* ends with the lover's face ablaze, as if he were the manifestation of the Sun God himself (discussed in more detail below), it is not farfetched to conclude that the film works in part as a reclamation of the heathen elements of Christmas. We should note that Duncan, even in his most casual correspondence, echoed Anger's conflation of Christ with the Sun God. In a holiday letter to Robert Creeley, Duncan wrote, "And to your family our as ever benedictions for Christ's (the Sun's) birthday all round." Duncan and Anger evoke Christmas primarily to remind their audience that the origins of the holiday lie in a dissident, pagan cosmology.

As *Fireworks* uses the pagan Christmas tree in an overtly phallic manner and combines the pagan aspects of the tree with the ritualistic cleansing force of fire, so Duncan begins his poem "The Torso" with

> Most beautiful!   the red-flowering eucalyptus
>   the madrone, the yew (63)

What can we make of the trees mentioned here?[5] Significantly, the eucalyptus, madrone, and yew are all evergreens. The fact that the "red-flowering eucalyptus" is "most beautiful" is especially compelling. Eucalyptus leaves are often used to make Christmas wreaths — this nod toward Christmas becomes especially interesting when we consider that eucalypts are renowned for their ability to regenerate quickly after fire. The finale of Anger's ritual in *Fireworks* that ends with "the initiate's virile power . . . restored" thanks to the cleansing force of fire is, in Duncan's overtly homoerotic poem, echoed in the beginning of "The Torso" with the introduction of the eucalypt, itself a symbol of regeneration and resistance.

The eucalyptus has a particularly personal resonance for Duncan as well in terms of its role in the pagan harvest festival Lammas (also known by its Gaelic name, Lughnasa). Lisa Jarnot points out in her forthcoming biography of Duncan:

> In Celtic tradition, August 1 marks the Lammas Tide, a celebration of the first harvest of the autumn. It was a date that fascinated Robert Duncan. . . . It had been on August 1, 1919 that Fayetta Philip told her sister Minnehaha Symmes [Duncan's adoptive mother] of the conversation that had transpired in the Philip & Philip pharmacy on that day [a conversation about Duncan's

birth-mother's death during labor, and Duncan's availability for adoption]. The following day the Symmeses made arrangements to see the Duncan child for the first time, and on August 4, six-month-old Edward Howe Duncan was placed in the custody of Minnehaha and Edwin Symmes.

Given that Lammas was significant for Duncan, we should note that eucalyptus is used as a "correspondence" during Lammas celebrations — for example, eucalyptus oil is applied ritually to the body or eucalyptus is burned on the Lammas altar. During Lammas festivities, it is also customary for bonfires to be set and for "fire magick" to be practiced. As there is a natural link between harvest festivals and fertility generally, it is not surprising to learn that Lammas is commonly associated with unbridled sexuality. Festivals in Wales, the Isle of Man, and Ireland found young people celebrating Lammas by enjoying "sexuality in the open air" (Monaghan 296–97). The links in Lammas between fire, renewal, and liberated sexuality that are evoked through Duncan's use of the word "eucalyptus" are all the more striking when viewed in the overall context of Duncan's references to Anger's *Fireworks* — itself a ritual marked in part by fire and the ceremonial/sexualized use of the pagan evergreen.

Lughnasa is named after the Celtic Sun God, Lugh. "He is sometimes described as a solar divinity because of the *brightness of his face*" and is described as "a god of arts and crafts." Lugh was known generally as a "fertility god" and as a "harvest god" (ibid. 297). He was also associated with fire, light, and metallurgy, and he was the protector and defender of the weak and ill. Lughnasa assemblies connected Lugh with a whole host of pagan figures: "About the first of August in very old times a gathering took place on the hill and fruit and flowers were strewn round the 'stricken' at the hilltop. In the evening a bonfire was lit and young people danced on a flat near the top. 'Fry-chawns,' flowers and fruit were left for the unseen residents in the hill, i.e., Donn-Fírine and his host as well as leprechauns and fairies" (MacNeill 205). Anger was versed in such occult and pagan mythology even at the age of seventeen (when he directed and produced *Fireworks*). "It's about the angel-demon of light and beauty named Lucifer," Anger explained, "And it's about the solar deity. The Christian ethos has turned Lucifer into Satan. But I show it in the Gnostic and pagan sense. . . . Lucifer is the Rebel Angel behind what's happening in the world today. His message is that the Key of Joy is disobedience" (qtd. in Sitney, *Visionary Film* 113). Anger designed the sailor whose head emanates light at the end of the film to represent a host of alternative gods including Lucifer (whom Anger repeatedly referred to as his

Kenneth Anger and sailor, from *Fireworks*. Courtesy of Anthology Film Archives.

"Angel of Light") and Lugh himself. When we illustrate how Duncan's "The Torso" alludes to Anger's film and to the Lughnasa festival, the interdisciplinary conversation between text and film becomes rich and complex.

The second stanza of "The Torso," *"So thou wouldst smile, and take me in thine arms / The sight of London to my exiled eyes / Is as Elysium to a new-come soul"* (*Bending the Bow* 63), is an almost direct quote from Christopher Marlowe's *Edward the Second*. Given the homoeroticism that drives *Fireworks*, one might suggest tentatively that such an image is used here by Duncan to evoke one of the more famous still images reproduced from *Fireworks* of Anger being carried tenderly in the arms of a sailor with just the barest hint of a maternal smile. While such an image of a submissive male being taken up in the arms of a stronger figure is a homoerotic chestnut evident in any number of American poems from Whitman and Crane through O'Hara and beyond, and while Duncan would in no way wish to limit the field of associations such an image might invoke, the fact of "The Torso" succeeding and preceding poems that take up themes specific to Anger's *Fireworks* invites us to read this stanza alongside Anger's screen.

The ritual aspects of "The Torso" are introduced in succeeding stanzas as the speaker promises rhapsodically, "If he be Truth / I would dwell in the illusion of him" (ibid. 64). Using sexuality for antinomian ends, Duncan here echoes Christian prayer in a remarkably transgressive way. The "He" here is not the Truth of the Son but the truth of a nascent and promisingly illuminating same-sex love. Duncan writes in subsequent lines, "His hands unlocking from chambers of my male body / such an idea in man's image / rising tides that sweep me towards him / . . . *homosexual?*" (ibid.) As *Fireworks* performs what Carel Rowe described as a "reverse transubstantiation" "turning essence into substance,"[6] so Duncan appears to use the ritual of the sacrament to sacralize homosexual love and lust. Here, the speaker is not made in the image of God but in the image of another man. "He" represents sexual love of man *for* man, "*homosexual.*"

Subsequent lines make much of orality, the passing of the higher power into the mouth of the supplicant, though, as in Anger's *Fireworks*, this is a reverse Eucharist that finds both Lord and host benefiting from the oral exchange: "and at the treasure of his mouth / pour forth my soul / his soul commingling" (ibid.). The body of the man becomes the vessel through which the speaker will attain a Paradise of distinctly earthly delights: "I thought a Being more than vast, His body leading / into Paradise, his eyes / quickening a fire in me, a trembling // hieroglyph" (ibid.). Duncan here insists resolutely on the body as an inscribed surface rich with meaning, what Cary Nelson describes as "a signifying field or a sacred text constituted by an alternative, celebratory naming" (134). Following stanzas then decode the hieroglyph: "*the nipples*, for the breasts are like sleeping fountains of feeling in man"; "*the navel*, for in the pit of his stomach the chord from / which first he was fed has its temple"; "*the pubic hair*, for the torso is the stem in which the man flowers forth and leads to the stamen of flesh in which his seed rises"; and so on (ibid.).

As the young dreamer in *Fireworks* achieved virility and strength only after plumbing the depths (and I use "plumbing" here as a pun, considering that the dreamer was beaten by a gang of sailors in a men's toilet), so the speaker in "The Torso" acknowledges of his object of desire that "He has brought me into heights and depths my heart / would fear without him" (ibid.). The poem suggests that to be loved necessarily requires one to be initially scourged. In subsequent lines the lover's look "pierces my side" with (significantly in light of this reading) practically demonic "*fire eyes*" (ibid.; emphasis added).[7] Continuing to challenge binaries and echoing Anger's reassessment and redefinition of the Prince of Darkness as Angel of Light, Duncan grants a voice to his lover who, we discover, is a practically Miltonic Lucifer-like figure:

> I have been waiting for you, he said:
> I know what you desire
>
> you do not yet know   but through me.
>
> And I am with you everywhere.   In your falling
>
> I have fallen from a high place.   I have raised myself
>
> from darkness in your   rising (ibid.)

In this potentially eerie section of the poem, Duncan appears to align homo-sexuality with magic — the act of sexual love between men results in a kind of resurrection ("rising") of the lover with "fire eyes" that leads to self-knowledge of both lover and loved. Subsequent lines add weight to this interpretation. The lover with fire eyes promises, "wherever you are / my hand in your hand seeking the locks, the keys / I am there. Gathering me, you gather / your Self" (64–65). The lover in "The Torso" and the sailor/lover/Lugh in *Fireworks* are both invoked through a ritualized narrative centered on a consecrated erec-tion: "I have raised myself / from darkness in your rising." Communion with the daemon lover results not in damnation but in a resolutely queer salvation marked by "integrality": "I am with you everywhere."

In light of all the echoes of *Fireworks* in "The Torso" (and given that Dun-can is about to begin Passages 19 and make the first overt reference to the film), it is tempting to read the final two lines of "The Torso" as analogous to the film's final moments. Again, near the end of Anger's work we see the young dreamer lying in bed next to the sailor whose face is emanating magi-cal sparks. In the final two lines of "The Torso," we find a corresponding image in the assertion, "For my Other is not a woman but a man" followed by the petition, borrowed from Marlowe, *"the King upon whose bosom let me lie"* (65). Significantly, as Hewett points out, this quotation is a misread-ing of Marlowe's text. "Here, startlingly, even Marlowe's 'The king, upon whose bosom let me *die*' is revised or misread for Duncan to create his own specific mystical king and visionary masculinity" (542). The appearance of the "mystical king" in Duncan's poem complements the ending of Anger's film, as both the speaker in "The Torso" and the Dreamer in *Fireworks* lie next to their invoked Other. Anger's God of Light and Duncan's "King" are raised "from darkness" to achieve Oneness with the initiate speakers — as Duncan puts it, "Gathering me, you gather / your Self." In both poem and film, this ritual is enacted primarily through the transformative sacrament of homosexual sex.

JETS OF BLOOD, MILK, AND RAIN: *FIREWORKS* IN
ROBERT DUNCAN'S "PASSAGES 19"

Duncan's poem "The Earth, *Passages* 19" is the first instance in *Bending the Bow* where Anger's images are directly invoked. Duncan names the ritualistic bodily fluids so crucial to Anger's film: "the jets of blood, milk, and rain / commingling / in the moving picture / [Fireworks, Kenneth Anger, 1947]" (67; brackets in original). The liquids correspond to a scene in *Fireworks* where the dreamer is attacked by a group of sailors. "From above we see fingers shoved into the dreamer's nostrils, and blood shoots out of his nose and mouth. A sailor twists his arm, and he screams hysterically. A bottle of cream is smashed on the floor. With a broken piece a cut is made in his chest. . . . Cream poured from above flows over it into his mouth. Cream washes his bloody face; then it flows down his chest" (Sitney, *Visionary Film* 87).

Interestingly, the opening lines of the poem strain against their boundary on the page:

Incidents of me   the eye sees

a leaf among many leaves   turning upon the stream, the screen,

the words upon the page   flow away into   no hold I have

What did it say? (66)

Duncan's use of the phrase "the screen" invites the reader to engage in a dialogue with the cinema. The disjunction achieved through the use of enjambment and typographical spacing suggest each word cluster is conceived of as a single frame, the movement of which the speaker of the poem wishes to release from the page to the unbounded atmosphere. Although a self-reflexive formal statement, "the words upon the page flow away into no hold I have" speaks the language of film as much as it does the language of poetry. Unlike the "words upon the page," the moving image, projected onto "the screen," is very much animate due to its nature as moving, living light. Considering that the printed word is materially chained onto the page, it appears that Duncan in these lines wants to liberate text so that it moves or "flows," ideally turning it onto "the screen." There is a kind of freedom that film has materially in terms of its autonomy — "no hold I have," writes Duncan, as if to remind us that what is recorded on the surface of celluloid is in a sense liberated when projected. (Duncan's appreciation for the material autonomy of the filmic image should not be underemphasized. In a fall 1952 letter to James Broughton, Duncan isolates "the achievement" of films as predicated precisely on their freedom from becoming objects, unlike, say, the printed

word or sculpted artwork: "The achievement of the movies is exactly that
they are works of art without being objects; we cannot own them, yet once
seen in a way they own us.")

After alluding to film in the first three lines of the poem, Duncan asks,
"What did it say?" Duncan then quotes a section of Jacob Boehme's *Aurora*:

> (A PASSAGE)   Kraftgänge
> ... for the stars have their kingdom in the veins of the body which are cunning
> passages (and the sun has designd the arteries) where they drive forth the form,
> shape and condition of man

This quotation is designed to blend into the *Passages* series as a whole, not
merely because it is literally in Passages 19 but because it corresponds to
Duncan's agenda of replacing binary models with a more fully integrated
vision. The excerpt from Boehme's *Aurora* works towards conflation and
coherence — the veins of the human body are linked formally to the stars,
the holy is in evidence in the carnal. As a passage linked to other passages,
Duncan's "Passages 19," assisted in part by Boehme's *Aurora*, fits in thematically with the series through its evocation of what Kenneth Anger referred
to as "integrality."

Notebook entries of December 1964 show Duncan was reading *Aurora* at
the same time as he was composing Passages 19 and 20:

> 3/112: Nor is this my *natural will*, that I could do it by my own small ability, for
> if the spirit were withdrawn from me, then I could neither know nor under-
> stand *my own writings*.
> 4/37. For when the powers spring up in God they *touch* and stir one another,
> and move one in another, and so there is a constant harmony, *mixing* or con-
> cert, from whence go forth all manner of colors.
> 4/55. (Lucifer) by his proud elevation in his kingdom, *kindled* the qualities or
> the divine Salitter out of which he was made and set it on fire.
> 7/8. Whose depth we cannot sound or reach with our sense, *all* this place or room
> together was one kingdom, and *Lucifer* was king therein. ("Notebooks")

Note that Duncan isolates passages in Boehme's work that address the subject of Lucifer — we should recall that Duncan made a fairly uncharacteristic
reference to Lucifer in his introduction to *Bending the Bow*: "Lucifer 'falling'
is the circumference or boundary of the need for Creation" (viii). In Hegel's
understanding of Boehme's work, Lucifer plays a crucial role in man's understanding of self: "The 'other' of God is thus the image of God. . . . This is the
connection of the devil with God, namely other-Being and then Being-for-

self or Being-for-one, in such a way that the other is for one; and this is the origin of evil in God and out of God" (Hegel). Duncan and Anger composed ritual pieces that functioned as methods to call up "the evil in God and out of God." Such ritual invocations result ideally in a new order that challenges or even seeks to harmonize the distinctions between gazer and gazed, dream and reality, good and evil. Rejecting Cartesianism in an effort to experience "integrality," as Anger sought to do in his films and Duncan in his poetry, is a positive development in that such a rejection leads to reconciliation and communion between conventionally established binaries.

After Duncan's quotation of Boehme, the poem continues with a reference to a section of Hesiod's *Works and Days* that describes a "golden race of mortal people, who existed at the time of Cronus, when he was *basileus* in heaven. They lived like gods with woe-free spirit, apart from and without toils and grief; wretched old age did not hang over them, but unchanged in feet and hands, they delighted in festivities beyond all evils" (Hesiod 67). In Duncan's telling, the "golden race" is characterized as follows:

They live in a place apart from men,

    at the ends of the earth

along the shores of the deep roaring Ocean   their campfires

    their circles of great stones   their gold crowns of hair

        untoucht by sorrow

                having no guilt
                (*Bending the Bow* 66)

Duncan provides the reader here with a markedly homosocial, if not overtly homosexual, lyric. The figures around the "campfires" are engaged in a kind of male bonding that suggests acts of resistance — "untoucht by sorrow / having no guilt." Such resistance is then heightened by Duncan's queering move when Duncan adds:

    For those who love us   must be heavy with sorrow

   We ourselves can know no good apart
        from the good of all men (ibid.)

Metaphorically speaking, the gift of homosexual union and same-sex love ("no good apart / from the good of all men") is here akin to the gift of fire, in that it brings with it both joy and "sorrow."

In light of the fact that Duncan refers directly to Anger's *Fireworks* in this poem, it is certainly possible that informed readers are invited to consider the above stanzas in light of *Fireworks*. After all, "They," like the "Angel of Light" at the end of *Fireworks* whose head is emitting sparks, have "gold crowns of hair." Duncan continues to establish connections between poem and film after his citation of Anger's *Fireworks* ("the jets of blood, milk, and rain / commingling / in the moving picture / [*Fireworks*, Kenneth Anger, 1947]") by providing the reader with a reading list ("*Aurora*, Jacob Boehme; Hesiod, *Works and Days*; / *Rewards and Fairies*, Rudyard Kipling"). The reference to Kipling is particularly telling. *Rewards and Fairies* begins with the story of two children, Dan and Una, meeting Puck "*alias* Robin Goodfellow, *alias* Nick o' Lincoln, *alias* Lob-lie-by-the-Fire, the last survivor in England of those whom mortals call Fairies" (xiii). Duncan echoes Kipling by introducing "Puck":

"I said to my Mother in the morning, 'I go away to find a thing for my people, but I do not know whether I shall return in my own shape.' She answered. . . . "

"True," Puck said. "The Old Ones themselves cannot change men's mothers even if they would." (*Bending the Bow* 67)

Again, *Fireworks* specifically and Anger's films generally can inform our understanding of this particular section of the poem. In the context of a series of poems that in part provides an insurrectionary model of homosexuality, the very reference to Kipling's *Rewards and Fairies* is rich with double meaning. Literally speaking, both Anger and Duncan believed in the existence of fairies. Anger himself was keen to return to — or reinvigorate — a self-consciously Romantic agenda that aimed aggressively to overturn hegemonic ideologies imposed on him in the name of reason, and he found in the purported existence of fairies a model wholly apart from rational discourse. In a letter to Duncan and Jess written during the height of the Vietnam War, Anger wrote, "I've been reading Blake too, Robert; this has been a summer for returning to sources. Have spent a cantie day climbing the heathered correi and have found one of the fairies lairs beyond bank, bush and scare. Even to our sight the images advance." With absolutely no irony intended, Anger establishes his belief in fairies as he locates Blake's visionary poetics as a "source" for his own aesthetic.

Duncan appears to share Anger's fascination with the possibilities fairies offer him in terms of conceiving of alternatively gendered subjects. The gender-ambiguous "I" quoted above acknowledges that his/her body might very well transform into another shape after his/her quest, and, thanks to the reference to Kipling's book, we sense that such a metamorphosis would occur as a result of a mischievous fairy's spell. Duncan then shifts to the next stanza with a quotation from Puck, adhering to the theme of metamorphosis when Puck affirms, "The Old Ones themselves cannot change men's mothers even if they would" (ibid.).

The figure of Puck was crucial to Kenneth Anger's own self-fashioning. Anger included images of and allusions to Puck throughout his work—he named his company Puck Productions, embossed his personal correspondence with an illustration of Puck, and so on. Indeed, a Puck-like figure features prominently over the fireplace in *Fireworks*. Puck helps Anger and Duncan to create gender trouble of all kinds. As Robert Haller explains:

> Transfiguration and transformation are themes, working materials, that Anger has continued to explore in all of the years following his departure from Beverly Hills. . . . One of Crowley's central maxims was "Do what thou wilt shall be the whole of the law." For Anger, too, this is a primary premise. We can see evidence of this in his adoption of Puck in his film logo. Puck is described as "the name of a fancied, mischievous or tricksy goblin or sprite, called also Robin Goodfellow and Hobgoblin." Puck is also a figure in the Reinhardt-Dieterle *A Midsummer Night's Dream*, and a rebellious trickster who can additionally be associated with Lucifer, another classic figure Anger has embraced (classic in the canon of John Milton and *Paradise Lost*, not the Christian sense) (*Kenneth Anger* n.p.).

Haller's reference to "transfiguration and transformation" is particularly important. Metamorphoses are consistently presented as liberatory in Duncan and Anger's work—the transformation of the lovers at the end of "The Torso," the sailor become Angel of Light or Lugh in *Fireworks*. Puck, a popular character in English folklore variously described as faerie, goblin, devil, or imp, was a shape-shifter. "Puck travels to England from Athens and back in a few minutes" and is able to turn "himself into a Will o' the Wisp, a horse, a headless bear, a roasted crab-apple, a three-legged stool" (Briggs 45). Given this typology, Duncan's use of Puck in "Passages 19" is designed to usher in representations of troublemaking as it simultaneously refers the knowledgeable reader to Kenneth Anger's oeuvre. Throughout the Passages series as a whole, Duncan consistently inserts references to "rebels" like Puck in order to situate the poems as transgressive, order-defying texts.

PASSAGES 20: FOR KENNETH ANGER

And what of "An Illustration, *Passages* 20 (Structure of Rime XXVI)," dedicated "*for* Kenneth Anger?" In the "Notes" section ending *Bending the Bow*, Duncan refers to the poem as "*An Illustration*, Structure of Rime XXVI, Passages 20: Maeterlinck, *The Blue Bird*. The poem illustrates a collage by Jess now in the collection of Kenneth Anger" (68). However, we can see that Anger's *Fireworks* itself forms one of the sources for the imagery found in the poem. In the first prose stanza alone, for example, we are introduced to the by-now-familiar burning Christmas tree "in whose branches our lives are continually kindled," along with the substances "Fire, Water, Bread and Milk."

The stanza contains other subtle references to film. The final phrase, "and the Children set out with Fire, Water, Bread and Milk — animated Things — on a progress thru the stories of the house they live in" works to emphasize movement and visuality in the poem (68). As with the titular phrase "*AN ILLUSTRATION*," " — animated Things — " highlights the visual aspects of the text. "Animated" is often used in relationship to film (i.e., the animated cartoon). More importantly, "animated" reflects back on the process of serial composition in poetry, particularly as Duncan practices it here. When we consider that an animated cartoon or film is made by photographing a series of images in order to give the illusion of movement, the conversation between poem and film is all the more apparent. Duncan, working against his "modernist shame," does not seek to juxtapose static images for the Poundian purpose of encapsulating an "intellectual and emotional complex in an instant of time" (Pound "'A Retrospect'"). Rather, Duncan seeks to animate the static image, to make it move within a serial sequence that spools from poem to poem, book to book.

As I mentioned earlier, we are almost immediately introduced to the Christmas tree, and accordingly our attention is drawn outside the poem to the texts preceding it as well as to *Fireworks* itself. This connection is established further when we consider the significance of "Tyltyl," mentioned in the first line of the poem. Tyltyl is a character in Maurice Maeterlinck's play, *The Blue Bird* (1919), which tells the story of Tyltyl and his sister Mytyl, who, after falling asleep following a disappointing Christmas (significantly, given Anger's focus on "American Christmas") have a dream in which a fairy sends them on a quest to find "the bird that is blue." Importantly for the purposes of our reading, in 1940 Maeterlinck's play was adapted for the screen by director Walter Lang. Featuring Shirley Temple, the film version was widely understood to be Twentieth Century Fox's response to MGM's *The Wizard of Oz* (1939). (References to the Oz books, if not the film, abound throughout the Duncan/Anger correspondence). Shirley Temple features prominently in Anger's mythology, and it is widely known that Temple was Anger's dancing partner when they were both children. "As a preteen from an upper-middle-class home, [Anger] was sent to an exclusive cotillion club, where his foxtrot partner was Shirley Temple. Curly Shirley, then 10 or 11, was already over the hill and, for Anger's money, as scintillating as a hard-boiled egg: 'She was not' he said, 'my most unforgettable experience'" (Calende 113). Given that *The Blue Bird* contained elements echoed in *Fireworks* (i.e., Christmas, a quest narrative occurring in the context of a dream, metamorphoses, fairies, and so on), we find that Duncan's reference here is a rather camp in-joke designed, as he acknowledges in his dedication, for Kenneth Anger. Once again, the languages of cinema, myth, poetry, and historical friendship interact in a highly complex fashion, one that is, however, not devoid of an almost lighthearted humor.

In the second prose stanza, we find Duncan conflating *Fireworks* with *The Blue Bird* as he continues to cause gender trouble:

> From the boy's slight form the bride goes up to the closed
> room to open the one door she was forbidden to open. She turns
> the essential key of the story she seeks. In the gloom of the red
> chamber she spies upon the hanging corpses of life after life.
> From the moaning body of the boy the man he is breaks like a
> wrathful husband his fiery torso. (*Bending the Bow* 68)

Duncan appears to be paraphrasing the moment early on in *Fireworks* where the Dreamer gets up from his bed and opens the magic door marked "GENTS," a door that, informed by our reading of "Passages 20," is perhaps meant to evoke all the magic doors typical of children's stories from *Alice in Wonderland* through the Narnia series. Additionally, while a cursory reading might suggest Duncan is granting both the male and female genders distinct presence in the poem, Duncan here blurs the boundaries between prose, poetry, and film as he complicates any essentialist reading of gender. The "bride," after all, "goes up" "*from* the boy's slight form." There are a number of ways that we can read this. The bride may, most prosaically, simply have gotten up after resting against the "boy's slight form." However, the ambiguous syntax suggests the bride actually emanates from the boy, that female is combined with male.

That Duncan dedicates this poem for Kenneth Anger helps us consider the

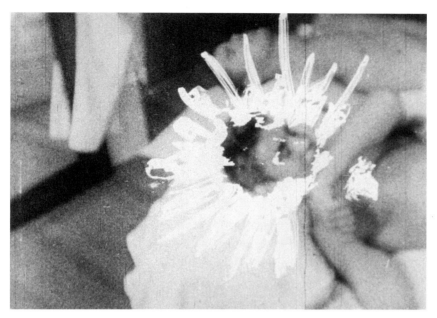

"This is the Lucifer brother, you see, the Unknown Angel side," from *Fireworks*.
Courtesy of Anthology Film Archives.

"bride" in light of *Fireworks*. After all, the Dreamer's role as he is carried in the arms of his heroic savior can certainly be interpreted to represent an iconic "lady in distress." Other relatively clear references to *Fireworks* in "Passages 20" include the evocation of the restoration ritual via the "body of the boy" breaking into "the man he is"; the phrase "his fiery torso," which reverberates with "Passages 18 (The Torso)"; and phrases in succeeding stanzas, including "The fire in the hearth," "Death by fire," and "Fireblast and flood."

Unlike his literary predecessors Pound and Eliot, Duncan's use of formal techniques including seriality, pastiche, pronominal shifts, and disjunction was not in the retrospective service of mourning the rupture of a coherent tradition. Rather, as we see in exploring the conversation between Duncan's films and Anger's *Fireworks*, Duncan believed his work could be in the service of progress, not bereavement. And unlike contemporary avant-gardists, Duncan wished to integrate opposites as opposed to playfully foregrounding the materiality of the signifier. As I've argued throughout this chapter, Duncan had Kenneth Anger's *Fireworks* as a model for such a project. Regarding the overall trajectory of the Magick Lantern series, Anger explained, "The last shot in 'Fireworks' is me in bed, and there is another boy in bed but his face is all bursting with white flames or light. This is the Lucifer brother, you see, the Unknown Angel side. In my own drama as an artist, I am always looking for him, that angel side, you know, the Lost Angel side. And it came out then, of course, much more clearly, in the 'Invocation of My Demon Brother,' only here it's the Dark One. And now, in 'Lucifer Rising,' I am trying to find the angel again, the Angel of Light" (qtd. in Mekas, "Movie Journal," May 17, 1973). Anger uses his cycle to achieve "integrality"; to summon forth the Angel of Light; to reconcile Good with Evil. Duncan was involved in much the same undertaking. Duncan used the *Passages* series in an effort to effect, if not successfully or finally, something we can call transcendence. Duncan, like Anger, was "always looking," and the *Passages* series appears to be his way of carrying out that search.

three

The Conversation between
Stan Brakhage and Robert Creeley

Gangulay: Looking back over 40 years of filmmaking,
    what matters most now?
Brakhage: That I believe in song.
("Stan Brakhage: Correspondences" 114)

THAT I BELIEVE IN SONG: STAN BRAKHAGE AND THE POETS

Perhaps no filmmaker was quite as invested in the conversation between film and poetry as Stan Brakhage. Brakhage found in the poetic avant-gardes a radical reassessment of the functions and possibilities of language — one that resisted narrativity as it emphasized instantism, materiality, and a practically physiological understanding of language's relationship to the body. For a filmmaker who famously distrusted language,[1] going so far as to wonder, "How many colors are there in a field of grass to the crawling baby unaware of 'Green'?" (*Essential Brakhage* 12), poetry was the only language art able to expand the boundaries of consciousness and the senses: "Poetry is enabled to make new grounds for interpretive sense precisely because at scratch it eschews any such usage as currently common sense of the language, opts rather for right brain's neuron song . . . rummaging the left hemisphere for only that language which will suffice rhythmically/texturally in orchestral support of the song schema" ("Stan Brakhage: Correspondences" 59). The poetic line itself, conceived of as sung utterance rather than page-bound text, was an analogue to the projected light of film: "But film and poetry relate rather closely for this reason: poetry is dependent upon a language that is in the air" ("Poetry and Film" 219).

As R. Bruce Elder and others show, the writings of Stein, H.D., Williams, and Pound were especially important to Brakhage's development:

> The sense that the self dies and is reborn continually is the deepest implication of Pound's paratactical forms—as it is of Stein's use of repetition with difference. It is also the deepest implication of . . . Brakhage's "perpetually regenerating structures." Such a self has neither a past nor a future, however. Hence, the time of the continually altering self is the continuous "now". The continuous "now" is also the time of the body, for the body knows only pulsations, movement, and energy, and nothing of the continuities of mental life. The push to provoke this sense of time is the deepest connection between paratactical forms of poetry and the concern with the body that is so evident in the works of Stein, Pound, and Brakhage. (68)

When Brakhage moved to San Francisco in the early 1950s, his interests in the work of modernist predecessors including Stein and Pound grew as his social connections to the contemporary poetic communities circulating around him became established. "Well, there was also a poet that saved me a lot of time. And how I came to meet this man is just a long story that I don't think maybe it's worth telling but it's one of those mysterious stories where I happened to meet very shortly, after I moved to San Francisco, Robert Duncan. And then as it happened after I came back to San Francisco, after a summer in Colorado, I had no place to live and they were looking for someone, that is, Robert and his life-long companion Jess, the painter, were looking for someone to help take care of their house, and sweep and do dishes and things like that and they offered me a basement room in exchange for these services, so I had this plus I got supper always, which was really a very good deal on my side" (qtd. in Varela 4). It was at Duncan and Jess's home that Brakhage was introduced both to a wider world of poetry and a scene that connected filmmakers with poets: "[In] the evenings Robert would come home and hold forth on poetry himself or related subjects for oh, sometimes all through supper and for hours afterwards, or, as was often the case, he would invite people over so that I was enabled to meet Louis Zukofsky, at a very young age . . . Kenneth Anger, incidentally. . . . Through Duncan I also met Michael McClure, who strangely was a contemporary of mine, he's about my age . . . but I had never gotten to know him or his friends Bruce Conner, or Bob Branaman, two other filmmakers that again came through Duncan and McClure. . . . And of those poets that I've been privileged to know, certainly Charles Olson would be the main inspiration,

I'd like to hope, and absolutely an influence, upon all my life; and Duncan, and Creeley, McClure, Zukofsky" (qtd. in Varela 4–5).

Other people associated with the group included Ruth Witt-Diamant, director of the Poetry Center at San Francisco State University, who was a close friend of filmmaker Sidney Peterson. The poet Helen Adam (one of the few women included in Donald Allen's 1960 anthology, *The New American Poetry*) was also an associate of Duncan's, godmother of James Broughton's son, and was herself a filmmaker, producing a rarely seen work entitled *Daydream of Darkness* (1963).[2] Filmmakers Kenneth Anger and Jordan Belson, poets and artists including Wallace Berman, Michael McClure, and Philip Lamantia, composers including Harry Partch were a rich community indeed for the young Brakhage to draw inspiration from and document through his own filmmaking, as we see in some of Brakhage's early films, including *In Between* (1955), which featured Jess, Duncan, "and the three household cats Pumpkin, Princess, and Kit Kat" (Jarnot).

Brakhage's reminisces of legendary filmmaker Christopher Maclaine are a window into a time when film was wholly entwined with the burgeoning literary scenes that were to become a part of what we now know as the Beat Generation and San Francisco Renaissance:

> Maclaine . . . sang and read poetry in the bars. He read poetry with jazz when that became popular toward the end of the Beat movement in the late 1950s. He always thought of himself as a poet. . . . The two men most often considered as the exponents of "Beat" were Allen Ginsberg and Jack Kerouac. Ginsberg had been to San Francisco and had written the great Beat poem "Howl." Jack Kerouac finally produced the great prose statements of the Beat generation with *The Subterraneans*, *The Dharma Bums*, and *On The Road*. But this was all long after the fact. With Maclaine, we are going back to the source of the Beats; he was the filmmaker who chronicled the movement as it happened and created a center of one of the aspects of the Beat myth seven or eight years before the grand epic of "Beat" became nationally known with Ginsberg and Kerouac. (*Film at Wit's End* 116–17)

Maclaine's place as a San Francisco filmmaker engaged with both poetry and film proved inspirational to Brakhage. Maclaine's rarely screened but highly influential films, including the apocalyptic *The End* (1953), *The Man Who Invented Gold* (1957), *Beat* (1958), and *Scotch Hop* (1959) combine traceable narrative psychodrama with gestures of total abstraction that anticipate Brakhage's direct scratching and painting on film. The films are tied intimately to the poetry scene in San Francisco, both overtly through voice-over (as we find in *The End*, where a voice intones, "All his life John had wanted to be a poet. Then one day it had come to him that he had nothing to offer poetry. . . . He turned into entertainer, clown, and he was brilliant at first") and through visual and verbal cues that point indirectly to the San Francisco community. Maclaine's *The Man Who Invented Gold*, for example, works practically as a satire of the mystical elements in the poetry community, complete with a Robert Duncan/Kenneth Anger–type character who learns the secret of alchemy and is repeatedly mocked by hipster caricatures.

For a budding filmmaker and failed poet such as Brakhage, San Francisco generally, and his place in the Duncan household particularly, proved useful in forging real aesthetic links between the two genres. Regarding his early relationship with Duncan, Brakhage recalled: "For one thing, I assumed I was a poet from the age of nine years old and that's all I ever wanted to be. . . . And when I made films, it was a poet making films, in the tradition of Jean Cocteau, and/or others. But then I gradually, painfully, came to learn through the association of these great poets like Robert Duncan, *et al* that I was not a poet. And so they taught me that I was not what I supposed I was, right in the midst of my deep loving of what they were and were able to make. Because I've always cared for poetry more than any other art" (Johnson 48). Responding to a question about whether poetry "worked its way into [Brakhage's] sense of rhythm as [he] structured images," Brakhage responded, "Unquestionably. I started where everyone else did with, you know, narrative drama. But then very quickly poetry became the guiding light" (ibid.). Though it is true that Brakhage (like Maclaine's "John") came to realize "that he had nothing to offer poetry," he continued to look toward poetry and poetics as a source for his own developing practice.

Duncan's insistent link of poetry and film must have proved inspirational. In Duncan's *H.D. Book*, for example, we find the poet framing literary inheritance as a kind of hermetic transmission passed down through the ages and — most importantly given our focus on Brakhage — repeatedly discussing modernist poetics after imagism within the context of the "moving picture": "H.D. did not stand alone but her work, like that of Pound and Williams belonged to a nucleus of the poetics in which I had my own beginnings. . . . After a handful of imagist poems, the poets were interested in movement. The sequence of images is what tells in the *Cantos* of Pound, and, scene juxtaposed to scene, line juxtaposed to line, the poem is built up like an Eisenstein film in the cutting room. In the passing of image into image, person into person, in H.D.'s War Trilogy too we are reminded of the transitions and montage that developed in the moving picture."

LANGUAGE IS A DAMNATION

By the mid-1960s Brakhage had repudiated "his epic ambitions after he had made *Dog Star Man* (which, of course, itself established him as a major artist of the epic form), and [accepted] his status as a lyric poet" (Elder 72).[3] *Dog Star Man* (1961–1964), which "portrays a solitary individual who, pitted against the forces of nature, struggles to reach the mountain top" (Elder 144–45), gives way to a series of films that reject such epic reach in favor of more discrete "home movies" documenting, albeit in a radically disorienting manner, friends' visits, childbirth, lovemaking, and highly subjective representations of what Brakhage terms "hypnagogic visions," the patterns of light and color we see when our eyes are closed.

The impulse behind such serial work was based on Brakhage's effort to rid his art of the elements of closure implicit in narrative or what Brakhage more prosaically called "story." As Brakhage wrote in a letter to poet Ronald Johnson, "I once said that story, like melody, was unavoidable in a continuity art; but my making since then has been especially devoted to the obliteration, or at least avoidance, of story. I suppose that in this sense I'm an artist a bit like Anton Webern who composed music which seems (at his best) to turn on itself, like a mobile, and resist ALL sense of 'continuity'" ("Stan Brakhage: Correspondences" 29). Rejecting narrative was not merely an aesthetic refusal of resolution, but a wholly political intervention into what Brakhage understood to be the hegemonically determined and latently violent discourse implicit in and disseminated by "narrative drama": "Narrative drama, as a form that's unchanged since the Greek, is a trap that's loaded people with the dice that makes it very possible that the Third World War will be in Jerusalem and all the apocalyptic visions of drama will be fulfilled. People will move to try to fulfill those prophecies if we don't move to get out of the three-act play" (ibid. 36). For Brakhage, only poetry offered a way of rejuvenating language in the face of the horror: "Except for poets, I think language is a damnation of human sensibility and in the blind mouths of politicians is destroying us all" (ibid. 33).

Brakhage's hostility to "story" was not employed in the service of an art that problematizes referential stability or breaks with "tradition" per se. Much of Brakhage's work through later projects, including *The Dante Quar-*

tet (1987) (a film that aims to evoke the stages of the *Commedia*, and which is composed of layers of paint and scratches over old stock) and *The Dark Tower* (1999) (a painted film that Brakhage describes as "an homage to all the dark towers in literary history"[4]), self-consciously extends early Renaissance and Romantic themes. And, despite some of his comments to the contrary, narrative of a sort had a place in his aesthetic — in a 2002 interview with Bruce Kawin, Brakhage described *The Dante Quartet* as "a story. Those are four stages that are crucial in a little narrative that I think is crucial to comprehend, to feel that film all the way through" ("The Dark Tower"). Overt links to a privileged literary tradition went hand in hand with Brakhage's repeated positioning of his work within realist frameworks. Brakhage aimed to expand the visual language and possibilities of what we might call realism, a realism that could reflect, however abstractly, the process of a mind thinking, synapses crackling, the colors and forms that we see when our eyes are tightly closed. "And so in that sense, all of what other people would call my abstract films, which as you know I don't regard as abstract at all, are the most concrete pieces of my making, because they come most directly from my synapses and my thinking" ("Stan Brakhage: Correspondences" 33).

Clearly, Brakhage's intention agitates against academic conceptions of what constitutes abstraction, textuality, anti-referentiality, and endlessly disseminating meanings. Brakhage appears instead to be committed to a subjectively determined "greater realism," one that emanates (as Brakhage would have it) organically from the artists' own thought processes, movements, breath, and so on. Ken Kelman's discussion of Brakhage's *Anticipation of the Night* (1958) is pertinent to what we are talking about here. "The emphasis with Brakhage is . . . toward the 'expressionistic,' the use of time to suggest, to investigate uncommon experience, the unknown" (234). Kelman later proposes that Brakhage identifies filmmaking with his own physical body: "Sustained insistence on identification of camera lens with film-maker's eye, camera movement as film-maker's gesture, camera as film-maker incarnate, rather than recording instrument, is found as early as Brakhage's *Desistfilm* . . . Brakhage's technique at all times is that of the artist vehemently imposing his feelings, his presence upon the material, in the most direct, indeed violent way" (275).

It is at this juncture that we sense Brakhage's commitment to so much of the physiological, essentially neo-Romantic discourse attributed to the New American Poetry. Examples abound: Olson's insistence that "the line comes (I swear it) from the breath, from the breathing of the man who writes, at the moment that he writes, and thus is, it is here that, the daily work, the WORK, gets in, for only he, the man who writes, can declare, at every moment, the line its metric and its ending" (19); Allen Ginsberg's "mind is shapely, art is shapely" ("Notes Written" 231); Jack Kerouac's "sketching language is undisturbed flow from the mind of personal secret idea-words, blowing (as per jazz musician) on subject of image" ("Essentials of Spontaneous Prose"); and Robert Creeley's discussion of Whitman's poetics as a "process" that "permits the material ('myself' in the world) to extend until literal death intercedes" ("Three Films" 70). Like the poets to whom he was so committed, Brakhage posits disruptive formal techniques as practically organic extensions and representations of his self "in the world."

I would like to focus now on the conversation between Brakhage and Robert Creeley. I am isolating Creeley for a variety of reasons. In terms of the physiological impulse behind Brakhage's fragmented forms, we find a corollary in Creeley's well-known practice of radical enjambment evident in practically all of his work, which is employed in part to mirror Creeley's own performed hesitations, near stutters, and emotive qualifications. As an example, note the slightly anxious, nervous tone tinged with rueful bitterness engendered not just through content but by the line breaks in Creeley's early poem "Like They Say" (here quoted in its entirety), included in his collection *For Love*:

> Underneath the tree on some
> soft grass I sat, I
>
> watched two happy
> woodpeckers be dis-
>
> turbed by my presence. And
> why not, I thought to
>
> myself, why
> not. (50)

As we are informed by available recordings of Creeley's readings, these line breaks are composed not to point away from or problemize the site of their authorship — that is, Creeley himself — but to reflect more closely the way the historical Creeley enunciated his lines during performance. Creeley's disorienting practices hover uneasily if productively between expressive subjectivity on the one hand and a more dialogic disruptive textuality on the other. As Charles Bernstein pointed out in a conversation with Creeley, hearing Creeley's line breaks points to an "anguish" that underlies much of the content in the poetry: "Reading [your poetry] on the page it seems a very formal way of breaking apart the syntax, and at the same time when one hears you read something else happens. There's an emotional valence . . . there's a kind of existential quality, a temporal quality, moving from moment to moment, almost in anguish at times in the way the words break" (Creeley, "Conversation" 6).[5]

I want to highlight Bernstein's use of the term "existential quality," particularly in terms of our conversation about Brakhage's work. As I've already pointed out, what looks like a foregrounding of disjunctive formalism in the films is consistently, even aggressively, positioned by Brakhage as a kind of extreme realism. Such "realism" is employed to document Brakhage's vatical subjective eye, one that promises to enact insight not only into the "nature" of his domestic life but into a state of consciousness that is practically prelinguistic. Such a stance perhaps suggests one major reason why Brakhage's work lost a measure of its favor following the emergence of identity politics on the American Left alongside the linguistic turn in the academy. As J. Hoberman has pointed out, "Both political and aesthetic left-wingers regard [Brakhage] with hostility. However radical his film practice or inventive his film language, Brakhage's work can be seen as romantic, obscurantist, and patriarchal. . . . The fact, I think, is that for Brakhage all of his work is representational. The flow of images corresponds to the stream of his consciousness. Even such nonillusionistic devices as scratching or painting the film are meant to represent hypnagogic states (or what he calls 'closed eye vision')" ("Duplicitously Ours" 45–46).[6]

Given Brakhage's repeated insistence that he is "not abstract," I want to revisit what looks like Creeley's increasingly denatured line (in evidence in a line like "woodpeckers be dis-" and, most exceptionally, in his book *Pieces* [1969]) in order to determine how Creeley was influenced in part by film practice generally and Brakhage's work specifically. Taking a look at Creeley's work in this context will, I hope, reveal a persistent if consistently knotty subjectivity informing Creeley's most disorienting work, a subjectivity moreover characterized by suggestively spiritual concerns. I acknowledge that choosing Creeley as my focus may seem somewhat arbitrary, considering the fact that Brakhage was in close contact with poets including Allen Ginsberg, Robert Kelly, Ronald Johnson, and Michael McClure. That said, the social and aesthetic exchanges between Creeley and Brakhage, and what looks undoubtedly like Creeley's enduring legacy as a major American poet of the postwar era, plays a large part in my motivation here. I certainly hope that my analysis of Creeley's and Brakhage's work offers fresh perspectives on Creeley's poems.

Perhaps more importantly, I hope that this study serves as a step toward a wider consideration of the rich, complex, and fascinating exchanges between Brakhage and poets affiliated with the New American Poetry.

ALMOST CONTINUALLY WITH BOTH BOB AND BOBBY

By the spring of 1962, Brakhage was becoming close to Creeley and his family. In a letter to James Broughton (April 25, 1962), Brakhage expresses his own affection for the Creeleys as he provides us with a picture of the poet engaged with the work of the New American Cinema generally:

> Well, since then we've been almost continually with both Bob and Bobby Creely [sic] and never more quickly were four people so deeply friends. Both of them have great love for you, James, and were thrilled at the picture of you in the ruins — and all of us have been spending some of the time talking of your greatness as well as playing with the magic toys you sent — and then, as to the rest . . . well, you'll understand immediately (out of your "When you have lived out and resolved your personal and *familial* struggles") the magic of Creeley coming into my life at this time. When telling him of your recording I suddenly thought to call Western Cine; and all this morning we were there, myself sitting in the room and he reading so very directly to me out of his understanding of the child-birth film and "Wedlock House: An Intercourse," recording the greater parts of "For Love" to make the 4th in the series of records.

The "child-birth film" Brakhage mentions refers either to *Window Water Baby Moving* (1959) or *Thigh Line Lyre Triangular* (1961), both of which document his wife Jane Brakhage in labor and giving birth. *Wedlock House* (1959) depicts Stan and Jane variously having sex, smoking, and gesturing in a way that suggests deep conflict between the two protagonists. These films are, despite their subject matter, in no way narrative representations of the Brakhages' lives. Rather, adherence to chronological time is rejected in favor of a far more subjective, impressionistic style that simultaneously foregrounds its own status as film. *Window Water Baby Moving*, for example, "begins with images of late pregnancy. The first shots are of a window, framed diagonally, intercut with flashes of blackness. Throughout the film Brakhage uses black and white leader to affirm the screen and the cinematic illusion as one of several tactics for relieving the dramatic tension built up as the moment of birth approaches" (Sitney, *Visionary Film*, 169). The film continues in a fairly splintered fashion, intercutting representational forms with pure blackness, flashing back, and so on, and ending "with shots of the parents and the baby spaced amid flashes of white leader following the rhythmic pattern at the film's opening" (ibid.).

That Creeley is recording his own *For Love* in between discussing Brakhage's films provides us with an early moment where the two artists turn the correspondences between their respective genres into a social event. Poems in *For Love* repeatedly approach the most extreme and intimate aspects of being in a relationship — yet do so in ways that are often disorienting and concerned more with generating mood than with telling a story. As Brakhage's *A Wedlock House* evokes an argument between the filmmaker and his wife through images shot in negative, wildly tilted camera angles and the like (rather than laying out the causes, effects, and resolution of the fight), so Creeley provides the reader with a series of poems that use disorienting effects independent of linearity to suggest not all is well in the house of Creeley. Note, for example, "Goodbye," included in *For Love*:

GOODBYE
She stood at the window. There was
a sound, a light.
She stood at the window. A face.

Was it that she was looking for,
he thought. Was it that
she was looking for. He said,

turn from it, turn
from it. The pain is
not unpainful. Turn from it.

The act of her anger, of
the anger she felt then,
not turning to him. (63)

I cite this poem not to propose that Creeley and Brakhage had already influenced each other formally at this point. Rather, I want to suggest that by the early 1960s both Brakhage and Creeley had begun to recognize shared formal techniques between their respective genres. The hesitant repetitions and fissures in Creeley's lines had their visual correspondence in Brakhage's practice.[7]

Social and aesthetic interaction between the two artists became so strong so quickly that Brakhage started borrowing Creeley's oft-used phrase "etcetera" in writing to the poet, as we see in this letter dated May 25, 1962: "Never in *my* life anything like our friendship, and Jane reflectively starry-eyed also. . . . Oh, I'd give a great deal to be talking to you right now, all of us sitting around the round table or across each other making angled conversation over the kitchen table, etcetera." Creeley returned the compliment. As Robert Duncan reveals in a letter (June 14, 1962) to Brakhage: "Creeley's recent letters have been filld [sic] too with how rewarding your visit there was for them. 'I've never really been close to anyone before working with film,' [Creeley wrote] 'and have not in fact seen much of anything either—but I was very struck by what he does and had happily chance to see a good deal of it. Selfishly, it helps me very much with problems of "continuity" in the novel [*The Island*].'" Influence didn't stop at *The Island*, of course: Creeley became a vocal supporter of Brakhage's work as he linked Brakhage's serial practice to his own development as a writer of poetry. In his essay "Three Films," Creeley discussed (among other works) Brakhage's *Anticipation of the Night* (1958):

> As you see this film, you might think too of its title—although far better to put such preoccupations out of your mind. They are appropriately left to the occasion of afterthoughts in this case. But the film is, nonetheless, a particular experience of "history" and of "western history" in particular . . . You will certainly see many things that you'll recognize very simply. Colors, surely—forms, movements, even places and things. You'll be interested, I hope, by the *pace* of their interaction and by their divers contents more singularly. In short, you'll be seeing a specific rhythm of visual activity which is itself an obviously definite information. Much as in the case of poetry, these rhythms and the pace thus defined will have a very significant role. (127)

Creeley advises us to forget about the film's manifestly ominous title in order to focus more clearly and single-mindedly on how lyrical elements ("a specific rhythm") combine with film ("visual activity"). As with poetry, it is the cadences (rhythm) of film that generate the material from which we gain information and pleasure. To be burdened by the title (particularly as *Anticipation* ends with a shadow-image of the protagonist hanging from a noose) is to *reduce* what's actually happening on the screen in favor of containing Brakhage's radical practice within the context of a story featuring a tortured soul who ends his days with suicide. Significantly, Creeley continues in this essay to discuss Robert Duncan's analysis of "all the ways in which *rhyme* might occur in poetry," advising his readers, "Again you might consider how visual instances of rhyming are used here" (ibid. 127–28). Film is organized rhythm and rhyme; it is poetry.

Why might Creeley counsel us this way, only to then go on and insist that *Anticipation* "nonetheless" deals with a specific aspect of history — namely, that it tells a "story"? I suspect that Creeley resists our using the title as a framing device for the film so that we might develop new eyes and ears, as it were. Creeley's commitment to *melos* as a sense-making proposition independent of transparent signifying practices is extended to his appreciation of Brakhage's film, where the story implicit in the title *Anticipation of the Night* recedes in favor of experiencing the film as a series of rhythmic and visual gestures, or "visual instances of rhyming," as he put it. Visual information becomes song and is simultaneously liberated from its slavish role as illustrator of story. "If the usual situation of literary narrative is then imposed on the activity of film, expectably the visual activity becomes a support of the story otherwise the case — as in a play or usual movie. Brakhage tells a story without exception, but my point is that it is a story of visual information, not of literary details" (ibid. 127). Brakhage himself was tremendously excited by Creeley's foregrounding of "visual activity" over and above the narrativity of the earlier films. In a letter dated July 2, 1978, Brakhage details his response to a recording of a lecture that was to result eventually in the essay "Three Films": "Your history of the divestature (is that a word?) of Narrative, along a path of 'Desistfilm' thru 'Anticipation,' spooning 'em first off that clear plate of road-signs, is itSELF a whole intact and absolute thesis of inestimable value; and the introduction of Duncan's rhyme ways in correlation to 'instances of rhyming' in film gives me MORE significant parallel (to other art) for attention than Music even has afforded — a great break-thru in my thot [sic] (on how to speak, at least) in this matter. . . . You've counterbalanced ALL the shit I've taken from other poets on the SUBject of Film all these years (a kind of magic necessity in that sense too)."

THE ASSHOLE OF STRUCTURAL AESTHETICS

The serial form of Brakhage's films was particularly important to Creeley. "Film, as poetry, as the language arts more generally, is a serial art. One thing 'comes after' another: words, images" ("Three Films" 124). We can envision Creeley recognizing the potential relationship between the serial poetry typical of his contemporaries (Duncan's "Passages" sequence, McClure's *Ghost Tantras*, Spicer's "Letters to Lorca," and Olson's *Maximus* come to mind) and Brakhage's work. The borders distinguishing so many of Brakhage's films tend to blur via devices including visual rhymes, thematic repetition, rhythmic consistency, and the like. As there is no conceptual "end" in the serial works of poetry that we associate with the New American writers, there is no end to Brakhage's commitment to highlighting the procedural nature of making a film in the service of a fixed series of themes centered on the primal experiences of birth, sex, love, death, and the nature of seeing. Creeley argued that "the factual, physical situation of a film is . . . to be insisted upon. I know that Brakhage likes to remind us that a 'moving picture' is a sequence of rapidly changing single, static images. If presently we are flooded with preoccupations of this kind, seeming — I am thinking of the didactic, actually self-dramatic, insistence on process and its physical occasion — do recall that Brakhage is revealing the *means* of the film (much as Méliès asked Pathé to do), not the *ends* possible, which he has also so brilliantly shown us (ibid. 125). Foregrounding "means" does not obviate using film in the service of recollection, soliciting emotion, and the like, as we see in *Anticipation of the Night*; in that film, after all, we are able to detect a very real, tortured protagonist preparing for his own death even as that character is constructed through highly discontinuous and disorienting filmic strategies that emphasize their own *film-ness*, their own "means," to use Creeley's word.

Given Creeley's implicitly critical comment on artists who foreground procedural technique as an end in itself ("the didactic, actually self-dramatic, insistence on process and its physical occasion") it is important to note that Creeley's and Brakhage's own commitment to displaying the materiality or "means" of the given form they were working in should not be taken to suggest they were participating in a structuralist aesthetic independent of what they perceived to be their own lived experience.[8] Brakhage in particular was careful to separate his work from the increasingly popular structural film of artists like Michael Snow, Ernie Gehr, Paul Sharits, and Joyce Wieland, whose work was gaining increasing attention in the late 1960s (around the time of the publication of Creeley's *Words* [1967] and *Pieces*) and who were ultimately to achieve a measure of institutional security (if not Hollywood stardom by any means) by the 1970s. In a letter to Creeley dated December 1, 1977, we find Brakhage has had enough of film for film's sake, or, as Gene Youngblood put it in his discussion of Michael Snow's film *Wavelength* (1967), in which "there is no dependence on an idea or source of motivation outside the work itself" (ibid. 126):

> I finally walked straight into the dragon's mouth of Millennium Film Workshop in N.Y.C [sic] and had at it, opening my statement with: "After all this struggle, finally Film has Achieved an ACADEMISM [sic], that very thing

which tortured all my poet friends nearly to death when we were young."
Annette Michelson screamed back at me from the audience, as did many
others. You'd have thought I lanced a boil, the pus did so begin to flow . . .
the SILENCE, the A.M.A. type colleague-protecting non-criticism all these
teacher film-makers harbor for each other is stifling thought and THAT the
entrenched teaching of Structural Film is precluding recognition of the VARI-
ETIES of film-making going on, trying to go on. . . . I've yet to come to Buffalo
to deliver this babe; and Buffalo is, surely, the asshole of Structural aesthetics.
Strange that this ideology of a film being primarily about its self being existing
and come-into-existence, or vice-versa, is most rooted in the two cities with
(in the first case literally) the least sunlight in the nation: Binghamton & Buffalo . . . under ironic banner of S.U.N.Y.

The "ideology" of a wholly autotelic film, rejected so strongly by Brakhage
in favor of maintaining film as not merely a form for "self-expression"
but as a manifestation and enactment of self and symbol, resonated with
Creeley. Practices that worked against narrativity and highlighted film as
film — scratches in the celluloid, leader, and the like — were seen by Creeley
as particularly suited for what we might tentatively call visionary insight:

> Not so very long ago it was characteristic to associate film with dramatic or
> with narrative art. We *saw* the images, so to speak, but we tended to place
> them as a story, a continuity necessarily involved with a message that either a
> novel or a play might otherwise convey. Something flashing, or stuttering in
> a myriad of colors, might alter our attention, but it was at best, we thought,
> an effect used in support of the actual purpose: to get on with the story itself.
> . . . In contrast to this presumption, a film by Stan Brakhage wants to push us
> out, to force us, in fact, to **see** as the activity of light itself permits us to. One
> mutual friend may object that he is "ruining our eyes" but I would emphasize
> that it is in the defense of those eyes, and their possibility, that his work takes
> on its most real and singular character. Therefore I interrupt myself and these
> notes to look again at a beautifully simple and precise instance, *Mothlight*.
> What do I see?
>
> > *pulsing —*
> >   *kinetic — flicker*
> > *tones brown, green*
> >   *details of (moth) wing, other parts —*
> > *occurring between light source — and*
> >   *the light now on the wall —*

scale — as detail of "size"
the presence (present-s as he would say)
of what occurs in the light.

And I find myself seeing the "blank" film
at the end as particularized now — dust bits,
scratches, something in the light. ("Mehr Licht" 22)

Note the language Creeley uses in describing Brakhage's work: "in the defense of those eyes," "their possibility," "most real." This is the kind of language that artists and writers affiliated with surrealism and abstract expressionism had used earlier in defense of what an uncomprehending audience considered to be, respectively, inchoate and radical juxtaposition and pure abstraction. Bizarre dream imagery, a razor slitting an eyeball, drips of paint covering the surface of a canvas were not simply highlighting, exaggerating, or foregrounding the materiality of form, nor were such strategies employed primarily to reassess and revise the relationship between art, artist, and audience. Rather, these were expressive gestures signifying spiritual and subconscious depth so that the audience could, to co-opt Creeley's words, get a sense of life at its "most real."

And what of *Mothlight* (1963), which Creeley writes a kind of impromptu poem about? *Mothlight* was "a film made without camera. It was accomplished by pasting between strips of mylar tape a line of moth wings and bits of plants that was then run through an optical printer. The result is a fluttering light collage that Brakhage likes to say is 'what a moth might see from birth to death if black were white'" (Renan 122). *Mothlight* manifests the fundamental possibilities of film in minimalist fashion — photography isn't even used, let alone paint, sound, actors, and so on. And yet we find Brakhage insisting yet again in situating this film not within a structuralist context, but within a recognizably neo-Romantic visionary mode wherein the enchanted maker can imagine and ultimately insinuate himself into the life cycle of a moth dreamed in negative. As Brakhage explained to Robert Kelly in a letter (June 19, 1963), "I am putting moth's wings, minute plants, leaf transparencies, flowers, etc. between strips of scotch tape, which is sprocketed, to be used directly as original film. The search is wondrous (in a way that makes me think of 'necromancy,' 'alchemy') and the form is developing beautifully." Such faith in the innate magic of projected images appears to have rubbed off on Creeley, particularly when we find him asserting *Mothlight* is significant in part for the way it invokes "*the presence (present-s as he would say).*" Instantaneity leads to the visionary, "*something in the light.*"

"Tones brown, green / details of (moth) wing, other parts —," from Stan Brakhage's *Mothlight*. Courtesy of the Estate of Stan Brakhage and Fred Camper.

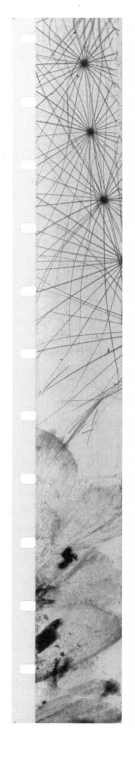

Let us not overstate the case, however. Clearly, Creeley's and Brakhage's poetics lend themselves to interpretation via structuralist and poststructuralist paradigms, and Creeley has written, "I know that [Brakhage] has also deep concern with 'what things mean' and with basic human relationship—but light, in all its modality, as 'seeing sees it' is much more to my own mind his insistent preoccupation" ("Mehr Licht" 22–23). Additionally, as Mary Nesthus points out, "Brakhage was grappling with what he sensed were the changing requirements of the time, and intuiting that Creeley, within his recent work [in *Pieces*], had done the same. He sensed a diminishment of the Creeley persona, a greater directness within the work" (143). That said, for Brakhage and Creeley, procedural and serial techniques do in fact have a center grounded in the quotidian world of the author and, by extension, in a kind of visionary tradition. As Creeley put it when describing Brakhage's *Songs* sequence, "The *center* of what we were seeing was the very possibility of sight itself. We saw the light" ("Mehr Licht" 23; emphasis added).

BRAKHAGE AND CREELEY IN *PIECES*

Outside of Creeley's collaborations with visual artists, *Pieces* is his most visually arresting work. Even the table of contents is striking, filled as it is with a blend of capitalized and noncapitalized titles, em-dashes, quotation marks, and italicized words that serve collectively to position the text on the page as a practically sparkling, shimmering visual event. Following the table of contents, a quote from Allen Ginsberg's poem "Song" serves as the book's epigraph: "yes, yes / that's what / I wanted, / I always wanted, / I always wanted, / to return / to the body / where I was born." Before the book even officially begins, then, we find Creeley framing the visually disruptive text in the table of contents through Ginsberg's own mystical confession. The book proper extends the optic elements so far discussed. Individual poems, and stanzas within single poems, are demarcated with three-period or single-period ellipses respectively; capital letters jump out at us; prose passages visually alter and disrupt the stanzaic patterns of Creeley's lyrics. The ellipses are particularly evocative of the space between film frames, both in terms of how they work to demarcate space between stanzas and in terms of highlighting the material fact that *Pieces* is a work composed out of discrete fragments that run together to evoke a whole. The visually engaging nature of the book works hand in hand with content to suggest a book-length work aching to escape its place on the page — to be, as Brakhage would have it, "in the air" like the light streaming out of the projector.

Creeley would come to emphasize the intertwined nature of film and poetry. "Writing is not, finally, some limited situation of dogmatic intentions," Creeley insisted, adding, "You must remember that film-making also wants to play, pun, echo, mistake, start over" ("Three Films" 123). Such an assertion helps us understand *Pieces* in part as an attempt to synthesize the genres of film and poetry, both because the book itself is an ongoing, constantly interrupting, reiterative, qualifying, and manifestly playful work, and because, as I have discussed, it appeals so insistently to our eyes. Indeed, repeated references to cinema add to our understanding of the book's latent desire to become multisensory spectacle, as the following selection suggests:

> It began, it
> ended — was
> forward, backward,
>
> slow, fast, a
> sun shone, clouds,
> high in the air I was
>
> for awhile with others,
> then came down
> on the ground again.
>
> No moon. A room in
> a hotel — to begin again.
> . . .
> The which it
> was, form
> seen — there
> here, re-
> peated for /
> as / — There
> is a "parallel."
>
> .
>
> When and/or if, as, — however, you do "speak" to people,
> i.e., as condition of the circumstance (as Latin: "what's
> around") a/n "im(in)pression." "I'll" *crush* you to "death"—
> "flying home."
>   . (54)

"It began, it / ended — was / forward, backward" embodies a plaintive melancholy engendered in great part by the awkwardly broken enjambed lines. Retrospectively considering the film projector's ability not just to begin a story/film and end it, but to manipulate time as it is represented in film through the mechanisms of the rewind, the fast-forward, variable speeds (slow, fast) and so on, Creeley summons the projector to underscore ironically the limitations of his own craft. Unlike film, words cannot flicker, visually go backwards and forwards, transport the audience through the vagaries of time in a space that is temporarily if artificially marked by its independence from linearity. The page is not a screen, the book is no film theater — indeed, the act of reading emphasizes our own time-bound trajectory as we work our way from left to right, letter to letter, word through word, whereas the space of the film theater and the mechanisms of cinema work their magic *on* us. Cinema can swoop us up to the "clouds, / high in the air" where we experience this giddy freedom in company "with others." And yet, given that the evocation of film is taking place on the page, Creeley yanks the reader away from a rewinding, fast-forwarding movement toward transcendence to focus once more on the self, "down on the ground again." With this rueful acknowledgment of the self alone in space and time, we find existential pathos allegorized through the removal of light — "No moon." In the dark now, the speaker finds himself alone in a "room in / a hotel."

And yet, given that this poem is a part of an ongoing serial piece, the liveliness inherent in the constantly unfolding and expanding echo chamber of a series project is not to be forsaken. The speaker allows he will "begin / again" and graphically marks the shift through the frame-like insertion of triple-period ellipses. What follows, however, resists the "story" intimated by the preceding stanza. What we get instead is a wholly disorienting series of words and phrases — any sense of syntactical order is disturbed by the violent insertion of backslashes, broken-up words ("re / peated"), and especially disruptive line breaks.

Nevertheless, "There / is a 'parallel,'" as Creeley insists at the end of this seven-line cyclone, redirecting our attention to the preceding poem and its relatively clear-cut depiction of a solitary subject in a hotel room. How is there a "parallel" between the two texts? Is Creeley inviting us to consider that our experience in and through language simultaneously points us toward coherence, some semblance of subjectivity, as it undermines that very coherence by virtue of language's basic arbitrariness? I ask this question particularly because the third poem on the page continues in the disorienting, article- and conjunction-heavy vein ("When and / or if, as,") only to then break suddenly into sense ("—however, you do 'speak' to people"). Lived experience is like this, Creeley seems to suggest. Even as we insist on organizing our lives by telling our stories, living in relation to others, speaking to people, we recognize the chaos—the slippages, the dreams, the miscommunications, the visions, all the unexpected turbulence attendant to daily experience—that parallels such stabilizing actions.

TWO: CREELEY / MCCLURE

The aesthetic that links formal disruption to the near-narrative order evident in *Pieces* has a corollary in any number of Brakhage films from the mid-to-late 1960s, particularly the series of films Brakhage titled *15 Song Traits*, which were filmed intermittently from 1964 through 1969. Guy Davenport describes them: "Inspired by books of poetry, meant to be returned to, shown to friends, commented on (their silence invites talk), collected, they are definitely home movies—in a double sense: Brakhage frequently enlists the preoccupations of the amateur photographer, taking as prime source (like Picasso, like Bonnard) the utterly familiar; and the Songs are not meant to brave the public, who have just left TV and are out to have their sensibilities soothed rather than wakened" (10). In these films we typically find relatively straightforward representation interspersed with disorienting visual effects. One of the most successful *Songs* is entitled *Two: Creeley / McClure* (1965). The film "is a portrait of two poet friends (and in reduced-to-8mm form is part of *15 Song Traits*). The McClure segment consists entirely of single frame shots" (Renan 123).

What we see initially during the title sequence of *Two: Creeley / McClure* is typical overall of Brakhage's attempts to present his images as essentially organic. The word "Two" appears in Brakhage's characteristic signature. We then see the word "Creeley" dissolving slowly into the word "McClure" —these names shimmer and waver nervously, pointing to the way we'll encounter the poets as flickering images and reflecting their practically physiological poetics. (As Michael McClure put it in his statement on poetics in *The New American Poetry*, "the emotions push me to discoveries that afterwards I recognize intellectively to be truths. Glimpses of my physiology" [423]). Creeley first appears in a series of superimpositions. He walks towards a chair, and there is a slow dissolve followed by a series of overlapping images featuring Creeley dissolving into Creeley dissolving into Creeley. The sense of the film's rhythm is created in great part through the superimpositions, by switching between negative stock and positive stock, and by going in and out of focus in sequence. Manifesting Brakhage's investment in Stein's cubist poetics, we see Creeley shown both in his entirety and in parts — hands, shoes, ear, mouth, torso, sitting and ruminating with a cigarette. At points during the film, Brakhage uses chemical flares as rhythmic accents between a series of superimpositions that switch back and forth between positive and negative. We see Creeley clasping his hands just before the camera swings to focus on his head. Creeley rubs his forehead, again in negative and positive, followed by a cut that finds Creeley sitting in the corner of a room in the twilight — a moment that alludes to the neurotic melancholy embodied in so many of the poet's lines. As the film reaches its end, the camera moves away from its close-up on the poet. There's a flicker effect of Creeley on the chair, followed by more superimpositions that show Creeley laughing. The film ends with a series of close-ups on Creeley as the pace of Brakhage's editing quickens.

Creeley / McClure was made in Placitas, New Mexico, when Brakhage and his wife, Jane Collum, went to visit the Creeleys. Having filmed McClure in San Francisco just before leaving the city,[9] Brakhage ended up filming Creeley in order to create a kind of diptych. It's worth quoting Brakhage at some length describing the process of making *Two: Creeley / McClure*:

I know "TWO: CREELEY / MCCLURE" is a film and I wish to make a world which is built out of what has passed thru my experience of those two fine men. And to approach each of them with all that I have of my experience of each of them. In both cases it happened to involve much more time spent reading their poetry than sitting around talking with them. I know it's me reading poetry — it isn't a great books compendium survey of how people read Michael McClure or Robert Creeley, it's my reading of them that's informed my life. Who else I can speak for. And that shapes the rhythm of which these films are compounded; along with, and in a dance with each of them moves, which in many ways is contradictory, the poetry rhythms actually on the page, unless you look closer. . . . In relationship to Creeley . . . well, he's a man who didn't come to full sentences until he was 11 or 12 years old, and he stumbles into speech with great hesitancy and enormous power and fantastic delicacy. He's New Englandish; shy, he's incredibly shy. Bob seems like one of those people born old — an old soul you could say. And I saw him that way. Also he commands a kind of attention where the eyes can become saturated, so engaged and reaching out to help him to come to speech that you get a reverse action. I'm sure all of you are aware if you watch a light bulb that actually at

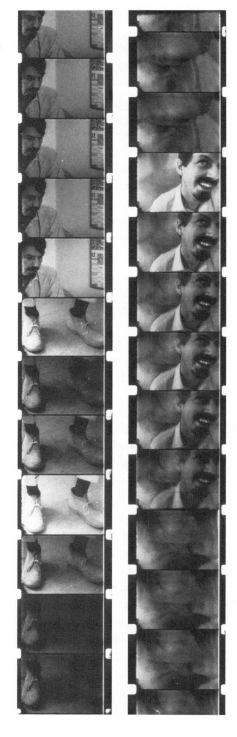

Robert Creeley in Stan
Brakhage's *Two: Creeley/
McClure*. Courtesy of the
Estate of Stan Brakhage
and Fred Camper.

some point, if you're relaxed, that light bulb can be impressing the optic nerve so much that it turns black. Closing the eyes will leave a blue light bulb, usu-ally, drifting off into the void, which is a reversal color of yellow. In the will to give out, it has to be relaxed, at least in my experience; a person can shift from positive to negative. That is, the values can reverse, the eyes are saturated and go to the opposite. So I'm always in that sense after equivalents of things I've seen. My experience isn't exactly like it appears on film, but it's an equivalent. And this reversal of light-value vision happens very often to me when I'm with Robert Creeley. So it seems necessary in the film to seem true to my experience of him. ("Poetry and Film" 227–28)

Once again we find an effort to achieve what Kenneth Anger called "inte-grality." That Brakhage insists "a person can shift from positive to negative," and that the film is understood as "always in that sense after equivalents of things I've seen," suggests Brakhage's attempt actually to merge light and dark, Jekyll and Hyde — almost prosaically, he realizes this effect by film-ing Creeley using both positive and negative film stock. Sitney insists this formal decision on Brakhage's part is "an intensely subjective image with a presentiment of aging" (*Visionary Film*, 217),[10] while Guy Davenport sug-gests that the manner in which Creeley is presented is "an evocation of the poet's tense sincerity" (11).

And yet in viewing this film, particularly in light of Brakhage's career-long attempt to show us what might be called an essential vision perceived through what he called "the primordial mind,"[11] I suspect that *Creeley/McClure* is an attempt to go beyond impressionistic portraiture. Rather, the Poet is used as a symbol by Brakhage representing that figure that, in the Ro-mantic tradition, is able to provide us with a holistic ethos wherein opposites reconcile and become generative.[12] While Brakhage's retrospective reminis-cence of making the film might suggest a more conservative reading along the lines of Sitney and Davenport, a letter Brakhage wrote to Creeley (June 1, 1962), during the period when the film was being edited, points to a far grander project: "Editing is coming along on 'portrait of Creeley' or what-ever it is to be called when finished. You start out very much in the realm of Aelf-Scin; but I foresee depths of dark reached also — a kind of absolute *and* relative working in inter-relation . . . as in a Bach fugue." The reference to "Aelf-Scin" is certainly telling here, given what we have been discussing regarding Brakhage's efforts toward "integrality." The Old English word *ælf-scýne*, which might be translated roughly into "shiny / beautiful like an elf/ fairy,"[13] is found, according to Alaric Hall, "only in poetry, twice in *Genesis A*

and once in [the Old English poem] *Judith*" (89). Hall adds, "*Ælfscýne's* generic element, *scyne*, principally means 'beautiful' both etymologically and
throughout medieval English. Like *beautiful* it is used in a wide variety of
contexts, but almost invariably of women rather than men (except that it is
often used of angels, which may afford a parallel to its association with *aelf)*"
(92). Thus, we find Brakhage clearly engaging with a "both/and" model that
positions Creeley simultaneously as magical shiny elf; as beautiful woman;
as mortal and angel; as a manifestation in which the "absolute" and "relative"
engage in a dynamic relationship; as metaphorical light (with its attendant
connotations of good) and metaphorical darkness (with its connotations of
evil and despair); and, finally, as a figure through which the figurative light
of insight and the fairy glow of film engage in play.

Brakhage's Romantic understanding of the poet finds both a visual and
textual corollary in Creeley's *Pieces*. The visually striking interconnected
poems in the book, composed as they are of narrative fragments, puns, ob-
servational detail, practically nonreferential grammatical games, and sustained lyric meditations on recognizable themes, including the speaker's beloved, all work as a single serial piece that serves to investigate the tensions
in being singular as that singular aches for a state in which singular and
plural converge. The following selection from the sequence entitled "Numbers (for Robert Indiana)" is typical of the many instances throughout the
book where Creeley sets up a kind of unresolved dialectic:

Two
When they were
first made, all the
earth must have
been their reflected
bodies, for a moment —
a flood of seeming
bent for a moment back
to the water's glimmering —
how lovely they came.

   .

What you wanted
I felt, or felt I felt.
This was more than one.

   .

This point of so-called
consciousness is forever
a word making up
this world of more
or less than it is.

  .

Don't leave me.
Love me. One by one.

  .

As if to sit
by me were another
who did sit. So

to make you
mine, in the mind,
to know you.
    . (22–23)

A recognizably spiritual diction permeates the first stanza, one that re-imagines and in part retells the story of Adam and Eve's presence in the Garden. Creeley relies on an almost ecstatic tone to heighten the conflation of bodies with material earth ("all the / earth must have / been their reflected / bodies, for a moment"). Might we read Creeley's work as inspired in part by William Blake's visionary project? We can recall Blake's "The Book of Urizen," chapter 4, in which the development of Urizen's body (his spine, his rib cage, his eyes, ears, nostrils, etc.), as distinct from an idealized "Eternity," is presented by Blake as a tragedy that results in "The eternal mind, bounded":

In a horrible dreamful slumber,
Like the linked infernal chain:
A vast Spine writh'd in torment
Upon the winds; shooting pain'd
Ribs, like a bending cavern
And bones of solidness, froze
Over all his nerves of joy.
And a first Age passed over,
And a state of dismal woe. (148)

As Urizen's body is formed, we find Blake associating the process with the loathed demarcations instituted by Cartesian rationalism. All our problems begin thanks to the ever-metastasizing power of reason/Urizen, a power that consistently separates time from eternity, mind from body, and so forth. Creeley's merging earth with bodies points to a synthesizing urge that is not just prelapsarian but, for all intents and purposes, free from conceptual, temporal, and physical distinctions instituted by Urizen.

Creeley—albeit far more qualifiedly than Blake—presents us with a vision of mystical cohesion that is in great part underscored and induced through the power of Eros. Note, for example, that the Robert Duncan–style punning which Creeley and particularly Brakhage were so fond of is evident in the line, "a flood of seeming." Given the trajectory of the lines, particularly as this stanza ends with "how lovely they came," it is clear that "seeming" contains "semen" as part of its desired signification. It is here, then, that Creeley's anxiety comes to the fore. At once aching for and skeptical of Blakean cosmology, Creeley consistently moderates his ecstasies. The absorption of semen into the word "seeming" emphasizes the artificial nature of language in terms of what it attempts to administrate. Language is always "seeming," always provisional regarding its relationship to the outward phenomena it catalogues. That "semen" (the material evidence of sexual bliss and temporary transcendence) is punned by Creeley into "seeming" highlights Creeley's overall angst regarding language.

Such angst is extended in the subsequent stanza. The power of Adam and Eve's communion, in evidence through the flood of semen/seeming and the loveliness of their mutual orgasm, is tentative—"What you wanted / I felt, or felt I felt. / This was more than one." Adam at first insists on his ability to feel the female's desire (perhaps a nod towards Blake's hermaphroditic ideal), only to then temper his claim by emphasizing his own subjectivity and separateness. He doesn't so much "feel" it as feels he feels it. The melancholy strain enters the poem as division between the subjects is made manifest. We are not "one," but "more than one."

As Adam's isolated self is introduced into the poem, Creeley moves on to point to the role language plays in determining subjectivity and its parallel quality of apart-ness. "So-called" "consciousness" is "forever / a word making up / this world of more / or less than it is." For all of Brakhage's and Creeley's ambivalence and, in Brakhage's case, hostility toward "structural aesthetics," these lines display a practically structuralist understanding of the role of signification in determining how we interact with our "reality." "Consciousness" is, ultimately, a word that has significance only because of an arbitrary system of conventions we associate with it—we cannot break free from the strictures inherent in an ordering system of signs to reach some idealized "outside" free from the boundaries in and of language. While such bitterness is consistently ameliorated by the speaker's petition to the other to become an idealized "one" — "Don't leave me. / Love me. One by one" — it is also almost automatically reiterated, as we find in the end of this section that features a manifestly ambivalent speaker conceptualizing (rather than feeling) the other in terms of absorption and a practically patriarchal ownership: "to make you / mine, in the mind, to know you."

Given that *Pieces* as a whole is Creeley's most visually arresting work, and that the book was conceived of and published during a period when Creeley was becoming not just friends with Brakhage but a subject and supporter of Brakhage's film, it is tempting to connect the two artists' work, particularly as they both radically interrogate the efficacy of language to embody what Creeley variously called a visionary-inflected "outside." We should note that Creeley saw even in the most mainstream of films a possibility for breaking through the strictures imposed on us by language. Describing childhood experiences in the local movie theater, he reminisces, "It was that miraculous 'outside' coming into one's sight, scrunched down in seat, stuffed with popcorn, kids again in that insistent impulse of, 'what's going to happen *now*?' . . . An art, any art, would seem to me to have to be *interesting*, so to speak. And what, among other things, would seem so is that fact of a revelation" ("Three Films" 120). Crucially for our discussion so far, Creeley continues this particular train of thought by referring directly — and critically — to Descartes's maxim: "'I think, therefore I am. . . .' Many ways now active in thinking, feeling, proposing, *using* 'the world' can contest his assurance, and the ego, the castle of this proposition, has long since been made to yield" (ibid. 121). Reason, then, through its acts of delineation, closes off access to what lies beyond the ego, beyond limits, outside the "I."

Creeley consistently linked visual arts, and in particular film, to an essentially mystical understanding of serial form, in which the act of viewing was in the service of revelation independent of reason. As Creeley perhaps more succinctly put it, "thus I'd want to say, look first, think later — and of course I want it to the ends of the world" (ibid. 125). Film, because of its materially procedural nature — and particularly as it was wedded to Brakhage's anti-Cartesian seriality and mysticism — appears to have played a role in inspiring Creeley's most formally challenging work, one that eschewed the relatively conventional narrative endings in poems included in preceding and succeeding books in favor of foregrounding the process of its making.

"Do recall that Brakhage is revealing the *means* of the film (much as Mélies asked Pathé to do), not the *ends* possible, which he has also so brilliantly shown us," Creeley insisted (ibid. 125). For Creeley and Brakhage, highlighting "means" ultimately was a way of seeing (as Wordsworth put it in his poem, "Tintern Abbey") "into the life of things."

four

The Conversation between Frank O'Hara and Alfred Leslie

Answering the question "What's your response to the postmodern aesthetic that seeks to break down the boundary between art and pop culture — in essence, that anything can be art?," Stan Brakhage replied with the single word "Hogwash," adding later,

> Created by a lot of lazy people who want to have their childhood kicks and have it sanctified as it was something tremendously serious. It's not church-worthy. And they have infiltrated the colleges to an enormous extent where they're even more pernicious because they know perfectly well that how to become a popular professor is to give all their students the sense that they can have all their easy movies, where they can escape and bug out, while at the same time having a profound art experience. The students lap it up, and both of them serve each other, sitting in lazy land. You know, art is a hard pleasure, and that's the beautiful thing about it. The appreciators are as hard-working as the maker to comprehend and unravel the enigmas and the complexities of a poetic cinema. (Johnson 48)

Imagine, then, Brakhage's reaction to Frank O'Hara's statement in his mock manifesto "Personism," in which O'Hara asserts, "Nobody should experience anything they don't need to, if they don't need poetry bully for them. I like the movies too. And after all, only Whitman and Crane and Williams, of the American poets, are better than the movies" (*Collected Poems* 498). Reading through O'Hara's *Collected Poems*, we come across odes and tender references to James Dean, Lana Turner, and "Ginger Rogers in Swingtime"; we encounter what are by now practically canonical lines, including "Mothers of America / let your kids go to the movies!" ("Ave Maria" 371)[1], "I'd have the immediacy of a bad movie, / not just a sleeper, but also the big, / over-produced first-run kind" ("My Heart" 231), and "Roll on, reels of celluloid, as the great earth rolls on!" ("To the Film Industry in Crisis" 233). As Jim Elledge points out, "Fifty-four poems in O'Hara's *Collected Poems* rely on film in varying degrees. . . . O'Hara incorporated film in central, if not primary, roles, illustrating or fortifying major points or suggesting themes, especially about love" (350).

But where is the "poetic cinema," to use Brakhage's term? O'Hara's appreciation for mainstream and B-movie cinema is a self-evident part of his overall poetics, one that suggests a postmodern sensibility anathema to Brakhage. O'Hara delights equally among malteds, Lana Turner, hot dogs, Rachmaninoff, Heine Pollock, Johnny Weismuller, and Pierre Reverdy as he expresses that delight through a formal approach informed by filmic practice. And yet, might we revisit O'Hara's poems and explore how O'Hara in fact reinscribes certain elements of popular culture in terms that might not be as far away from Brakhage's position as we might generally think? Is O'Hara always hilariously ironic in his undermining of "high" and "low" cultures? Is O'Hara "church worthy?"

Throughout his poetry O'Hara reframed actors like James Dean for his own brand of queer dissidence, one that offered a refreshing counternarrative to the adamantly heterosexual histrionics typical of dominant male poets of the 1950s and early 1960s like Robert Lowell, W. D. Snodgrass, and Louis Simpson. The dead Dean becomes the Adonisian object of O'Hara's affections, one who can be reanimated by O'Hara "as long as the beast in me maintains / its taciturn power to close my lids / in tears, and my loins move yet / in the ennobling pursuit of all the worlds / you have left me alone in" ("For James Dean" 229). In the significantly named section "A Ceremony for One of My Dead" from his poem "Four Little Elegies" (devoted to James Dean), O'Hara uses the lyric to affiliate himself with keening female gypsies mourning their beloved: "the sad tires pound along the highway, whining, shrieking, / and beating like so many gypsy girls who fell dead / for love at their tar-haired lovers' polished feet" (229). Photographs of Dean turn into manifestly biblical "parchment" and, using William Carlos Williams's inherently elegiac variable foot measure, O'Hara suggests Dean is more Prime Mover than movie star: "I can't really tell / that I'm alive, except / I name the world" (250). Too good for mere mortals, Dean ascends from his place as Hollywood superstar and tragic hero to become both a wholly sensuous being and He who names the world.

O'Hara's gestures seem designed to co-opt or recuperate certain aspects of mainstream culture for outlaw ends, including liberated sexuality, disaffiliation from consensus society, and the like. Consider, for example, O'Hara's friendship with poet and Underground film star Taylor Mead, who was chosen by O'Hara to play the starring role in O'Hara's play, *The General Returns from One Place to Another* (1969), on a double-bill with LeRoi Jones's (Amiri Baraka's) *Baptism* (1967).[2] O'Hara's published dedication of the play—"To Vincent Warren and to Warner Brothers and Taylor Mead"—is a rich little line indeed, in that we find O'Hara integrating his real-life love interest, Vincent Warren, with a major Hollywood studio, only to then further queer his invocation by adding fey Taylor Mead to the overall mix. It's a three-way: Warner Brothers is the Lucky Pierre here, practically and progressively contaminated by being sandwiched between such evocatively faggy proper names.

Apart from reframing the content of the Hollywood industry to suit his own queer ends, however, how might we see O'Hara complicating the insistent and predictable formal narrativity we associated with the vast majority of his named films? I ask this question particularly because, as Andrew Epstein pointed out, "O'Hara is profoundly intrigued by the formal qualities of film, by the fast visual jumps and dislocations it makes possible, because his own poetics is based on a hatred of 'all things that don't change' and an enduring fascination with 'quickness' and 'transience'" (94). Marjorie Perloff makes much the same case when she argues that O'Hara, in his poem "Music," adapts "the techniques of film and action painting to a verbal medium. For one thing, the poem is framed as a series of cuts and dissolves, whether spatial, temporal, or referential" (*Frank O'Hara* 121). Regarding O'Hara's poem "To Hell with It," Perloff insists, "Photographs, monuments, static memories . . .—these have no place in the poet's world. We can now understand why O'Hara loves the *motion* picture, *action* painting, and all forms of dance—art forms that capture the *present* rather than the *past*, the present in all its chaotic splendor" (ibid. 21).

And yet despite the fact that the predictably narrative form of the movies O'Hara mentions bears little to no resemblance to the variously fragmented, serial, non-narrative, and generally far more complex forms of O'Hara's poems, most critical work on O'Hara and film asserts a thematic and formal harmony between mainstream film and avant-garde poem. As Mark Goble points out, "Many critics . . . take for granted a basic equivalence between certain techniques of film editing—jump cuts, swish pans, fade-outs, cutaways, and wipes—and some of O'Hara's signature techniques for directing readerly attention. Furthermore, the few critics who have looked closely at what O'Hara's interest in film signifies thematically or what historical importance it might have for postwar American culture have presented a picture of almost total consonance between O'Hara's poetry and the culture of cinema" (58).[3]

Critical work on O'Hara and cinema tends to move from a brief consideration of the formal aspects of O'Hara's filmic poetics to an emphasis on how the movies' content informs O'Hara's work—thus, enlightened by O'Hara's references to specific films, critics position O'Hara as postmodern poet par excellence, queer poet par excellence, urban poet par excellence, love poet par excellence, and so on. Goble comments that "O'Hara is said to share with many of the films he mentions a preoccupation with dramas of desire and romance, dramas he often appropriates for homoerotic fantasies. Alternatively, O'Hara's 'urban sensibility' is said to possess a natural affinity for 'cinematic form.' Even critics interested in O'Hara as a gay poet . . . align him in a productive agreement with film, tending to see him in terms of 'the gay camp fascination with Hollywood'" (58–59).

Apart from Olivier Brossard's essay on *The Last Clean Shirt* (1964; a film discussed in detail below), critics interested in the role of film in O'Hara's poetry—Sarah Riggs, Lawrence Goldstein, Andrew Epstein, Marjorie Perloff, Jim Elledge, even Mark Goble, to name a few—do not make much if any reference to O'Hara's work and interest in the New American Cinema scene. This is unfortunate, cementing as it does the disconnect between "mainstream" and "avant-garde," a disconnect that O'Hara worked to eliminate through his enthusiastic embrace of any number of filmic approaches. Consider, for example, O'Hara's friendship with, and participation in the films of, Rudy Burckhardt. O'Hara played a real role in Burckhardt's films, from playing piano in some of Burckhardt's efforts from the 50s; to advising Burckhardt on what kinds of scores would be most appropriate; to suggesting cuts, edits, and the like. Yvonne Jacquette recalls:

> Frank gave Rudy advice on what music to include. The music in "Lurk," for example, after Rudy showed the film to Frank, who would then say, "Oh try Wagner there, try Grieg there." Rudy loved Frank's poetry; he was very familiar with all of it. When Rudy had a film that was almost together he'd call people over to show it to them, painters, poets, whoever, and they could say what they felt, and Frank would come over all the time and give his opinion. The word would go out and people would show up. Frank would say things like "I don't like that shot so much," or "you might want to use this Schoenberg

piece." The way things were in New York those days, the space between a filmmaker and a poet and a dancer and an artist was very short . . . it was so mixed
up . . . it doesn't seem to happen so much anymore . . . then it was so easy . . .
New York was so easy, cheap lofts, whatever, people come and go, there was a
tremendous interaction. (personal interview)

Beyond playing a part in Burckhardt productions, we can also note that
O'Hara wrote screenplays for filmmakers Andy Warhol and Alfred Leslie.
Joe LeSueur, O'Hara's longtime friend and roommate, remembers that "in
the mid-sixties I used to run into Andy Warhol at some of Kenward Elmslie's
parties on Cornelia Street. . . . One night I drunkenly suggested [to Warhol]
that for a change he make a long movie with lots of plot. He seemed intrigued, so I dreamed up the idea of asking all the poets and writers I knew
to contribute episodes; I would supply the continuity, and the movie would
be called *Messy Lives*, a title Bill Berkson gave me. I mentioned all of this
to Frank. Before I decided what the movie's frame would be, he wrote an
episode called *Love on the Hoof* with Frank Lima" (O'Hara, *Amorous Nightmares of Delay* xxiv). O'Hara's script for Alfred Leslie (a surrealist, libidinal
mélange titled "Act & Portrait, Al Leslie Film") is interesting, especially for
the way it seems to echo aspects of Leslie's *Pull My Daisy*: there is a long-
suffering woman called "Dorothea" who gets "the children ready for school"
as the bohemian protagonist wonders, "John the Baptist or John the Beloved? I was thinking about all of that"; rapscallion beatnik friends including
"Miles" who "wouldn't leave, I had to force him. We didn't want the children
to see us playing children's games"; a "bishop"; and so on. I will not consider
these two texts in detail here as the scripts were never fully realized, though
one can certainly refer to them as supplementary evidence of O'Hara's participation in the experimental film scene.

O'Hara also made tantalizing references throughout his poetry to New
American filmmakers and film sites. O'Hara's poem, "Vincent and I In-
augurate a Movie Theater," for example, comically laments Ginsberg's and
Orlovsky's peripatetic nature as it situates the reader firmly within the Lower
East Side Underground film scene—the Charles Theater on the corner of
East 12th Street and Avenue B:

Now that the Charles Theater has opened
it looks like we're going to have some wonderful times
Allen and Peter, why are you going away
our country's black and white past spread out
before us is no time to spread over India. (*Collected Poems* 399)

The Charles was a place that, J. Hoberman states, "effectively put underground movies on the cultural map" ("Explorations" 34), and at which, as Jonas Mekas recalls, "[premiers] of Ron Rice's *The Flower Thief*, Brakhage's *Anticipation of the Night* and my own *Guns of the Trees*, all dutifully reviewed by the *New York Times*, took place there. . . . Jack Smith was one of our ticket sellers for a while as was the publisher of *Mad* magazine" ("A Few Notes" 98). The Charles showed revivals and classics during regular opening hours and, after closing for a couple of months, reopened with a new mission. Beginning in October 1961 the Charles featured midnight shows curated by Jonas Mekas, who screened films by Gregory Markopoulos, Marie Menken, Ken Jacobs, Larry Jordan, and many others. Hoberman's description of the theater's programming might just as well serve as a description of O'Hara's diverse range of reference: "The Charles's program was an eclectic mixture. Astaire-Rogers rubbed shoulders with Italian Neorealism, Edgar G. Ulmer was celebrated along with the Marx Brothers, *Touch of Evil* was advertised as Orson Welles's masterpiece. . . . Langford and Stein recruited Jonas Mekas . . . to organize some additional screenings. Significantly, these were to be on weekends at midnight, giving them a ready-made aura of cultish exoticism" ("Explorations" 22, 34).

Despite these indications of O'Hara's participation in and affection for the Underground, the New American Cinema pretty much doesn't exist in O'Hara's world as it has been constructed by contemporary critics. Consider Elledge's reading of O'Hara's poem "Fantasy" (dated 1964, just after the period that *Flaming Creatures* hit downtown and other screens).[4] "[In] 'Fantasy,' O'Hara is '*actor*.' At home, O'Hara drifts in and out of reality, in turn speaking to an ailing Allen Ginsberg, who never responds to him, and fantasizing himself into a role in the 1943 anti-Nazi romance/adventure film *Northern Pursuit*" (355). Elledge adds later that O'Hara "asserts, 'The main thing' for film to do 'is to tell a story. / It is almost / very important.' The story is the ideal, the romance, the fantasy — what holds viewers' attention, keeps them paying 'a quarter' for admission, and enables them to recall at will the film in time of need" (357). Apart from not really exploring the significance of the manifestly ambivalent "*almost* / very important," Elledge does not point out that the poem reads more like a fractured collage of filmic references than it does an easily consumable "story." Opening the poem with a conversation, "How do you like the music of Adolph / Deutsch? I like / it, I like it better than Max Steiner's. Take his / score for *Northern Pursuit*, the Helmut Dantine theme was . . ." (O'Hara, *Collected Poems*, 488), O'Hara immediately collapses any semblance of narrative coherence with ellipses followed by the cartoon-like lines, "and then the window fell on my hand. Errol / Flynn was skiing by." The poem continues by jumping from a reference to a submarine, "fantasies of snow farts," medical advice for an ailing Allen Ginsberg, and so on. True, the poem is loosely held together by repeated references to *Northern Pursuit*, but such references tend to highlight the very gaps in the "story." The story is not "the ideal," as Elledge would have it, but rather the problem that O'Hara solves by exploding it.

Epstein, while providing us with some fascinating insights into the role of the filmic in O'Hara's work, also tends to avoid the possibility that, as Mark Goble suggests, O'Hara is arguing with film rather than merely celebrating it. Epstein refers to the "movies" based on a tacit agreement with readers that "movies" are always and only part of "popular culture." As he writes, "By context, I mean both how O'Hara's movie poems can be seen as an integral part of his rebellious response to the rigid orthodoxy of the literary establishment in the 1950s, and how they can be seen as a reaction to the ongoing intellectual debates, waged in the postwar period, over the value and place of popular culture" (96). Epstein adds, "We must recognize that O'Hara's work is driven by a sophisticated and influential engagement with popular culture and the images it creates" (97).

It is this analysis that ultimately drives Epstein's readings of such poems as "An Image of Leda." Epstein writes: "By modeling this poem about the movies on an encounter between the divine and the human, O'Hara adopts a mock-heroic stance that is certainly meant to deflate seriousness with irony. After all, an afternoon at the movies is hardly a brush with the divine!" (99). This assumption is problematic, given the precisely mystical possibilities associated with an "afternoon at the movies" that filmmakers and poets aimed to associate with both popular and non-narrative cinema since at least the turn of the twentieth century. Certainly, artists affiliated with the French modernist avant-garde—whose output was so foundational to the development of the New York School of poets—saw in any number of films a possibility for apprehending a practically Keatsian "truth" and "beauty." In writing about cinema, critics and poets isolated visual and rhythmic moments independent of story to underline their belief that radical juxtaposition could lead to the temple of psychological and spiritual insight. In a review of Douglas Fairbanks's 1915 film, *L'Aventure à New York* (*The Mysteries of New York*), for example, critic Louis Delluc insists the film embodies "that which you glimpse on the street in a face, in a sign, in a color, everywhere and incessantly, and which a 'metteur-en-scène' can isolate explicitly. Landscapes, horses, dogs, furniture, glasses, a stair, a lamp, a hand, a jewel, all take on an element of the fantastic. And the true. True, but you would not have seen it, almost no one knows how to see the beauty of things the cinema sometimes forces one to see" (qtd. in Abel, "The Contribution of the French Literary Avant-Garde" 27).

Such an awestruck and spiritually tinged response to "the movies" was not limited to the French modernists. Aspiration for the "divine" was at the heart of the moviegoing experience for American poets and filmmakers alike. Goldstein states that "[Vachel] Lindsay saw at once what other writers did not see for many years, that movies would take on the same aura of spirituality that formerly belonged to poetry and song. Movies would do so by sponsoring a mythology of iconic figures that would eventually rival the ancient legendry favored by poets before Edison and Griffith. This mythology would become a source of tactical allusions for poets who required at key moments in their verse both deep and superficial images shared by the literate community" (7). Hart Crane, Eugene Jolas, O'Hara's beloved Pierre Reverdy, and related modernist literary figures, while acknowledging the sheer entertainment value in "mainstream" actors and films, simultaneously took such value very seriously indeed. From Cocteau's definition of his relationship to making the film *Blood of a Poet* as "that of a cabinetmaker who puts together the pieces of a table whom the spiritualists, who make the table move, consult" (4); to Maya Deren's description of her films as enacting a "ritualistic form" that could create "fear, for example, by creating an imaginative, often mythological experience" (Nichols, ed., *Maya Deren* 20); to Stan Brakhage's belief that film could take us to a practically precognitive, preverbal level where "our eye does not respond to the name of everything but which must know each object encountered in life through an adventure of perception. . . . Imagine a world before the 'beginning was the word'" ("The Camera Eye" 211); to Kenneth Anger's attempt to achieve a mystical "integrality" between good and evil, a huge part of spending an "afternoon at the movies" for independent cinema figures has been aimed precisely at providing viewers with a "brush with the divine."

It is this approach to film that seems to discomfit O'Hara aficionados like Lawrence Goldstein. While Goldstein provides us with a fascinating analysis of the role "movies" have played in modern and postmodern American poetry, he nevertheless seems to suffer from the same cultural shortsightedness that afflicts other devotees of O'Hara's work, namely, their dismissal of avant-garde cinematic practice as an influence in O'Hara's work. Goldstein goes so far as to insist that "O'Hara's indifference to experimental film, so often the province of the homosexual artist such as Andy Warhol, Jack

Smith, and Kenneth Anger, and so often self-consciously hermetic in its narratives, has much to do with his sense of Hollywood movies as a fantasy lifeline to the majority culture" (162). Before showing that O'Hara was indeed
interested in these figures, we should address the misreading of the work
of the "homosexual artists" that Goldstein names here. Doing so will serve
two functions. We will help dispel Goldstein's assertion about the purported
inaccessibility of "experimental film," and we will set ourselves up to rethink
the formal and thematic interactions O'Hara's poetry might have with a
variety of cinemas.

Clearly, much of New American Cinema lifted sources from "the majority culture" — including bubblegum pop and Hollywood and B movies
— to inform its practice. Anger's use of music in *Scorpio Rising* (1963) is a
case in point. Edited into an ominous thirteen segments, with a series of
songs including Bobby Vinton's "Blue Velvet," The Surfaris' "Wipe Out,"
Ray Charles's "Hit the Road, Jack," and Elvis Presley's "Devil in Disguise,"
Scorpio Rising aims to continue Anger's project of "integrality" by disclos-
ing the subversive potential inherent in popular culture. This subversion is
especially effective when illuminated via images that consistently juxtapose
and ultimately aim to reconcile Christ with the Devil, pain with pleasure,
normative sexuality and a markedly violent queer sexuality.[5] Popular culture
is not mocked or treated in a wholly parodic fashion here. Rather, by Anger's
yoking mainstream culture to his series of images, the Eros and Thanatos
drive within even the most supposedly banal of ordinary cultural sources
are joyously, if at times terrifyingly, revealed. To anyone who has seen *Scorpio Rising*, Elvis will never sound merely safely racy again.

We might also look to Anger's legendary book *Hollywood Babylon*, particularly as it consistently folds lurid biographical details of major Hollywood
stars into Anger's overall cosmogony. Pictures of actors including Shirley
Temple, Montgomery Clift, Frank Sinatra, and Charlie Chaplin are yoked
to quotes from Aleister Crowley and references to polytheistic black magic
practices. Given our focus here, it is significant that, as Bill Berkson points
out, "Frank certainly knew Anger's book HOLLYWOOD BABYLON"
(O'Hara's). That O'Hara read Anger's book shows, at the very least, that he
was willing to consider the conflation of the hermetic with the popular that
Anger so consistently aimed to effect in his works.

Goldstein is certainly correct in stating that some New American Cinema work is self-consciously "hermetic." In Anger's case such a definition
is literal, as his films have their narrative roots in the hermetic traditions
represented by Aleister Crowley, The Hermetic Order of the Golden Dawn,

William Blake, and beyond.[6] That said, Anger consciously leavens the potential insularity of his focus by incorporating "the majority culture" into his work. Popular music, rock and roll stars including Mick Jagger, evocative visual allusions to 1930s film fantasies, Mickey Mouse, and more all feature in his films. This is not to say that these facets of popular culture exist in Anger's films as a metaphorical "lifeline" that saves his films from sinking into a little-viewed avant-garde swamp. Rather, Anger sees majority culture itself as already permeated by the hermetic forces of darkness and light he was so intent on revealing in his films.

Jack Smith's transformation of postal worker Rene Rivera into Mario Montez — who acted under the name "Dolores Flores" in Smith's *Flaming Creatures* and as Mario Montez in Smith's film *Normal Love* — is another indication of how "experimental" cinema looked to mass culture in both its Hollywood and "trash" manifestations to inform its own practice. J. Hoberman says that "as P. Adams Sitney would be the first to observe, *Flaming Creatures* made manifest what Smith found 'implicated in [B-movie film actress] Maria Montez and von Sternberg's films, and without the interference of a plot. What he brings to the fore is what has been latent in those films — visual texture, androgynous sexual presence, exotic locations'" (*On Jack Smith's Flaming Creatures* 20). Maria Montez's role as foreign exotica in films produced by Universal and 20th Century Fox and Montez's appearances in less stellar B-movie vehicles were read by Jack Smith as rich in avant-garde potential, a potential he would realize in his own wild variations on stardom, gender, and place in films including *Flaming Creatures*, *Scotch Tape*, and *Normal Love*.[7] Hoberman's take on Smith's film is especially illuminating, particularly given the manner in which he stresses Smith's ability to transgress boundaries of genre, economy, and taste: "At once primitive and sophisticated, hilarious and poignant, spontaneous and studied, frenzied and languid, crude and delicate, avant and nostalgic, gritty and fanciful, fresh and faded, innocent and jaded, high and low, raw and cooked, underground and camp, black and white and white-on-white, composed and decomposed, richly perverse and gloriously impoverished, *Flaming Creatures* was something new under the sun. . . . *Flaming Creatures* proposed an entirely new form of cine-glamour — one that owed everything and nothing to Hollywood's" (ibid. 10).

I mention Smith's films here both for the ways in which Smith's recuperation of Hollywood sources for libidinal, practically polysexual ends rhymes with much of O'Hara's practice,[8] and to point out that Smith's actors played a real role in O'Hara's world as well. For example, Judith Malina, who played the role of "The Fascinating Woman" in *Flaming Creatures*, produced several of O'Hara's plays for the Living Theatre; O'Hara mentioned John Wieners lovingly in poems including "To John Wieners"; Diane di Prima worked as stage manager for the Living Theatre production of O'Hara's play *Awake in Spain* (1960) and published O'Hara in the journal *The Floating Bear*;[9] Gerard Malanga, a link for O'Hara to the growing group of younger poets that so adored him, played a role alongside Smith in Ron Rice's *Chumlum* (1964); and so on. In a letter to Larry Rivers in April 1964, O'Hara complained that "all the queer bars except one are already closed, four movie theatres have been closed (small ones) for showing unlicensed films like Jack Smith's *Flaming Creatures* and Genet's *Un Chant d'Amour* [1950] (Jonas Mekas has been arrested twice, once for each)" (qtd. in Gooch 424). These facts are listed here if only to evoke the interrelated spheres of friendship that linked O'Hara socially and aesthetically to the filmmakers of the early and mid-1960s. I would propose, however carefully, that there was a mutually beneficial exchange of ideas between poet and filmmakers, one that is visible in the fragmented forms and daring content of many of O'Hara's later poems and the visual sumptuousness and erotic frisson of Smith's films.

In a 1965 interview with Edward Lucie-Smith, O'Hara discussed the very idea of an "Underground" in film. Referring to Jonas Mekas's Cinematheque, O'Hara rather blithely dismissed the idea of a filmic "Underground" as just so much warmed over romanticism, though he then went on to proclaim his deep appreciation for the New American Cinema:

> OH: There's a whole Cinematheque on Lafayette Street to show those movies. They have their own. . . . Even most Hollywood producers don't have their own showcase in New York. They have to farm it out to the Albee-Fox and so on. They're dependent on managers, business managers, to do it. I don't think that's being very underground. I don't mean that I'm saying that it isn't a good thing; I think it's terrific. But it is not being underground; that's a lot of romantic nonsense.
>
> L-S: I think it is romantic nonsense myself. But I think that it puts extremist art in a new position. That you have for the first time a deliberately extremist art with a ready-made audience, with an acceptive [sic] audience.
>
> OH: Yes, I do too.
>
> L-S: And what difference do you think this makes?
>
> OH: I think it makes it, it puts it back . . . I would think that if I were, if I had been. . . . Ah, that's too silly a thing to say but I'll say it anyway. If you were an Athenian, let's say, and you saw, if you went to the studio and you saw the

eyeballs being painted and the nipples being painted and so on, I should think it would be just as sensational as if you were invited to a private showing of *Flaming Creatures* of Jack Smith. (Lucie-Smith 8)

Far from being indifferent to experimental film, O'Hara went so far as to compare watching *Flaming Creatures* for the first time in a coterie setting to what it might have been like for someone to witness the birth of illusion-ism in classicism. O'Hara's appreciation for Smith's work specifically should not be glossed over. As Bill Berkson, O'Hara's close friend and the subject of many of O'Hara's best-known poems, recalls, "Frank often spoke of Jack Smith, and of FLAMING CREATURES in particular, with admiration. The admiration he felt for Warhol may have developed around that time, too. But then Frank had watched Andy Warhol's rise carefully; what Joe Brainard says in *Homage to Frank O'Hara* (1988) rings so true, that Frank attacked Andy one day and the next would 'defend him with his life.' I don't think Jack Smith occasioned the same ambivalence, partly because Smith was so clearly thoroughly 'underground' (downtown) and Andy carried this residue of the uptown fashion world" (e-mail).[10]

Berkson suggests O'Hara's admiration of Smith's work was predicated in part on Smith's underground status. This is certainly a compelling note on which to end this section. I say this because we are about to explore O'Hara's participation in an adamantly "underground" film — Alfred Leslie's *The Last Clean Shirt* (1964). This film, roundly despised at the time of its production and meager distribution, is the clearest indication we have that O'Hara, far from being ambivalent about experimental film, was in fact a participant and collaborator in the New American Cinema community. That O'Hara transferred many of his more familiar lines from his poems into the film, thereby transforming them into subtitles, suggests *The Last Clean Shirt* is worthy of literary study as it reveals O'Hara actively participating in the conversation between New American Cinema and Poetry.

ALFRED LESLIE PLUS EZRA POUND EQUALS KING KONG

Born in New York in 1927, by the late 1940s Alfred Leslie was grouped among the younger members of an emerging generation of artists, taking his place alongside painters including Joan Mitchell and Larry Rivers. His relation-ship to the New York School poets began in 1952, when he had his first solo show at the Tibor de Nagy gallery. Tibor de Nagy was a kind of home base for O'Hara, Ashbery, and their painter friends. The gallery's director, John

Bernard Myers, first published the poets and bestowed the name "New York School" upon them. In 1960 Tiber Press published a set of four volumes of poetry by Kenneth Koch, John Ashbery, Frank O'Hara, and James Schuyler, illustrated with original silkscreen prints by Alfred Leslie, Joan Mitchell, Michael Goldberg, and Grace Hartigan. Leslie would be affiliated with the New York School poets throughout his career.

As with so many of the filmmakers affiliated with the New American Cinema,[11] Leslie found a trace of a filmic aesthetic in modernist poetry that resonated with his developing practice:

> Pound connected to my sensibility. I was brought up in a literary sense in the movies. To me one of the greatest juxtapositions was one of Pound's unintelligible Chinese ideograms followed by a reference to the nobility of a certain class of Chinese emperors . . . and then all of a sudden he quotes from a letter of Thomas Jefferson and says "what I require is a light-skinned slave who is clean and who is a good cabinet maker and who can live in the house and play the oboe." And I thought, "this is unbelievable." Why should this touch me? I think it touched me because I crawled under the seat when King Kong was released. Cinema brought all that into my head at a time when I was just part of that generation — the touch of modernism when it came into public life perhaps. We had Irwin Piscator, Brecht's associate in Germany, he was brought over to the New School in the 40s. That sense of cinematic *layering*, it was given by that transformative generation at the cusp of the 20th century, it was given over, and I got it! (personal interview)

Leslie's reference to Pound's montage practice as "cinematic layering" certainly corresponds to recent critical work that explores the connections between Pound's imagist theory and Eisenstein's notion of montage as informed by the ideogram and hieroglyph.[12] Bruce E. Fleming has observed that "in the Kabuki theater [Eisenstein] saw example after example of 'pure cinematographic method'; in Japanese painting it was the possibility of picking out the detail that intrigued him. And the ideogram was offered as an example of the infinite number of cinematographic traits present in all of the Japanese culture — save, he thought, in its cinema" (88). Susan McCabe historicizes the emergence of the modernist lyric by aligning it to the development of "experimental montage." The "renovation of the lyric coincided with the beginnings of experimental montage. Imagism with its ideographic roots anticipated Eisenstein's theory of montage as 'copulation (perhaps we had better say, combination) of two hieroglyphs.' Eisenstein, like Pound, turned to the lyric forms of haiku and tanka as 'montage phrases' or as 'shot forms.'" McCabe provides us later with an elegant reading of Pound's "In a Station of the Metro," which illustrates her theory of an image-based poetic as fundamentally cinematic: "Pound's poem approximates a long shot to clear a visual pathway for the sake of a brief close-up and then withdraws" (32– 33).

The crucial difference here between Leslie's appreciation of Pound and Leslie's own practice in *The Last Clean Shirt* (1964) is that Leslie scampers away from Pound's reputedly grander project, one that aimed to employ "layering" in a scheme that would result in imagistic and thematic synthesis achieved through juxtaposition of conventionally disparate objects. Pound "was fascinated by those ideograms which seemed to combine two *distinct* elements or drawings into a *single new meaning*, such as the ideogram for 'west,' composed of a circle (the sun) half-superimposed on (and thus 'caught' in) a series of vertical strokes indicating trees: the setting sun. And he offers as a second example an explanation of the creation of the ideogram for 'red,' which consists of simplified pictures of four objects that are red (rose, cherry, iron rust, and flamingo); this resembles nothing so much as Eisenstein's consideration of how a series of shots of white things can produce the indication of 'whiteness'" (Fleming 89–90; emphasis added). While Leslie appreciates Pound's disjunctive formalism, he nevertheless willfully misreads *The Cantos* by highlighting the pleasure of "layering" as primarily surface-oriented. Leslie does not emphasize how Pound attempts to create a transnational model of social order through his juxtaposition of Chinese potentates and practically deified Founding Fathers. Rather, Leslie is interested primarily in the *pleasures* of the juxtapositions, the way they intimate that the artist is free to use whatever strikes him to create new sensations and ideas that are not necessarily tied into some overarching vision. We sense this when Leslie links his appreciation for Pound's montage work to that moment when he "crawled under the seat when King Kong was released." Joy here is not centered on creating juxtaposition that leads to insight, to (in Pound's own oft-quoted words) an "emotional and intellectual complex *caught* in an instant of time" ("Pound's 'A Retrospect'"; emphasis added). Leslie's joy is one that revels in experiencing new sensations created out of unexpected and funny recombinations and juxtapositions. What is produced is a thrilling disorder that does not, however, preclude intellectual delight and wonder nor, as I will argue below, preclude progressive political change.

Pound's radical montage practice offered artists including Leslie and O'Hara new models for art making, even as both Leslie and O'Hara rejected Pound's cultural/economic program and the attendant vision of the artist as Manichean seer. Kenneth Koch's comments on Pound define why he and other New York School affiliated writers took only so much from *il miglior fabbro*: "Pound has this very quirky way of talking, very conversational. He gives you all these pleasures — a very flat, spoken style mixed in with unexpected quotes and other languages. I think I, and John [Ashbery] and Frank [O'Hara] were all influenced by Pound's way of referring to all kinds of things all at once. But Pound did it to make some kind of point, whereas I think we did it because we just liked the splash of it, having everything in" (Koch 96). O'Hara's field of reference, which arguably is as encyclopedic as Pound's, is, according to Lytle Shaw, "far more quotidian than most other famous attempts by modern poets to synthesize or monumentalize cultural knowledge. . . . Though O'Hara was unquestionably affected by reading *The Pisan Cantos* . . . his response is anything but admiring" (Shaw 64). Ultimately, Pound's philosophy behind his montage practice was just too unnecessarily serious as far as O'Hara and his cohorts were concerned, even if his poetics were positively adaptable.

As Alfred Leslie suggests, it is exciting to leap from subject to subject, particularly if those leaps are represented visually. Instead of using Pound's montage poetics to extend a transcendent model for being and thinking in the world, however, Leslie adapted Pound's work to produce his own affirmative, unanchored aesthetic, one that delighted in creating practically random juxtapositions and connections between, say, King Kong and Thomas Jefferson. Pound's modernism, as Leslie states, "was given over, and I got it!" An analysis of Alfred Leslie's film, *The Last Clean Shirt*, produced collaboratively with Frank O'Hara, is a wonderful way for us to understand not just how Leslie and O'Hara "got it," but what they did with it.

PUT ON YOUR LAST CLEAN SHIRT

What "happens" in *The Last Clean Shirt* is perhaps at the furthest end of Poundian monumentalism — a black male driver and white female passenger drive a car up Third Avenue, make a couple of turns, and park uptown around 34th Street and Park Avenue. This scene is then repeated three times, and the film ends. As Olivier Brossard describes it, "The road trip begins on Astor Place in Manhattan: the car goes one block south, makes a U turn at the level of 6th Street (it goes around Cooper Union) goes up Third Avenue, stays on Third Avenue until it hits 34th Street, turns left on 34th Street until it hits Park Avenue, makes a right and parks on 34th Street and Park. . . . The film repeats this scene three times. In the first part of the triptych, we can hear the woman talk to the driver in Finnish gibberish. . . . The second part of the film has us go back to Astor Place and start again, but this time we get the subtitles which tell us what the woman is saying. The third part is yet another return to Astor Place, the subtitles now expressing the silent driver's thoughts. There is no action in the movie beside the gesticulations and verbal outpouring of the woman sitting in the car."

Leslie describes the rather hilarious and fascinating process of making the film:

> In Sweden, March 1962, during a preposterous ride in the back seat of a convertible, the combination of the wino, the motor roar, the Swedish language, and my already faulty hearing produced what turned out to be the final notes for THE LAST CLEAN SHIRT. I made a rough draft of the film in around October 1962 on returning from Europe, using as its basis the car ride, LIFE AND TIME, and the outline of a scene I had written for Mr. Z [a film Leslie wrote "especially for Zero Mostel"].
>
> In 1963 SHIRT was filmed. In the first days' shooting the camera was focused and tied and left to operate independently in the back seat of a convertible. In the second shooting I tied the camera to the knees of a friend who was then strapped into the back of a station wagon. Knowing what the camera would see at that angle and position I simply drove around looking for things to shoot through the rear view mirror of the car. When something looked right I yelled "Shoot" and the camera would be turned on.
>
> Later I was given the use of a record called THE LAST CLEAN SHIRT, written, produced, and released by Jerry Lieber and Mike Stoller. Because I liked it so much and because the music and lyrics had so much to do with the ideas in the film I named the film after the song.
>
> When the composite print was complete I screened it for Frank O'Hara to see if we could work out a way for him to write the sub-titles for what would be reels two and three. O'Hara and I had considered doing a few things earlier: an animated film based on an idea of Joe LeSeur's called MESSY LIVES, an animation of some poems, and also the staging of a pornographic tape of mine called THE FLOWER GIRLS. None of these had ever worked out because the production time seemed too immense to coordinate with our respective work schedules. But this project seemed measurable, and we worked out this method of collaboration. O'Hara would write whatever he wanted. I would adapt the transfer, the timing, and the word and letter spacing of the sub-titles on the screen. I could also repeat any line or lines as frequently as I wanted, as long as they remained in the original sequence.
>
> I burned the title in at Titra, and a complete version of the film was screened

at the Museum of Modern Art in San Francisco in the summer of 1964. The showing there was the only sympathetic viewing of the film I have ever known of. More usual was the hissing, booing, slow clapping, and foot stamping that greeted the film at the New York and London Film Festivals.

A description of the London screening appears in a very complete and sympathetic review by Philip French in an issue of ENCOUNTER MAGAZINE, 1964. A piece about the film in THE CATHOLIC FILM REVIEW saw the film as a search for truth, and eventually the film won an award in Bergamo, Italy. It then was ignored. ("Letter to Peter" 8)

As Leslie indicated, *The Last Clean Shirt* was not popularly received in the one place we would expect it to be adored — the Underground film scene in New York. Soon after the fire in Leslie's loft destroyed much of the art he had produced up to that point, Leslie wrote, "Would like to show you other films. All were destroyed the the [sic] fire excepts [sic] The Last Clean Shirt. I have a print here and would be glad to ship it if you're up to it. It's a grueling film. ... When it was shown in the NY film festival of 64 the audience — including Jonas Mekas who was sitting in front of me — Robert Frank also — booed and hissed and walked out — that happened in London also and Dan Talbert of the NEW YORKER thethre [sic] showed it once and a guy chased him out of the projection booth into a supermarket where I suppose he hid behind a case of toilet tissue cause the gu [sic] kept shouting 'You Fucking asshole-you fucking asshole'" (ibid. 8).

The film has since followed a familiar narrative — that of the avant-garde film so ahead of its time that it would take decades for critics to recognize its importance. In 1984, for instance, Blaine Allan insisted Leslie's film was most fruitfully read as an anticipation of the structural film scene of the late 1960s and 1970s: "In premise and design and in its concentration on issues of language and speech, repetition and duration beyond boredom, Alfred Leslie's *The Last Clean Shirt* (1964) anticipates later influential films in the international avant-garde, including the works of Michael Snow (*Wavelength* [1967], *Rameau's Nephew* [1974]), Hollis Frampton (*Critical Mass* [1971]), Robert Nelson (*Bleu Shut* [1970]), and Joyce Wieland (*Solidarity* [1973], *Pierre Vallières* [1972]), as well as Jean-Marie Straub and Daniel Huillet's didactic *History Lessons* [1972]" (*The New American Cinema* n.p.). What on earth caused this film to be so roundly rejected during its own time, only to earn increasingly admiring reception later?

Admittedly, watching *The Last Clean Shirt* for the first time can be hard going. The film begins with a two-minute-long static shot of a Polish film logo — "Zléyiuz EDU Filméei" — as the sound of a howling wind plays in the background. Seconds into the shot, however, the viewer receives a crucial clue about the function of the film we are about to see — a non-diegetic, female voice is heard singing an adaptation of James Russell Lowell's poem, "The Present Crisis," to the tune of Thomas John Williams's "Ton y Botel":[13]

> Once to every man and nation, comes a moment to decide,
> In the strife of truth with falsehood, for the good or evil side;
> Then it is the brave man chooses while the coward stands aside,
> And the choice goes by forever, 'twixt that darkness and that light.

It is important to focus on the role "The Present Crisis" played in America in 1964 — the poem was, after all, written by Lowell in 1845 as a protest against America's imperialist war with Mexico. Lowell was an abolitionist and editor of the progressive magazine, the *Atlantic Monthly*, and the poem later inspired the nascent National Association for the Advancement of Colored People to call its institutional magazine *The Crisis*.[14] That Leslie chose to open his film with this song was sure to resonate with the fact that the only two people in *The Last Clean Shirt* are a mixed-race couple. For those politically aware members of the audience seeing the film in 1964, the sound of Lowell's poem might very well have been considered more generally in the context of the Civil Rights Movement and increasing American participation in the Vietnam War. Consider that the period around the production and distribution of Leslie's film saw the assassination of Medgar Evers and President John F. Kennedy; the March on Washington; the bombing of the Sixteenth Street Baptist Church in Birmingham; Freedom Summer; the passage of the Civil Rights Act; the murders of civil rights workers James Cheney, Michael Schwerner, and Andrew Goodman; and the Gulf of Tonkin incident, followed by U.S. bombing raids on North Vietnam. Certainly, any film that uncritically presented a laughing, affectionate, mixed-race couple prefaced by a poem linked to the Civil Rights Movement would have been viewed against the incendiary background of its times.

Leslie himself has read the film retrospectively as participating in debates characteristic of the 1960s: "As the Vietnam War escalated, Leslie says, people saw 'an American soldier [on TV] firing an M-16 into a man's head' while voice-overs told viewers 'something entirely different, and the people believed it.' Leslie wanted [*The Last Clean*] *Shirt* to force the question 'What the fuck is going on?' because 'to most people, reality is nothing more than a confirmation of their expectations'" (Baker). Lowell's poem, designed as it was to provoke the individual to ask "what the fuck is going on" and then

make the tacitly correct choice to join the "good" side, was a fitting introduction to *The Last Clean Shirt.*

The political connotations implicit in Lowell's stanza are further established in the opening scene, which features a shot of a stationary convertible
parked on Astor Place. The passenger door opens, and an animated young
white woman gets in speaking in gibberish. A young black man enters, tapes
an alarm clock to the dashboard while generally ignoring the laughter and
babble of the woman, and adjusts the clock's time from 11:10 to 12. (The way
this draws our attention to a specific time certainly evokes O'Hara's poems,
which situate the reader within a given moment — "it is 12:40 of a Thursday" ["A Step Away From Them," *Collected Poems* 257]; "It is 12:20 in New
York" ["The Day Lady Died," ibid. 325]; "It is 12:10 in New York" ["Adieu to
Norman, Bon Jour to Joan and Jean-Paul," ibid. 328], etc.) He then begins
the drive uptown that Brossard has already outlined. Within the first two
minutes or so of the drive, as the man makes a U-turn on 3rd Avenue and
heads north towards Cooper Square (while the white woman smiles and
laughs at the black man, at times leaning in closely to him), an aural collage
of car horns is heard that is artificially manipulated by Leslie to sound more
cacophonic and chaotic than usual.[15] We might argue that this moment
resonates, if elliptically so, with the evocation of the Civil Rights Movement
suggested by the Lowell poem and the inherent cosmopolitanism of the
mixed-race couple: the appearance of a benign and safe interracial relationship is implicitly threatened by the welter of car klaxons overwhelming the
woman's own babble.

As the road trip continues north, the viewer is struck by the fact that Leslie's New York is barely recognizable in terms of conventional ideas about
what constitutes the city's landmarks. There is no Brooklyn Bridge or Empire State Building, no bird's-eye views of teeming masses. Instead, we join
an anonymous, mixed-race couple in which the only speaking subject emits
gibberish, nursery-type songs, affectionate gestures, and laughter as she and
her friend make their way through some of Manhattan's more anonymous
and visually unremarkable avenues. (Even after the couple parks on Park
Avenue at the end of the film, one would be hard put to recognize it as such.
In fact, every time I watch the opening of the film, I am reminded of "The
City of New York vs. Homer Simpson" episode from the animated TV show.
The Simpson family arrives in New York in its car, and a cartoon montage
ensues that finds Marge exclaiming, "Wall-to-wall landmarks! The Wil-
liamsburg bridge! 4th Avenue! Governor's Island!")

That said, the apparent dullness of this particular stretch of road is not quite so dull when we consider the fact that this film is designed in part as a conversation with Frank O'Hara's poetry. While O'Hara's lines have not yet appeared in the film, we can nevertheless detect his presence in the very beginning, where we find the interracial couple driving north on Cooper Square between 5th and 6th streets. This juncture was a crucial spot for the developing countercultural scene in and around the Lower East Side. The first incarnation of the by-now legendary Five Spot bar, after all, was located on Cooper Square between 5th and 6th streets.[16] "In the late 1950s," Michael Magee reports, "O'Hara was introduced to the Five Spot, a downtown club that featured the live music of the new jazz avant-garde. . . . He would come to associate this music and the social milieu in which it was performed with other forms of egalitarian desire, including his own poetry and the Civil Rights movement" (130). At the Five Spot in the late 1950s and early 1960s, one could find a mixed-race crowd enjoying the new sounds of Ornette Coleman, Thelonious Monk, and others. Kenneth Koch and Larry Rivers held their jazz poetry nights at the Five Spot, and O'Hara himself referred to the place in poems including "The Day Lady Died" and "Poem Read at Joan Mitchell's." Indeed, in the third section of *The Last Clean Shirt*, O'Hara goes so far as to include the exclamation "Ornette!," serving to further identify the location of the film with the Lower East Side jazz and poetry scene he was a part of. (Ornette Coleman and his band performed at the Five Spot for a legendary ten-week stint in 1959.) In the 1950s and 1960s, Cooper Square between 5th Street and St. Mark's Place was an increasingly important if temporary site for a multiracial avant-garde. The apparently barren stretch of Manhattan territory, framed through the bodies of Leslie's biracial protagonists, becomes particularly significant when contextualized through O'Hara's references to this jazz-soaked location.

As O'Hara went uptown to work from his home in the East Village, so the couple in the film continue their drive by heading north. The woman becomes more animated, singing "la la la la lah lah lah laaaa" and so forth as the man variously ignores her, smokes his cigarettes, or smiles with a mixture of endearment and condescension. At points, the sound of police sirens and fire engines is heard, again inserting somewhat anxious notes into the otherwise lighthearted scene. The couple smokes together as they continue their way up the avenue. The sound of something like thunder is heard repeatedly, despite there being no sign of rain.

Then, suddenly, a voice-over is heard reading over the tolling of bells: "From dust thou was taken, and unto dust thou shalt return. Ashes to ashes, dust to dust." Directly after this intonation, Lieber and Stoller's song, "The

Last Clean Shirt," is played as a soundtrack while the car remains stationary. There's a closeup on a WALK sign, which serves as a kind of cue for us to finally remove our focus from the couple and onto the street itself. The camera cuts away from our subjects and is pointed backwards towards the street. The car begins to move again, but this time we see the street as if we were facing backwards — the lens iris of the camera is then driven closed to evoke a human eye.

The car backs up into a parking space, and the camera once again focuses on the couple. The man removes the clock from the dashboard and opens the door for the woman who then steps out. Both subjects then disappear from the frame. The section ends with "The Last Clean Shirt" playing over a static shot of the car, looking exactly as it did at the opening of the film. The end of the section is comically emphasized when Leslie presents us with more Polish film stock, reintroduces the sound of howling wind, and superimposes the sound of a crowd applauding and cheering wildly over the wind. The exact same scene will be repeated twice before the film is fully over, though it will take on different meanings predicated very loosely on point of view. (Olivier Brossard usefully describes the three parts of the film as a "triptych" and demonstrates how the subtitles for section two represent the woman's speech and, in section three, the driver's thoughts.)

Importantly, these fluid points of view are generated by a series of subtitles that begin during what could be described as an intermission between scenes one and two, where the lines are superimposed over film leader and stock. These initial "intermission" lines work to extend the political undertones of the film overall. Though the tone of the film has so far been generally comic, the political issues inherent in the Lowell song (and developed via the presence of the mixed-race couple, the countering of the woman's laughter and singing with abrupt and aggressive street sounds, and the funerary invocation juxtaposed manically against Lieber and Stoller's song) suggest Leslie and O'Hara were committed to displaying and celebrating a progressive — if lighthearted — politics.

The first subtitle we see in the intermission reads "Of course I resent / Bernice saying I have. . . . " The notion of the "personal" is here neatly contained in what sounds like the fragment of an overheard conversation referring to the problems one person has with his intimate other, Bernice. O'Hara's aesthetic is in full force even in this little fragment. The comically petulant tone we associate with many of O'Hara poems, for example, "a lady asks us for a nickel for a terrible / disease but we don't give her one we / don't like terrible diseases" ("Personal Poem," *Collected Poems* 335) — is contained

in the phrase "Of course I resent," with its implicitly stressed "course" adding a humorous patina to the fragment. The funny nostalgia of the archaic
proper name "Bernice," evocative as it is of twenties-era flappers and glitzy
nightlife, certainly resonates with O'Hara's general inclination to celebrate
flapper-era icons and films. (We can refer back to F. Scott Fitzgerald's short
story, "Bernice Bobs Her Hair," for an idea of where O'Hara plucked this
name from.)

However, the whimsical is almost immediately complicated by the serious
— a turn typical of O'Hara's poetics overall, where, to cite the most famous
example, one can list the quotidian and even banal details of the day only
to end in elegy where "everyone and I stopped breathing" ("The Day Lady
Died," ibid. 325). Read as a single sentence,[17] the two subtitles following the
"Bernice" line practically shock the viewer by their violence of contrast: "You
don't say that the victim is responsible" "for a concentration camp or a Mack
truck." Certainly, the presence of the "Mack truck" maintains the lighthearted tone of the "Bernice" subtitle, but nevertheless the personal is here
categorically linked to the political. One's wholly self-involved concern with
one's own Bernice is here put into perspective by a statement that invites
reflection on one of the major sources of existential trauma for the postwar
generation. The fact that humor is maintained even when referencing the
Holocaust invites us not to diminish the horror of the event, but to examine
our own complicity in pushing harrowing historical narratives outside the
boundaries of our own experience. If "the victim" is not responsible for the
concentration camp, then who is? And why are we still moved to smile, even
invited to do so, by the appearance of the Mack truck? Does that somehow
make the "concentration camp" less serious? And if so, what does that say
about us and the ways we look to comedy to alleviate suffering?

O'Hara wants us to ask these kinds of questions. As I stated earlier, the
intermission is followed by a repetition of the car ride uptown, but this time
the ride is framed by O'Hara's subtitles representing the woman's babble. At
one point in part two, we find the "concentration camp" lines are repeated
and followed up with a particularly trenchant assertion: "You don't say / that
the victim is responsible for a concentration camp / or a Mack truck. / You
know what I mean. / Breathing is not all about breath. / Peace not just the
absence of war." By recycling Spinoza's oft-quoted maxim, "Peace is not an
absence of war, it is a virtue, a state of mind, a disposition for benevolence,
confidence, justice," O'Hara plays off the basic content of the film by tacitly
suggesting we work toward something approaching social equity. As he did
in the first intermission of *The Last Clean Shirt*, O'Hara gently uses subtitles

in part two to encourage us to read political significance into the film generally, and the presence of the mixed-race couple driving together in 1964 specifically.

While we can laugh and wonder and even get bored at the apparently meaningless series of images so far experienced in this odd little road movie, O'Hara and Leslie nevertheless prod us into questioning why we are doing precisely that — why do we choose to consume a film, a poem, a ballet, and how do those choices reverberate with our other choices to ignore or merely report on the fact of the horrors outside our apartment doors? Such an imperative to question our political responsibility as readers in the face of a profoundly violent society is found in a number of O'Hara poems. We can return to "Personal Poem," for example, where, in the midst of "lunchtime," the "House of Seagram," and sexy construction workers we learn that "Miles Davis was clubbed 12 / times last night outside BIRDLAND by a cop" (*Collected Poems* 335). This is not to suggest O'Hara did not believe in joy — rather, I want to suggest that O'Hara's poetics connected the development of a political awareness to joy, much as Emma Goldman famously insisted on her right to dance as she staged revolution.

Alfred Leslie's comments in an interview with Brossard agitate against any reading of the film — and, by extension, O'Hara's poetry — as somehow "non-political": "This is a gun that's being put to your head like the Dada poets and threatening you and saying: 'you gotta pay attention to what's going on at the beginning of the turmoil in the country culturally and politically'. . . . 'You gotta pay attention,' I mean it means something, you read those newspapers and maybe you need to understand that what's being printed in those newspapers is not true and that you have to hold back a little bit" (Brossard). Leslie and O'Hara manipulate the very notions of stable genre associated with film and subtitle to enact formal disruption — O'Hara's lines, many of which are adapted from his poems, open up "the space of the subtitles, a well-defined format, to poetry. This opening up of the subtitle format to poetry is going to alter the nature of the film: the subtitles are not here to be mere appendixes to dialogues, they are not dependent on a preexisting meaning, they create a self-sufficient space which interacts with images on an equal footing" (ibid.). Film becomes poetry — or film interacts with poetry. Or poetry extends film. Or poetry becomes subtitle, thus yoking high culture to a kind of base functionality not ordinarily associated with the lyric. Such moves invite the spectator/reader experiencing the no-longer-autonomous work of art to "pay attention," to participate in making meaning in response to a form that no longer adheres to conventional definitions of genre as she or he negotiates the overtly political themes introduced by the interracial couple, the Lowell poem, and so on.

Out of the disorientation that results from watching and reading the film — its insistent repetition coupled with discontinuous intertitles and sub-titles — the viewer must decide to be "the brave man" who "chooses while the coward stands aside, / And the choice goes by forever, 'twixt that darkness and that light." Choose the light, O'Hara and Leslie quirkily implore us. Let us return for a moment to the first intermission of *The Last Clean Shirt*. Emphasizing the ethical nature of the film, the final intertitle we read before the second repetition of the car journey reads, "It's the nature of us all to want to be unconnected." Yes, we want to be unconnected — free — but the film has already begun to suggest, however lightly and humorously, that perhaps we resist that part of our nature in an effort to be connected members of a community, one which delights in the possibilities of urbane love, laughter, and a casual interracial accord.[18]

POLITICS, PLACE, REPETITION, AND IDENTITY
IN *THE LAST CLEAN SHIRT*

Prior to the second repetition of the trip uptown, we hear the Lowell poem/song one more time. After a short pause, we are back where we started from — the parked car on the street, followed by the entry of the couple into the car, followed by the identical ten-minute drive uptown. Olivier Brossard has already done us the favor of tracking many of the quotations and allusions to the corpus of O'Hara's work found within the subtitles that follow in the second and third parts of "The Last Clean Shirt."[19] I would add to Bros-sard's list the subtitle "We shall have everything we want and there will be no more dying," which is the first line of O'Hara's poem "Ode to Joy" (*Collected Poems* 281); a reference to the poems "Oranges" and "Why I am Not a Painter," evident in the subtitle "And Not of Grace and her Oranges"; a rephrasing of the lines "I don't know as I get what D. H. Lawrence is driving at / when he writes of lust springing from the bowels" ("Poem," ibid. 334);[20] the subtitle "A lady in foxes on such a day puts her poodle in a cab," from the poem "A Step Away from Them" (ibid. 258); the subtitle "My friends are roaming or listening to La Bohème," cut from O'Hara's poem "Thinking of James Dean" (ibid. 230–31); and multiple references to one of O'Hara's best poems, "In Memory of My Feelings."

A series of subtitles in the second part of the film offers the informed

"And not of Grace and her oranges," from *The Last Clean Shirt*
© Alfred Leslie. Courtesy of Alfred Leslie.

reader a rich social and literary world paradoxically playing against the dullness of the road journey:

> I was thinking about India just now . . .
> Big bags of sand . . .
> . . . birds swooping down and gulping . . .
> . . . helpful creatures everywhere . . .
> We could be alone together at last.
> Who needs an Ark? a Captains table?
> Anyway India should think about China.
> And the Chinese could build another wall.
> Maybe even bigger if they're feeling so ambitious.
> It would keep everybody busy.
> And the Africans can go on building dams.
> What I really would like to do is go to Havana . . .
> for a weekend —

Why might O'Hara be thinking about India — and, subsequently, China,
Africa, and Cuba — "just now," circa 1963 and early 1964, when *The Last*

Clean Shirt was being produced? It is probable that O'Hara was referring to his friend Allen Ginsberg's recent return from a well-publicized trip to India with his lover Peter Orlovsky, a trip that was discussed widely in the Lower East Side poetry community thanks to Ginsberg's indefatigable ability to maintain a steady stream of correspondence.[21] The association between Ginsberg and India was such that Jonas Mekas could make a casual reference to it in his "Movie Journal" column (June 29, 1961) without providing any explanation or context: "Some ideas are useless. If you want ideas, and the right ones, don't fool yourself: go to India or China, study Sanskrit. Go to India and get lost, as Allen Ginsberg says."

Such a reading is all the more likely when we consider that Ginsberg was considering going to Cuba around the time *The Last Clean Shirt* was produced.[22] Cuba was a cause célèbre for many in the downtown poetry scene. In his essay "Cuba Libre," written after his return from Havana and first published in the *Evergreen Review* in 1961, O'Hara's close friend Amiri Baraka (then Leroi Jones) made much out of what he believed to be an ideal socialist paradise. Alfred Leslie himself published Castro's 1960 Address to the General Assembly of the United Nations in his one-shot literary review, *The Hasty Papers*, a journal that also featured work by O'Hara, Ashbery, Orlovsky, Kerouac, and others.

Africa—a continent that of course was going through its own revolutionary stage in the fifties and sixties, with country after country rejecting the colonialist legacy—was a focus of attention for many of the Lower East Side poets, particularly for Baraka, the Umbra poets, and affiliated writers. In his autobiography, Baraka recalls participating with poets including Calvin Hicks and Askia Touré in a demonstration responding to the assassination of Patrice Lumumba (267). Downtown poet David Henderson also remembers that, following the killing of Lumumba, there were "demonstrations at the U.N. that we went to. Calvin Hicks and other Umbra poets were kind of instrumental in that" (personal interview).[23] Africa, Cuba, India, China—these were all countries very much "in the air" in O'Hara's Lower East Side, strongly engaged with as they were by an increasingly activist, biracial (if not yet militant) leftist avant-garde.

Of course, O'Hara's love for movies from the 30s and 40s surely played a part in the subtitles I've been discussing as well, especially in terms of his specific reference to Cuba. Brossard mentions that "there was a movie . . . called *Weekend in Havana* (1941) directed by Walter Lang which starred Carmen Miranda and Alice Faye." Given that O'Hara had addressed Faye in his poem "To the Film Industry in Crisis," we see that a rich and deliberately outrageous link is being made between a markedly progressive, even radical politics typical of O'Hara's downtown milieu and the kind of queer, urbane subjectivity that delights in watching "Alice Faye reclining, / and wiggling and singing, Myrna Loy being calm and wise, William Powell / in his stunning urbanity, Elizabeth Taylor blossoming" (*Collected Poems* 232). Unlike Jones's and Ginsberg's highly politicized analyses of and responses to the Castro government, O'Hara provides us with a typically lighthearted assertion that *his* — or rather, *her*[24] — trip to Cuba would be limited to a weekend jaunt that takes place in the imaginative and resolutely lavender world we associate with Carmen Miranda, Faye, and other glamour pusses of the 1940s.

As usual, O'Hara likes his revolution taken with a dash of bourgeois ease and comfort. This is not to say that O'Hara is attacking dissenting voices like Ginsberg's or Baraka's, which after all offered alternative and more complex ways of thinking about socialist governments than American consensus culture was capable of providing at the time.[25] Rather, by aligning his queer sensibility to socialist industry, O'Hara opens up the discursive field of revolutionary politics by suggesting the queer dandy can participate as well, on his or her own terms. We *can* have our revolutionary cake and eat it, too. The tacit suggestion in these subtitles is for more socialism, albeit socialism that in no way is hostile to a bit of camp.[26] (Such campiness is established further in part three of *The Last Clean Shirt* through the subtitles "When does the camp close?" and "The close never camps.")

As part of his marking an emerging social and literary field through subtitles, the selected subtitles above, when read in combination with succeeding titles, also lead readers to specific poems in O'Hara's corpus that highlight his participation in the Lower East Side poetry community and his acknowledgment that Underground cinema was part of the overall landscape. The third repetition of the car journey finds O'Hara calling upon the ringmaster of Underground film himself to show up to the party when the subtitle "Jonas Mekas where are you I'm worried" appears on the screen. "Jonas Mekas where are you I'm worried" allows O'Hara to lightly acknowledge that a social and aesthetic link between New York School poet and Underground film entrepreneur is potentially surprising but certainly welcome. The interplay of these various subtitles works to position O'Hara in active relationship with the Beat/cinema world, particularly when we consider that Allen Ginsberg wrote and narrated the text for Mekas's film *The Guns of the Trees* (1962), and that O'Hara addresses Ginsberg directly in part three of the film via the subtitle, "Allen I wish we were uptown doing the 'Bronx Tam-

"Jonas Mekas where are you I'm worried," from *The Last Clean Shirt*
© Alfred Leslie. Courtesy of Alfred Leslie.

bourine.'" O'Hara in part uses the opportunity afforded to him by Leslie's film to yoke the urbane New York School dandy to the bearded downtown bohemians he lived among. In *The Last Clean Shirt*, such sociability is often performed through a cut-up of O'Hara's earlier poems.

The subtitle "India! India! India!," for example, is succeeded by "I really am kind of worried Orange New Jersey . . . ," then by "My friends are roaming or listening to La Boheme [sic]." Consider that "India!" alludes to O'Hara's poem, "Vincent and I Inaugurate a Movie Theater," where O'Hara writes, "Allen and Peter, why are you going away / our country's black and white past spread out / before us is no time to spread over India" (ibid. 399); that "I really am kind of worried Orange New Jersey . . ." alludes to O'Hara's poems "Oranges: 12 Pastorals" and "Why I Am Not a Painter";[27] and that the line "My friends are roaming or listening to La Boheme," lifted from O'Hara's poem "Thinking of James Dean" (ibid. 230–31), can be interpreted as alluding to Ginsberg's and Orlovsky's "roaming." The reference to *La Bohème* further underscores our place on the downtown scene; Puccini's *La Bohème*, the beloved opera detailing the charmingly dissolute lives of artists and poets living in the kind of garret-type abodes that Lower East Side denizens would find familiar, would surely resonate with O'Hara's peers.

In these three charged subtitles, O'Hara creates connections between New York School sophistication, predicated in part on the kind of urbanity inherent in the gallery and loft scene depicted in O'Hara's poem, "Why I am Not a Painter," and the somewhat wilder Beat aesthetic championed by Mekas, Ginsberg, and others. From the mid-1950s, O'Hara had supported the work of poets including Gregory Corso and John Wieners, and Allen Ginsberg has said of O'Hara, "I was amazed he was so open and wasn't just caught in a narrow New York Manhattan Museum of Modern Art artworld cocktail ballet scene" (Gooch 280). O'Hara uses *The Last Clean Shirt* to continue yoking bohemia to his "artworld cocktail ballet scene" by reframing crucial lines from his poems as subtitles in a film that, significantly, begins in the Lower East Side and heads uptown. What results is a further blurring of the lines between uptown and downtown, New York School and Beat, disengaged aesthete and nascent revolutionary.

IT IS NOT REPETITION

Given the repetition with textual variation that characterizes *The Last Clean Shirt*, we might very well be reminded of Gertrude Stein's cinematically informed poetics of "loving repeating": "As I say what one repeats is the scene in which one is acting the days in which one is living, the coming and going which one is doing, anything one is remembering is a repetition, but existing as a human being, that is being listening and hearing is never repetition. It is not repetition if it is that which you are actually doing because naturally each time the emphasis is different just as the cinema has each time a slightly different thing to make it all be moving" ("Portraits and Repetitions" 179). "It is *not* repetition"; "Each time the emphasis is different." These references to the film medium are especially apt in considering Leslie's second and third repetitions of the car journey. While physically identical to what we witnessed initially, the subtitles illustrate how variation is inherent in repetition, how perception and truth are ultimately contingent on who is doing the looking, the seeing, the talking, and from what vantage points that looking, seeing, and talking are taking place.

In line with "Stein's admiration of Chaplin," which she linked "to her notion that the 'rhythm of anybody's personality' overrides the sentiment of narrative since 'events are not exciting'" (McCabe 68), Leslie and O'Hara reject the potentially obsolete aura attendant to narrative — the story, after all, is tied to a beginning, middle, and *end* — and choose instead to repeat. As "Stein's famous tag — 'A rose is a rose is a rose' — becomes a form of 'regularity,' a perpetual film loop of comedic and useless gesture (memorialized by Chaplin in countless films)" (McCabe 83), so O'Hara and Leslie repeat the same scene three times to at least hint at the sensation of endless possibility and variation within repetition.[28] McCabe's analysis of Stein's relationship to film is especially pertinent here:

> Stein praised cinema for its dual ability to focus and fragment attention through the continuous supplanting or erasing of one image by another, its ability to capture the temporal displacement of "existing." In cinema, every successive image "has each time a slightly different thing to make it all be moving. . . . With the relentlessly rolling picture, memory becomes a form of disintegrative erasure where one second was never the same as the second before or after." In the same vein, Jean Epstein . . . proclaims: "there is no real present . . . it is an uneasy convention. In the flow of time it is an exception to time.". . . "Cinema," he continues, "is the only art capable of depicting this present as it is." (McCabe 57)

O'Hara's impossible efforts to somehow enact the present moment, to embody that instant of time when "everything / suddenly honks: it is 12:40 of / a Thursday" ("Personal Poem," *Collected Poems* 257) are perhaps more able to be interrogated when text becomes film. Cinema only fully exists *in* the present, urged into being as it is through the whirr of the machine, the practically magical projection of light. Film makes it corporeally evident how "one second was never the same as the second before or after" even if — or, perhaps more appropriately, particularly if — what was being witnessed was the repeating mechanisms of a Chaplin skit or a road trip.

Perhaps it is because of film's ability to perform presence that O'Hara chose to reimagine the function his poems could play in the space of *The Last Clean Shirt*. Given the opportunity to attach his text to a form that could only exist in the moment, predicated as it was on "the continuous supplanting or erasing of one image by another," O'Hara used the second and third repetitions of the couple's trip uptown practically to cannibalize, restructure, collage, and goad into being lines from a number of his previously published poems. By chopping, cutting, and revising specific lines, attaching them to brand new phrases developed specifically for the film, and allowing his text to be absorbed by and inform an entirely new genre, O'Hara brought his work into a new kind of life that was mechanically predicated on the immediacy and instantism he so desired.

As I have been maintaining throughout this chapter, O'Hara's and Leslie's formal innovation was in part a manifestation of their political concerns. To this I would emphasize that the mixed-race couple in the film, represented as it is by O'Hara's cut-ups/subtitles, is further marginalized by being queered — that is, the already provisional status of the man and woman as racial outlaws is further extended because their language and thoughts are being denoted via O'Hara's gay cosmopolitan diction. This is an act of celebration, of multiplicity, particularly when we consider the many subtitles in the film that O'Hara adapted from his poem, "In Memory of My Feelings." Subtitles grafted from the poem into *The Last Clean Shirt* include "I am a girl walking downstairs in a red pleated dress with heels"; "I am a jockey with a sprained ass-hole"; "I am the light mist in which a face appears"; and "I am a dictator looking at his wife." By applying this fluid range of identity to a black male and white female — whose physical safety as a couple in mid-1960s America is threatened merely by the color combination of their skin — O'Hara and Leslie reject identity politics as manifested on both the left and right of the political spectrum. "You say I'm *this*?" O'Hara and Leslie ask implicitly throughout the film, only radically to resist and disperse any essentialized understanding of what constitutes identity through playful repetition and variation. "Dispersion and change," as Michael Davidson argues in his discussion of "In Memory of My Feelings," are "a kind of grace":

> Any celebration of multiplicity here is less a sign of self-revelation than it is an indicator of vulnerability. When each proposition of self comes with its own weapon, then the single voice — what O'Hara calls the "serpent" in his midst — remains locked in infinite reflexivity. Once the self is recognized as a "likeness," however, it can be manipulated to accommodate any occasion. And, while this may offer a degree of control in a homophobic environment, it may also lead to a sense of rootlessness and despair. O'Hara's only defense is to regard dispersion and change as a kind of grace. . . . These "identifications" may be sordid to the individual seeking a unitary center or ground, but for the gay poet in 1956 they may be necessary for survival. O'Hara opposes the totalized frame of the masque to the allegorical representations with it, the "cancerous statue" of the self to the multiple "ruses" it adopts. (*Guys Like Us* 111)

By dispersing the self — by continuously interrogating not just the nature of genre but the "nature" of race, of sexuality, of conventional social behavior — O'Hara and Leslie paradoxically create a liberating model for being in the world. While O'Hara and Leslie are certainly moving away from the self-expressive aesthetic evident in Kenneth Anger's and Stan Brakhage's work, not to mention the overt spiritualism in films like *Fireworks*, *The Last Clean Shirt* remains "church worthy" in its efforts to provide viewers with a fluid, inherently cosmopolitan model of identity that resists oppressive social forces aiming to keep people "unconnected."

five

The Conversations between Allen Ginsberg, Charlie Chaplin, and Robert Frank

In his poem "City Midnight Junk Strain," Allen Ginsberg's elegy for Frank O'Hara, Ginsberg celebrated O'Hara as a "chatty prophet" (*Collected Poems* 457), ending the poem by referring to O'Hara's "common ear / for our deep gossip" (ibid. 459). In these charming phrases we find some of the major themes evident in *The Last Clean Shirt* — the ability to synthesize the quotidian with the visionary, depth versus surface, the sense of community engendered by bitchy babble — coming into play. By the time he composed this poem (dated July 29, 1966), Ginsberg was moving away quite resolutely from the centered, visionary self he devised for himself in poems including "Howl" and "A Supermarket in California" in favor of a more diffuse (if still spiritually informed) understanding of what constituted identity. This move coincided with Ginsberg's participation in Robert Frank's *Me and My Brother* (1968) and, as I will argue here, resulted in Ginsberg's increasing politically dissident enactment within his poetry of the gaps between signifier and signified. This shift in Ginsberg's approach should not be ascribed entirely to his love for and participation in film. As with Duncan, Creeley, and O'Hara, influences for Ginsberg were eclectic and wide-ranging. Nevertheless, an analysis of Ginsberg's relationship to cinema will show the very real and significant influence film had on his growth as poet, as it will more generally illustrate the fascinating theoretical, cultural, and aesthetic concerns emanating out of the conversation between film and poetry.

A SKETCH ON ALLEN GINSBERG, "HOWL," AND "A LETTER TO CHAPLIN"

In his high-school yearbook, Allen Ginsberg was described as "'a fiend of Beethoven and Charlie Chaplin,' who 'indulges in music, politics, history, and literature'" (Schumacher 22). In an interview decades later, Ginsberg advised, "Read William Blake & Dostoyevsky; listen to old Blues (Leadbelly Ma Rainey & Skip James); learn classical Buddhist-style meditation practice; try everything; 'If you see something Horrible, don't cling to it,' sez Tibetan Lama Dudjon Rinpoche. See Charlie Chaplin Marx Brothers & WC Fields. Read PLATO's *Symposium*" (Interview with "Helen" 433). As is clear from this sentence, Ginsberg certainly acknowledges other comics, and throughout his work we can detect his affection for vaudeville traditions, Yiddish theater, and the like. Nevertheless, Chaplin appears to have been especially beloved by the poet. With Peter Orlovsky, for example, Ginsberg collaborated on "A Letter to Chaplin from Allen Ginsberg and Peter Orlovsky," a practically epic ode or "love letter" to Chaplin published in the spring 1966 issue of *Film Culture*. The poem featured lines including "Every few years / we dream in our sleep we meat you [sic]. Why don't you go ahead & make another picture & fuck everybody. If you do / could we be Extras. We be yr Brown- / ies free of charge" (7).[1] Ginsberg also wrote retrospectively on recording his seminal "Howl," "the whole first section typed out madly in one afternoon, a tragic custard-pie comedy of wild phrasing, meaningless images for the beauty of abstract poetry of mind running along making awkward combinations like Charlie Chaplin's walk" ("Notes Written" 229). Chaplin as formal inspiration for "Howl"; Chaplin in an orgy with the poets; or Chaplin alongside outsiders, visionaries, philosophers, and saints — Ginsberg consistently placed Chaplin in such company, seeing in the actor's practice a liberatory model that would inform him socially, politically, and formally. Why this admiration for Chaplin?

As I have indicated in previous chapters, innovative poets' appreciation for Charlie Chaplin specifically was not unprecedented. We can see Ginsberg building on a modernist cinematic inheritance that includes Reverdy's and related writers' love for "Charlot"; Hart Crane's poem "Chaplinesque";[2] Gertrude Stein's admiration of Chaplin; and any other number of paeans, poems, and articles written in celebration of the actor. Ginsberg's published statements on Chaplin overall suggest that he finds Chaplin anticipating the improvisatory, madcap, and nonconformist sensibility so crucial to the formation of what we can tentatively call the Beat aesthetic, one typified by Kerouac's writing slogan "first thought best thought," Ginsberg's own "spontaneous mind," and Neal Cassady's merrily itinerant lifestyle, extreme verbal play, and love of free association. Quoting Ginsberg's and Kerouac's poem "Pull My Daisy,"[3] Michael Schumacher points out, "[With Neal] Cassady around, [Ginsberg and Kerouac] dabbled with his crazy, improvisational wordspeak, best exemplified in a fairly lengthy poem/jingle they composed together, a humorous lyric that Ginsberg half-seriously considered offering to Charlie Chaplin or Groucho Marx" (105–6). "Crazy" and "improvisational" elements are something that Ginsberg understood to rhyme with Chaplin's and Marx's own practice. While Schumacher writes that Ginsberg "half-seriously" thought of sending Chaplin a copy of *Pull My Daisy*, Ginsberg was quite serious when it came to deciding who would receive gratis copies of the City Lights edition of "Howl": included on his list were e. e. cummings, W. H. Auden, T. S. Eliot, Ezra Pound, and Charlie Chaplin, the only comedian listed in Schumacher's account (ibid. 238). The fact that Ginsberg's first book was published as a City Lights imprint — *City Lights* (1931) being one of Chaplin's most famous movies — must have seemed especially significant to the poet.

Indeed, as serious as "Howl" purportedly is, we should refer back to one of Ginsberg's early performances of the poem in Berkeley in 1956 (included in *Holy Soul Jelly Roll*) in order to recuperate the comic elements in the text. I have always been struck by the laughter that greeted Ginsberg's recitation, particularly over lines I assumed previously should be received with seriousness, if not reverence. Why, I asked myself, were the poetry habitués laughing knowingly at lines like "who got busted in their pubic beards returning through Laredo with a belt of marijuana for New York" and "who vanished into nowhere Zen New Jersey leaving a trail of ambiguous picture postcards of Atlantic City Hall." Weren't such sentiments supposed to be taken as genuine anguished expression? And of all the recordings of "Howl" Ginsberg could have chosen for his retrospective CD, why this one? (Even decades later, in the context of a lecture in 1981 on Christopher Smart, Ginsberg insisted on characterizing his use of anaphora in "Howl" as leading naturally to the development of "funny humor lines" ["Allen Ginsberg Lecture on Expansive Poetics"].)

I find that rethinking Ginsberg's lines partly in light of the Chaplinesque influence (what Ginsberg referred to as "running along making awkward combinations") goes some way to helping readers see "Howl" as a comedic if simultaneously bardic work. Echoing the Beat/jazz fetishization of spontaneity and improvisation, Deleuze writes that Chaplin "is caught in the instant, moving from one instant to the next, each requiring his full powers

of improvisation" (169). This definition of Chaplin's movement reflects Ginsberg's improvisatory-seeming practice. So many of the lines in the first section of the poem, urged on by the anaphora "who," are characterized by long,
almost punctuation-free detonations of images and ideas that feel as if they
were composed on the spot for maximum shock effect, such as "who blew
and were blown by those human seraphim, the sailors, caresses of Atlantic
and Caribbean love, / who balled in the morning in the evenings in rose-
gardens and the grass of public parks and cemeteries scattering their semen
freely to whomever come who may" (*Collected Poems: 1947–1980*, 128). The
form that lines in "Howl" take is analogous to the Chaplinesque comedic
trajectory, where practically each step the Little Tramp makes boosts him
into a series of ever-expanding ridiculous situations that lead him to swerve
away[4] from anything approaching sensible linearity.[5] We can see a relationship between the increasingly uncontrolled and decentered careening driven
by Chaplin's literal way of walking and running and the uncontrolled and
decentered careening embodied in Ginsberg's lines.

We should also appreciate the many moments of inspired goofiness
throughout "Howl." Note, for example, characters in the poem who "bit detectives in the neck," who "plunged themselves under meat trucks looking
for an egg," who "threw potato salad at CCNY lecturers on Dadaism," who
"hiccupped endlessly trying to giggle." Now, while Chaplin may never have
been "fucked in the ass by saintly motorcyclists, and screamed with joy," the
excerpts above evoke any number of Chaplin's slapstick acts — from the early
Keystone comedies to later films, including *City Lights*, in which Chaplin ac-
cidentally swallows a whistle and ends up with a particularly tuneful attack
of hiccups. This is not to reduce "Howl" to mere Chaplinesque imitation, nor
to deny the possibility that similar moves by actors like the Marx Brothers
and Buster Keaton might have played a part in offering Ginsberg models for
composition, nor to suggest that we should all be laughing uproariously as
we read through the poem. Rather, it is a petition to readers to find in the
wildly digressive, formally disruptive first section of "Howl" a Chaplinesque
element that lends a welcome ludic note to the otherwise almost messianic
tone of this landmark poem.

Chaplin was a model for Ginsberg not just because of his slapstick form,
but also because of the way in which he managed as a public figure to represent a radical politics that ran counter to the dominant views of the times.
Chaplin was a lifelong leftist with Communist sympathies, even through the
Soviet invasion of Hungary. Beginning in the 1920s, the FBI spent over thirty
years filing reports on Chaplin's supposed connections to the Communist

Party. The years following the Japanese attack on Pearl Harbor were particularly difficult for Chaplin. After a speech Chaplin gave that was arranged by Russian War Relief, Inc., "J. Edgar Hoover and the FBI were back on his trail. The day after the meeting, a report was filed by an unidentified agent, who had posed as a sympathizer. He sent back a detailed transcript of Chaplin's speech, which included such enthusiastic and, in the Bureau's eyes, incriminating phrases as 'I am not a Communist, but I am pretty pro-Communist'" (Robinson 556). Chaplin was also, at least for the times, radical in his sexual politics as well, and was in fact hailed by surrealist groups as a model of unfettered sexual freedom. In the collaboratively written surrealist manifesto "Hands Off Love," Alexandre, Aragon, Breton, Eluard, Desnos, and others assaulted the rationale behind "Mrs. Chaplin's suit against her husband" for, among other crimes, fellatio, seduction, and encouraging her to seek an abortion (264–65). After attacking the hypocritical sexual mores of American culture, which "Mrs. Chaplin" apparently so revoltingly embodied, the surrealist group moved on to claim Chaplin as a kind of existential hero fighting bourgeois conformity and an attendant mainstream aesthetics.

In light of Chaplin as both literary model and model for being in the world as a sexual and political outlaw, Ginsberg's and Orlovsky's "love letter" to Chaplin mentioned above is worth further consideration. "A Letter to Chaplin" appears to serve a variety of hilarious and serious functions — as political commentary, as celebration of homosexuality (wherein the poets inform Chaplin, "Again we say you / got that personal tickle-tuch we like- / love"), as manifestation of sociability, as booster of misfit and outsider writers (such as Louis Ferdinand Celine, who "vomits Rasberries" and "wrote the most Chaplin-esque prose / in Europe"), and more. Interestingly, as we find in the nostalgic evocation of "summers in Coney / Island" and the populist "millions & millions of people / waveing hello," this poem is inflected throughout by a recognizable class consciousness. The beginning of the poem, with its image of the two poets in India, assigns an aura of exoticism and poetry to Chaplin, tempered by the inevitable poverty we associate with the very word "India." (Ginsberg's *Indian Journals: March 1962–May 1963* [1970] is informative here. His diary entries oscillate wildly between a kind of proto-hippie awe at the exoticism of India — the easy access to drugs, the tropical fruits, the cute monkeys, and so on — and a socially engaged horror at the visible signs of the continent's profound poverty and caste system.) The "little tramp," with all the peripatetic and economic significations we attach to that phrase, is here updated and joined to two other "little tramps" beating their way across the poverty-stricken subcontinent.[6]

Ginsberg, who famously ends his poem "America" by putting his "queer shoulder to the wheel," extends his affiliation of marginal practices to Chaplin by resolutely queering the Little Tramp. That "tickle-tuch" in "A Letter to Chaplin" is no benign cuddle, but rather a bit of foreplay leading up to a hoped for orgy: "make another / picture & fuck everybody. If you do / could we be Extras." Ginsberg and Orlovsky, of course, were not by any means inventing elements of Chaplin's character that weren't already there implicitly. As anyone who has seen Chaplin's films knows, Chaplin often cuddled up to, kissed, and embraced his male costars. (We can refer to *City Lights*, which finds Chaplin batting his eyes coquettishly at his boxing opponent or sleeping in the same bed as the rich drunk whose life he had saved.) The homosexual eros implicit in these gestures is certainly extended in Ginsberg's and Orlovsky's poem, as the two male poets announce their desire to tickle Chaplin's feet, join him in an orgy, and so on. Line breaks are used to humorously extend this male camaraderie. "We would like come / visit you" is certainly a creaking groaner of a double entendre, given the emphasis on liking "come" — one of those "it's so bad it's good" moments that add much mirth to the overall experience of reading this poem. "We be yr Brown / ies" serves a similar function, in that it focuses reader attention on the color "brown" and subsequently suggests the "brown" of the assholes that "Brownies" Ginsberg and Orlovsky will help Chaplin fuck.

Orlovsky's and Ginsberg's "A Letter to Chaplin" is packed with awkwardly enjambed lines; willfully misspelled words (due, no doubt, to Orlovsky's well-known dyslexia); qualifications, insecurities, and hesitations ("What else shall we say to you," "Why / didn't we ever do this before?," "Shall we let it go at that?"); and wild digressions that take us from the poets' commenting on Chaplin's films, to an unorthodox definition of Ganesha, to a suggestion that Chaplin read Celine, to an imagined screenplay featuring Chaplin as last man standing in a post-apocalyptic world. The visual nature of Chaplin's slapstick finds a textual parallel in the structure of the poem itself and reminds us more generally of the ways in which Ginsberg saw a partial model for his own practice in Chaplin's movements. "A Letter to Charlie Chaplin" breaks, hiccups, prances, and whistles wildly from start to finish, ending, as so many Chaplin films do, with a rapturous look and a promise of "love and flowers": "Okay I guess we can end it now. Forgive / us if you knew it all before. Okay. / Love & Flowers / Peter Orlovsky, Allen Ginsberg."

RADIO THE SOUL OF THE NATION:
GINSBERG AND THE POETICS OF DICTATION

In Ginsberg's poem "Kansas City to Saint Louis," we read:

" . . . I don't see any reason" says the radio
"for those agitators —
Why dont [sic] they move in with the negroes? We've been separated all along
why change things now? But I'll hang up, some other Martian might want
to call in, who has another thought." (*Collected Poems* 413)

This poem and other works written around the time Ginsberg composed "Wichita Vortex Sutra" show the Bard moving away from a model of composition predicated on inner revelation — which Ginsberg repeatedly evoked in any number of ways, from retelling his "Blake vision" in which he heard William Blake reading his poems "Ah Sunflower," "The Sick Rose," and "Little Girl Lost,"[7] to his advocacy of entheogenic drugs as pathways to mystical insight — to a poetics of dictation. Poetry no longer comes from "within," but is rather dictated to the poet through any number of media, including (as Cocteau had imagined it earlier in his film *Orpheus*, which Ginsberg very much loved) the car radio.

David Jarraway notes "a key rhetorical shift in Ginsberg's later writing," one that is tied in part to Ginsberg's putting "his long-standing addiction to Blake's visionary transcendentalism behind him around the time of 'Wichita Vortex'" (84).[8] Similarly, Michael Davidson and Tony Trigilio recognize that "prophecy 'no longer emanates from some inner visionary moment but from a voice that has recognized its inscription within an electronic environment'" (Trigilio, *Allen Ginsberg's Buddhist Poetics* 95). Such "later writing" (and I would include a number of Ginsberg's poems from "The Fall of America" section of the *Collected Poems*, including "Beginning of a Poem of These States," "Have You Seen This Movie," "These States: Into L.A.," and "Bayonne Turnpike to Tuscarora") provides us with an alternative model of Ginsberg that suggests a far more complex and linguistically innovative poet than the post-Romantic, shamanistic model allows: "Speeding thru space, Radio the soul of the nation," Ginsberg writes in "Beginning of a Poem of These States," ceding vatic authority to a disembodied mechanism independent of the poet's oracular stance (*Collected Poems* 369). Rather than foregrounding inner revelation, Ginsberg transcribes and riffs off what the radio spits out, presenting those transcriptions as essential constituents of meaning-making in the poem.[9]

"Wichita Vortex Sutra" especially allows for what Jarraway, in quoting from the poem, calls a more polyvalent reality of "conflicting language"

> proliferating in airwaves
> filling the farmhouse ear, filling
>   the City Manager's head in his oaken office
>   the professor's head in his bed at midnight
>   the pupil's head at the movies (86)

Despite containing many of the elements we associate with Ginsberg-as-mystic — his overtly religious diction, his positing spiritualism as an antidote to materialism, his almost hilarious inflated rhetoric ("On to Wichita to prophesy! O frightful Bard!" [*Collected Poems* 404]) — Ginsberg-as-author often disappears within the surfeit of textuality:[10]

> Turn Right Next Corner
>   *The Biggest Little Town in Kansas*
>   *MacPherson*
> Red sun setting flat plains west streaked
>   with gauzy veils, chimney mist spread
>   around christmas-tree-bulbed refineries — aluminum
>   white tanks squat beneath
>   winking signal towers' bright plane-lights,
>   orange gas flares
>   beneath pillows of smoke, flames in machinery —
>   transparent towers at dusk
>
> *In advance of the Cold Wave*
>   *Snow is spreading eastward to*
>   *the Great Lakes*
>   News Broadcast & old clarinets
>   Watertower dome Lighted on the flat plain
>   car radio speeding across railroad tracks — (ibid. 394)

The poet has yet to make an appearance in the opening of this poem. Instead, bits of information are dutifully noted and recorded in order to set up a scene characterized by signage, radio crackle, and moving landscape. The reader is provided with a close-up on the Macpherson billboard, followed by a panoramic shot of the "flat plains west." The poem continues much as a car tracking shot in a film: refineries, tanks, signal towers, and gas flares all whiz by us. The second stanza adds to the generally arbitrary and unsystematic feel of the opening. A radio announcer's weather report impinges itself upon the optic regime established in the first stanza, and so sound and image are unconditionally linked to position the poem all the more as modern filmic experience. The ordinary landscape then becomes surrealist spectacle — "News Broadcast" alongside "old clarinets." The seeing and speaking eye/I has yet to be designated as Ginsberg's own. Rather, the subject, as we detect it in the lines, "Watertower dome Lighted on the flat plain / car radio speeding acrost railroad tracks," is not the passenger in the car but the car radio itself, transmitting its seemingly random messages and visions onto the page.

Significantly, "Wichita Vortex Sutra" and related poems were initially recorded on a tape machine in the context of what we can now recognize was a kind of private multimedia spectacle — Ginsberg's road trip with Peter Orlovsky across the United States. (The journey was documented at times by filmmaker and photographer Robert Frank to create *Me and My Brother*, which I will discuss in detail below.) "Allen traveled across America in a Volkswagen Microbus, noting whatever struck him, from newspaper headlines to bits of conversation to billboards to music and news he heard on the radio. His composition technique was also influenced by a gift, a state-of-the-art, portable, reel-to-reel Uher tape recorder he received from Bob Dylan that same year. . . . As the radio crackled with news reports of the escalation of America's involvement in Vietnam, Allen journeyed on to Wichita" (Ginsberg, "Interview with Barry Farrell" 54). The tape recorder encouraged Ginsberg to transcribe environmentally specific language into the poem that was predicated not on his own internal will but on what was happening outside. "The machine not only afforded him the opportunity to record his thoughts instantly without even the slight intrusion of having to put them on paper but it also had the effect of providing him with an instant cut-up when the machine picked up all the sounds around him" (Schumacher 457).

In Ginsberg's interview with Michael Aldrich and others regarding this new compositional practice, Aldrich insisted that Ginsberg's method of arranging text on the page was "essentially a romantic, expressionistic way of organizing a poem. . . . It's not an intellectual logic or a narrative logic" (154). We can see in Aldrich's definition a reification of a clichéd Ginsberg as inspired, alogical visionary. Ginsberg retorted in part by insisting "I think it is an intellectual logic — because you're organizing it logically" (ibid.). Ginsberg links surrealism and his own poetics to the strategies of the cinema, all the while insisting on the inherently sensible nature of his project:[11]

AG: Montage is logical — montage was at first considered to be illogical, and
irrational, or surrealism was first considered to be irrational, until everybody
realized that what really was irrational was a rearrangement of the actuality
of mind consciousness into syntactical forms which didn't have anything to
do with what was going on in the head. (ibid. 154–55)

Rereading "Wichita Vortex Sutra" with Ginsberg's words in mind, we see how
Ginsberg's poetics of dictation progress into a poetics of montage. Transcrib-
ing bursts of radio noise, newspaper headlines, and billboard legends, Ginsberg continues in succeeding stanzas to entwine these aleatory texts with
carefully composed juxtapositions and scene-jumping cuts:

> Police dumbfounded leaning on
> > their radiocar hoods
> > While Poets chant to Allah in the roadhouse Showboat!
> (*Collected Poems* 394)

> While the triangle-roofed Farmer's Grain Elevator
> > sat quietly by the side of the road
> > > along the railroad track
> > American Eagle beating its wings over Asia
> > > million dollar helicopters (ibid. 399)

and "wires ranging from Junction City across the plains — / highway clover-
leaf sunk in a vast meadow" (ibid. 406). All the while, the radio, billboards
and newspaper headlines whisper their messages to the poet, who dutifully
lays them out on the page: "Approaching Salina, / Prehistoric excavation,
Apache Uprising / in the drive-in theater" (ibid. 396); "'Better not to move
but let things be' Reverend Preacher?" (ibid. 397); "You're in the Pepsi Generation" (ibid. 398); "Central Georgia's rust colored truck proclaiming / *The
Right Way*" (ibid. 404).

A fair enough complaint at this point might be that Ginsberg's transcription is merely an updated romanticism, one that finds the twentieth-century
poet stating his purpose and invoking the Muse to sing through him. However, Ginsberg's poetics of dictation are opposed to classical and Romantic
conceptions of the Muse, in that what is dictated to Ginsberg is unspecified,
open to randomness and chance — the previously quoted "*In advance of the
Cold Wave / Snow is spreading eastward to / the Great Lakes* / News Broadcast
& old clarinets" ("Wichita Vortex Sutra," ibid. 394), or "'For he's oh so Good /
and he's oh so fine / and he's oh so healthy / in his body and his mind' / The

Kinks on car radio" ("Hiway Poesy: LA — Albuquerque — Texas — Wichita," ibid. 382). Compare this dictation and reportage to previous invocations of the Muse — Homer's "Tell me, Muse, of the man of many ways, who was driven / far journeys, after he had sacked Troy's sacred citadel"; Milton's

> Of Mans First Disobedience, and the Fruit
> Of that Forbidden Tree, whose mortal tast
> Brought Death into the World, and all our woe,
> With loss of EDEN, till one greater Man
> Restore us, and regain the blissful Seat,
> Sing Heav'nly Muse;

Wordsworth's "The Waggoner" ("Rich change, and multiplied creation! / This sight to me the Muse imparts"); and so on. Such invocations are based on a framework that has already been developed and thematized by a poet summoning the Muse for assistance and inspiration in composition. This is a much different model of dictation than that offered by Ginsberg. Many of the poems included in "The Fall of America" section in Ginsberg's *Collected Poems*,[12] while certainly antiwar in theme, include sources that bear no immediate relevance to the "topic" of the work. Statistics, signs, and songs appear according to what happened to be unfolding outside the car window and playing on the radio at the time Ginsberg was taping, and subsequently Ginsberg organizes his materials through a juxtapositional aesthetic that oftentimes works to resist rather than extend a centered theme. "Wichita Vortex Sutra" in particular, Trigilio writes, "forecasts the aesthetic turn that would become the Language movement in U.S contemporary poetry in the following decade, where form *is* content rather than an extension of content. . . . Buddhism and the technologies of Cold War culture combine to create a boundary site that produces pacifistic language in 'Wichita.' The mantra simultaneously summons and subverts the referential power of language" (*Allen Ginsberg's Buddhist Poetics* 97–98).

This "aesthetic turn" seems influenced in part by the film world in which Ginsberg was a player. Indeed, Ginsberg emphasizes the significance of film by referring repeatedly to poets and filmmakers. In "Hiway Poesy: LA — Albuquerque — Texas — Wichita," for example, Ginsberg wrote, "Beautiful children've been driven from Wichita / McClure & Branaman[13] gone / J. Richard White departed left no address / Charlie Plymell come *Now* to San Francisco / Ann Buchanan[14] passing thru, / Bruce Conners took his joke to another coast" (*Collected Poems* 388). When visiting Wichita in January 1966, Ginsberg reminded the locals of filmmakers, including Bruce Conner,

Charlie Plymell, Robert Branaman, and Stan Brakhage, who grew up in its environs. Gary Scharnhorst reports that "Ginsberg was interviewed by the *Wichita Eagle* . . . on February 6, [1966], and he spoke his mind, to say the least [about city harassment of a local bookstore/café owner]. 'The city imposes a dark night on the soul of its youth,' he insisted. He again mentioned Michael McClure, Roxie Powell, Bruce Conner, J. Richard White, Stan Brakhage, Robert Branaman, and [Charlie] Plymell among the poets and artists native to Wichita who had fled the city rather than submit to its intellectual constraints" (Scharnhorst 374).[15]

Given Ginsberg's references to film and poetry in "The Fall of America" section of his *Collected Poems*, combined with a developing poetics that suggest film's formal influence, we should consider the final lines of Ginsberg's "A Methedrine Vision in Hollywood," where we find the poet asserting forcefully that what we understand as reality comes not from some core of privileged inner truth, but from an allusively cinematic and endlessly projecting outside

> Made of Ideas, waves, dots, hot projectors
> mirror movie screens,
>   Some what the Shadow cast at Radio City
>   Music Hall Xmas 1939
> gone, gone, utterly completely gone
> to a world of Snow
>   White and the Seven Dwarfs —
> Made up of cartoon picture clouds, papier-mâché
>   Japanese lantern stage sets strung
>   with moon lights, neon arc-flames
>   electric switches, thunder
> reverberating from phonograph record tape machine
>   Tin sheets of Zeus on
> the Microphone jacked to gigantic Amplifiers, gauge
>   needle jumping, red lights warning Other
> Dimensions off the overloaded public address Sound
>   Systems feedback thru blue void
>   echoing the Real of Endless Film. (*Collected Poems* 380–81)

Ginsberg's style here suggests what Laszlo Géfin calls "nontransitional methods." Referring to *Planet News* and "The Fall of America," in which many of the "auto-poesy" poems, including "Wichita Vortex Sutra," were included, Géfin notes, "In his search for a nonlogical, 'elliptical' mode of expression,

[Ginsberg] utilized all possible manifestations of the form, whether found in haiku, Williams, Cézanne, or surrealism. Absorbing and benefiting from the variety of nontransitional methods, Ginsberg in the 1960s arrived at his own poetics. He put them to use in an open sequence, begun in the volume *Planet News* and continued in *The Fall of America*" (279–80). To those "possible manifestations" of "elliptical" form, as I will now argue, I would add the New American Cinema as an important component to Géfin's list.

GINSBERG IN THE NEW AMERICAN CINEMA

Returning to the city in 1963 from his sojourn in India, Ginsberg saw the poetry scene morphing into a countercultural poetry-film scene:

> But what's happening now in the U.S.? Amazingly enough, MOVIES. After having been absent from the land for three years, I found on my return an excitement, a group, an art-gang, a society of friendly individuals who were running all around the streets with home movie cameras taking each other's pictures, just as — a decade ago — poets were running around the streets of New York and San Francisco recording each other's visions in spontaneous language. So now the present moment is being captured on film. This is nothing like the commercial film of banks distributors money-stars etc. This is the film of cranks, eccentrics, sensitives, individuals one man one camera one movie — that is to say the work of individual persons not corporations. As such naturally it's interesting depending upon the individual behind the camera — Ron Rice, Harry Smith, Jack Smith, Brakhage, Mekas, Anger, Connors [sic], others. Jonas Mekas is the genius organizer of encouragement and showings, and there is a Film-Makers Cooperative — which naturally has been attacked by the police. ("Back to the Wall" 8)

Ginsberg "became a familiar face in avant-garde movies by a variety of filmmakers, [and] he showed wide-ranging tastes in nonnarrative cinema, praising Andy Warhol's work and Barbara Rubin's audacious *Christmas on Earth* (1963), which he described as 'a lot of porn, beauty, in which she made an art object out of her vagina. I thought that was in the right spirit'" (Miles 334).[16] Ginsberg read parts of his poems "Death to Van Gogh's Ear," "Sunflower Sutra," and "The Fall of America" in Jonas Mekas's film *Guns of the Trees* (1962); he appeared as himself in Robert Frank's and Alfred Leslie's *Pull My Daisy* (1959); Barbara Rubin's *Allen for Allen* (1965), Piero Heliczer's *Joan of Arc* (1967), Conrad Rooks's *Chappaqua* (1967), and Robert Frank's *Me and My Brother* (1969); he read "Who Be Kind To" and "The Change" and chanted mantras in Peter Whitehead's *Wholly Communion* (filmed on June 11, 1965, Royal Albert Hall, London; released later in 1965); he performed his poems in Gregory Markopoulos's *Galaxie* (1966); he appeared in Mekas's *Walden* (1969); he horsed around with Bob Dylan in D. A. Pennebaker's *Don't Look Back* (1966); he was featured in Bob Dylan's *Renaldo and Clara* (1978); he participated (alongside writers such as William Burroughs, Peter Orlovsky, and Philip Whalen) in Stan Brakhage's *Tho't Fal'n* (1978); talked about his father in Nam June Paik's *Allan and Allen's Complaint* (1982); played the part of a shady lawyer in Jacob Burckhardt's *It Don't Pay to Be an Honest Citizen* (1985); and, as with so many of the poets we have considered here, he was part of the Warhol film scene, appearing in Warhol's *Couch* (1964), as a screen test subject for Warhol, and in Gerard Malanga's and Andy Warhol's collaborative book *Screen Tests / A Diary* (1967), discussed in more detail below.

Ginsberg's participation in these film projects invites us to more generally consider the effects of Ginsberg's decades-long relationship to filmmakers and Underground film stars. Exploring these exchanges in light of how the filmic influenced Ginsberg's developing poetics can show how New American filmmakers saw Ginsberg as a source informing their own aesthetics generally and as a way into creating an intermedia community that could blur the lines between text and image. It is my hope that this study will encourage others to explore the above-mentioned filmmakers and films related to Ginsberg. One could certainly analyze the ways in which Jonas Mekas engaged with Ginsberg's poetry in his film *Guns of the Trees*, for example, or consider the way surrealism and mythopoesis[17] influenced both Harry Smith and Ginsberg to experiment with disjunctive practices and dream imagery in an effort to achieve a kind of spiritual transcendence. The remainder of this chapter, however, will explore the ways in which Ginsberg's poetry intersected with, was influenced by, and informed the work of Ginsberg's close friend, the filmmaker Robert Frank. I will refer to letters between Frank and Ginsberg detailing their plans to make a film out of the poem "Kaddish" in order to set the stage for an analysis of Frank's film *Me and My Brother*, which — in its documentation of the trip that resulted in the composition of "Wichita Vortex Sutra," its use of poetry readings as dramatic events, its innovative editing, and its experimental and suggestively postmodern take on what constitutes subjectivity and authorship — will add greatly to our consideration of the conversation between film and poetry. I would like to reiterate, however, that the ways in which I read Frank's film and Ginsberg's poems forms only a small part of what is possible in thinking about Ginsberg's poetry as it played in and among the New American Cinema.

MAKING "KADDISH" INTO A MOVIE?

While Robert Frank's film *Me and My Brother* is relatively well-known (if not screened as often as it should be), what is not so well-known is that the film came about due to Robert Frank's and Allen Ginsberg's failure to transform Ginsberg's poem "Kaddish" into a movie. Ginsberg recalls

> Returning from India 1963 I was more or less broke, so Robert hired me to his house daily, I wrote a cinematic script for my *Kaddish* one scene a day — Robert paid me $10 an hour or so, or $15 a scene. A subsidy gratefully received, and under his encouraging direction I finished a model script, then at Robert's suggestion, wrote scenes from present time to be interweaved with original narrative, flashes forward. I hadn't thought of that. The poem was an account of my mother's nervous breakdowns and death in a mental hospital. But Robert couldn't raise money to film *Kaddish*, so he started shooting my roommate Peter and his mental hospital brother Julius Orlovsky in New York. ("Robert Frank" 467)[18]

That Ginsberg "hadn't thought" about the possibility to feature scenes "from present time to be interweaved with original narrative, flashes forward" is pretty fascinating when we take a look at his poetry from that period. We can return to "Wichita Vortex Sutra" and the "auto poesy" poems generally to find Ginsberg engaged in writerly practice that juxtaposes quotidian events with references to the Buddhist pantheon, Native American creation myth, and the Vietnam War. Note the following lines from "Beginning of a Poem of These States":

> Coyote jumping in front of the truck, & down bank, jumping thru river, running up field to wooded hillside, stopped on a bound & turned round to stare at us — Oh-Ow! shook himself and bounded away waving his bushy tail.
>   Rifles & cyanide bombs unavailing — he looked real surprised & pointed his thin nose in our direction. Hari Om Namo Shivaye!
>   Eat all sort of things & run solitary — 3 nites ago hung bear dung on a tree and laughed
>   — Bear: "Are you eating my corpses? Say that again!"
>   Coyote: "I didn't say nothing."
>   Sparse juniper forests on dry lavender hills, down Ritter Butte to Pass Creek, a pot dream recounted: Crossing Canada border with a tin can in the glove compartment, hip young border guards laughing — In meadow the skeleton of an old car settled: Loot To Jesus painted on door. (*Collected Poems* 370)

Of course, any number of poems from antiquity to the present day combine details of the present with allusions to the past and prognostications of the future. What is notable about Ginsberg's poetry around the time of his writing a screenplay for "Kaddish" and participating in the filming of *Me and My Brother*, however, is the way in which the writing is so manifestly cinematic. The first quoted line works much like a tracking shot as we are encouraged to follow the coyote's movement across the road and up the hill. But like a fabulist film combined with a Looney Tunes cartoon, the coyote quickly becomes something like Wile E. Coyote, a wholly anthropomorphized creature who looks at the poet and friends with an "Oh-Ow!"[19]

The subsequent line further disorients the reader by leaping to what we can presume is a Vietnam War battlefield where "Rifles & cyanide bombs" are "unavailing." The conceptual and visual confusion that results finds us unable to say with any certainty who is "pointing his thin nose in our direction." Is this still the coyote? A soldier, American or otherwise? A transhistorical Buddha evoked by the mantra "Hari Om Mano Shivaye"? The next scene — a cartoon-like discussion between Bear and Coyote — further anthropomorphizes the Coyote as it resists any attempts on the part of the reader to find a connecting thread. The narrative line has leapt from present moment to an imagined battlefield to cartoon to a dialogue between animals. This fractured series bubbles out of the tracking shot, an anchoring strategy predicated on notating, in a practically mechanical, dispassionate tone, what is seen from the window of a moving automobile.

As the line following "I didn't say nothing" indicates — "Sparse juniper forests on dry lavender hills, down Ritter Butte to Pass Creek" — the tracking shot is precisely the very mode that serves as a kind of base from which Ginsberg cuts, flashes forward, and flashes back. Film historian Kristian Moen suggests that the line beginning "Sparse juniper forests" works much like the prologues to Hitchcock's *Rebecca* and Orson Welles's *Citizen Kane*. In the opening to Hitchcock's film, the camera pauses at the gates of the Manderley mansion, then moves through them to work its way through the overgrown driveway to rest finally on a misty closeup of the ruined mansion. In Welles's *Citizen Kane*, as the script describes it, "the camera moves slowly towards the window which is almost a postage stamp in the frame, other forms appear; barbed wire, cyclone fencing, and now, looming up against an early morning sky, enormous iron grille work. Camera travels up what is now shown to be a gateway of gigantic proportions and holds on the top of it — a huge initial 'K' showing darker and darker against the dawn sky" (Welles and Mankiewicz). Of course, whereas Hitchcock's and Welles's scenes rest on a house, Ginsberg rests on a "settled" car, and a flashback to a "pot dream recounted" interrupts the flow of action. My point here is merely to emphasize the strikingly cinematic way in which Ginsberg uses text to practically work his way through a variety of visual environments.

As we find in reading correspondence between Ginsberg and Frank, Frank was particularly aware of the filmic possibility in Ginsberg's poetry. Writing to Ginsberg about his desire to create a film out of "Kaddish," Frank promised in a letter dated October 15, 1963, "I will try to send you next week a clear idea of what goes on in my head about Kaddish. I have talked to some people about Kaddish almost all think and believe intuitively that a film can be made. I haven't changed my mind it is only the departure from SF which stopped the project. Eddy calls me often and I assure him that I'm with it and that Allen will be with it too. I have just gotten this typewriter (found it in a house to be torn down) had it fixed and the machine looks like a black Bentley Car." Frank met some resistance from Ginsberg, as a letter written the following week (October 23, 1963) found him goading the poet to work on the project: "Dear Allen, Spoke to Eddy today, has told me about you working hard being fed up, agreeing, thinking and sometimes being happy to do it. What? That Kaddish will make a good movie if we start it." The race was on — Frank would write Ginsberg on a weekly basis during this period, variously encouraging him, steering him away from certain aesthetic choices, promising to back off and give Ginsberg space to think, and so on. A particularly remarkable letter from Frank (November 1, 1963) synthesizes all these dreams and concerns into one utopian expression of camaraderie through struggle:

Dear Allen. Nov. 1 got your letter agree with what you say. Will leave you alone so you can get out of bed mornings. Will just clarify certain thoughts in this letter. Because me too have been thinking and unable to arrive at any thing clear but some ideas have come and I need to encourage myself. First it is your Kaddish and in movie it will stay yours. Filling out scenes by yourself would not be good anyhow. Kaddish should not be done in Flashbacks alternating between present and past. One would weaken the other. It should be done with Prologue — Kaddish — Epilogue. Everyone has his own Kaddish I consider your lament (in the Epilogue) miraculous because you have not gone crazy you are not defeated you are yourself. In the Prologue the climate in which we (YOU) live (AMERICA) is to be felt — then Your Kaddish becomes everybodys [sic] — the miracle of surviving will move us and Your Kaddish becomes everybodys and don't worry about filling in scenes in Patterson [sic] nor anywhere else. . . . We should not be afraid. Where we will differ will be at the Epilogue as I do not have the same Ideals or dreams as you have. We will make the movie and stay friends.

Apparently, this letter did the trick. On November 18, 1963, Frank wrote Ginsberg again to inform him that "I am writing to you after a stretch of 21 hrs. of work on Kaddish. I think we are really getting somewhere." He *was* getting somewhere. That "somewhere," however, would not result in *Kaddish: The Movie*. Frank didn't know this at the time, but he was getting ready to make what would eventually become *Me and My Brother*.

ALLEN GINSBERG, ROBERT FRANK, AND *ME AND MY BROTHER*

In his fundraising proposal, "Prospectus for 'Kaddish': A 90 Minute Black and White 35mm Film, by Robert Frank," Frank concludes his bid with a description of the proposed film project, makes it clear that it would begin with Ginsberg's "narrative," and discusses how he will develop a parallel structure switching back and forth between telling the stories of Ginsberg's mother Naomi and Julius Orlovsky:

> The proposed 90 minute black and white film is based in part on Allen Ginsberg's narrative poem "Kaddish."
>
> The poem recounts Ginsberg's adolescence and his attempts to help his disturbed mother, Naomi. It takes place in Paterson, N.J. during the late 1930's and early 1940's.
>
> The fears of Naomi and her final breakdown have a parallel in Julius Orlovsky. Julius, who is thirty years old, spent fifteen years in Pilgrim State Hospital. He now lives with his brother Peter, and Allen Ginsberg, in New York City. This part of the film is what I imagine Julius to see, hear, say and dream. Julius is silent; he can not communicate with anyone. As he wanders around the city he becomes — through the experience of other characters in the film — a kind of unresponsive mirror of their own madness. These people are my contemporaries (photographer, stock broker, garbage collector, painter, actor, beatnik, dentist, model).
>
> Episodes in the film show the underside of their existence and the variety of relationships between them, real and imagined ("Prospectus").[20]

The end result of this project, however, resulted in the "Kaddish" aspects of the film getting scrapped in favor of focusing entirely on the interactions between Julius Orlovsky, Peter Orlovsky, Allen Ginsberg, and the "other characters" Frank refers to above. The film was both in black and white and in color. Frank served both as director and director of photography. Screenplay credits were attributed to Sam Shepard, Robert Frank, Ginsberg, and Orlovsky. The "Cast" included Julius Orlovsky (Himself); Joseph Chaikin (who doubled as Julius Orlovsky); John Coe (Psychiatrist); Allen Ginsberg, Peter Orlovsky, and Gregory Corso (playing themselves); Virginia Kiser (Social Worker); Nancy Fish (playing herself); Cynthia McAdams (Actress); and Roscoe Lee Browne (Photographer).[21] Seth Allen played the role of Peter Orlovsky (balancing out Chaikin's fictional turn as Julius) and a strikingly angelic-looking Christopher Walken played the role of Robert Frank.[22] Harry Smith appeared in a cameo as a bum on a subway who convinces a nun to sniff glue out of a brown paper bag.

What happened to Frank's original idea? Describing Frank's and his attempts to make this film, Ginsberg wrote, "But Robert couldn't raise money to film *Kaddish*, so he started shooting my roommate Peter and his mental hospital brother Julius Orlovsky in New York, in Central Park at night, in Kansas wheat fields and a Kansas City night rock club, actual life with improvisations including a scene in our apartment East 5th Street Lower East Side where I played a waiter's role. Joseph Chaikin played Julius for awhile when in mid-film Julius wandered away, lost — we found him months later in a provincial hospital north of Berkeley. Frank at that time, mid '60s, had a silent Arriflex movie camera" ("Robert Frank" 467).

Frank developed a film that confounded at least some of his contemporaries. As he wrote Ginsberg in a letter postmarked November 4, 1965, "I have shown Julius Film to some people. I know that it is by far the best film that I have ever done. The reaction to it is in that line and the criticism is that it lacks a definite Idea or the conclusion of a thought or even express (clear) of a thought. The film is criticized as being fragmentary — visions but not making a statement." *Me and My Brother* was finished in 1968. The first showing was in New York throughout the week of February 2–8, 1969, playing alongside a series of avant-garde films at the New Yorker film theater on Broadway and 88th Street.

The film tracks Julius Orlovsky's release from a mental institution to the care of his brother, Peter Orlovsky, and Allen Ginsberg. We first encounter Joseph Chaikin, playing the part of Julius, watching fictional versions of Peter and Allen having sex on camera for the benefit of a psychiatrist and cameraman making a film about homosexuality. Chaikin/Julius remains completely silent and withdrawn and is either unable or simply refuses to respond to anything around him.

The "real" Julius is then shown with the "real" Peter and Allen on the poetry-reading tour of Kansas that resulted in poems including "Wichita Vortex Sutra." As the film progresses, we learn that Julius has disappeared during a visit to San Francisco and, later, that Peter and Allen have found him institutionalized in a hospital north of Berkeley. We discover how Robert Frank (either heard offscreen or played by Christopher Walken) hired Joseph Chaikin to play the part of Julius, though the narrative repeatedly swings from one "Julius" to the other as conditions allow. Peter and Allen discuss how Julius received electric shock treatment and Thorazine. This treatment cycle appears to have enabled Julius to begin engaging verbally with people around him. Julius is again released in Peter's care, and the film ends with an interview between an offscreen Robert Frank and an onscreen Julius, who responds to a number of questions about his life, his feelings about acting and film, what he thinks about Ginsberg, and so on.

SAY IT THIS WAY: THE VORTEX IN *ME AND MY BROTHER*

Of course, such a description does not come close to approximating the highly disorienting experience of watching the film, particularly as that very disorientation is in many ways achieved by the manner in which the film intersects with the "auto-poesy" period of Ginsberg's career that resulted in poems including "Wichita Vortex Sutra." Much of *Me and My Brother* documents Peter's, Julius's, and Allen's trip through Kansas and features a number of scenes where Ginsberg reads versions of "Wichita Vortex Sutra" itself. In one scene, for example, we find the three men walking around on a field in Kansas as an aural collage superimposes itself over the scene: airplane announcements, non-diegetic sounds of Ginsberg and Orlovsky singing "Hare Krishna," Peter Orlovsky stating "We are driving down to Kansas City. At 8 pm there will be a poetry reading full of dirty words," and so on. Frank's visual and aural tapestry evokes Ginsberg's collagist gestures. As with Ginsberg's "Wichita," parts of *Me and My Brother* work as a bricolage composed out of close-ups on newspaper headlines ("BLAST KILLS 28: 100 MISSING," "35 KIDS ON WILD BURNING BUS: Crippled Boy Killed, 12 Hurt"),[23] airport departure and arrival announcements, disembodied voices, radio broadcasts, and the like.

Evocations of and quotations from mass media forms play a major role in the film, suggesting the influence of Ginsberg's dictation and transcription practices in "Wichita," along with the progressive politics such disruptive textual practices were designed to promote. For example, one particularly funny scene in *Me and My Brother* features the filmmaker and folk-song an-

Me and My Brother © Robert Frank.

thologist Harry Smith in a subway car drinking liquor and "making eyes" at a nun. The song "Wooly Bully" (played at tremendous volume) serves as this scene's soundtrack. Other sights and sounds that contribute to the setting include a radio announcer introducing Bobby Kennedy to a screaming audience, some indecipherable radio noise, and a young man unfurling a cloth tapestry of Kennedy (which we get glimpses of throughout the film). We then find Smith and the nun in what looks like a median park on Broadway in the Upper West Side of Manhattan. As Smith and the nun huff glue from a brown paper bag, we hear a radio voiceover of Senator Everett Dirksen's speech nominating Barry Goldwater for the Republican candidacy: "In that spirit let me tell you simply and briefly about a man. He is the grandson of a peddler. A peddler who was a proud, honorable and spirited man who left his ancestral country in Europe at an early age. And it is about his grandson that I will speak to you this afternoon. And that grandson's name is Barry Goldwater."

The contrast between the dissolute Smith and nun and the self-important grandiosity of Dirksen singing the praises of the right-wing, staunchly anti-Communist Goldwater parallels the way in which Ginsberg inserts media

speech into "Wichita Vortex Sutra" to point out the latent violence encoded
into anti-Communist ideology. Writing, for example, of the "Pale Indochi-
nese boys" who "came thronging thru the jungle . . . to the scene of TER-
ROR!" and the Marines "Drawn from the shores and farms shaking / from
the high schools to the landing barge / blowing the air thru their cheeks with
fear," Ginsberg then cites a variety of media as he thunders cynically

> Put it this way on the radio
> Put it this way in television language
>   Use the words
>   language, language:
>   "A bad guess"
> Put it this way in headlines
>   Omaha World Herald — *Rusk Says Toughness*
>   *Essential for Peace*
> Put it this way
>   Lincoln Nebraska morning Star —
>   *Vietnam War Brings Prosperity*
>   (*Collected Poems* 399)

Ginsberg illustrates how "truth" is really constructed from a hegemonically
determined arrangement of language. By emphasizing how open to desta-
bilization "fact" is — particularly in the furiously funny phrase "Put it this
way . . ." — Ginsberg shows us that "absolute knowledge once pure, positive,
priestly . . . becomes open to question, its own borders at last penetrated by
the contingencies of time, place, and circumstance" (Jarraway 82). Using
quotation and collage, Ginsberg in this particular case manifests the constructed nature of a "truth" that argues killing for peace as a way forward.

In turn, Robert Frank, by linking the "bum" played by Harry Smith with
the authority of the Church embodied by the nun, only to then juxtapose
them ludicrously against the pomposity and conservatism of the Barry
Goldwater introduction, visually and aurally represents Ginsberg's decon-
structive moves, which aim to show that "truth" is never fixed or essential.
By rearranging word and image in unexpected ways — that is, to simply *hear*
the paean to Goldwater as we simultaneously see the authority of the Catholic Church undermined by the glue-sniffing nun (who is herself eroticized
and possibly aroused by Harry Smith, the no-good bum) — is to point to the
possibility that power is vulnerable to progressive disruption. (We might add
that the nun's presence resonates with Frank's and Ginsberg's critique of the
role the American Catholic Church played in supporting the Vietnam War.

New York's Cardinal Francis Spellman famously bestowed the title "Soldiers of Christ" to American servicemen in Vietnam; Ginsberg referred obliquely in "Wichita" to Cardinal Spellman in his phrase "Cardinal Vietnam"; and, in *Me and My Brother*, Joseph Chaikin, his face pressed against an apartment window, shouts "IN VIETNAM! THEY'RE KILLING! CARDINAL SPELLMAN BLESSES IT! PEACE!")

If Ginsberg and Frank affirm repeatedly that "language, language" determines reality, thereby challenging the constructions of truth emanating out of the discourses of war and government, what are the implications for the poet's and filmmaker's *own* aesthetic, social, and political worlds? David Jarraway argues:

> As we internalize more and more of ["Wichita Vortex Sutra's"] borders we may begin to grasp the sense of a text in which "nothing is reconstituted, nothing recuperated," and whose bliss is more likely to be "absolutely intransitive." Ginsberg's relentless brief mounted against so many figures of authority throughout the poem, from President Nixon . . . on down through the ranks of Cardinal Spellman, J. Edgar Hoover, Secretary McNamara, Senators Stennis and Alexander, and any number of other "Idiot mayors / and stony politicians" — this unrelenting critique is certainly an important part of the intransitiveness of a discourse that, more often than not, fails to return to subjective authority the closure of passive objects reflecting the idealizations of masculine power and mastery. (84)

As Ginsberg refuses to accept the authority of those who would say "Toughness / Essential for Peace," he simultaneously denies transcendent status to his own self. The Ginsberg we see in "Wichita" is, as Jarraway so ably puts it later, an endlessly disseminating and wholly uncentered self: "Wichita is . . . given to us initially as a 'vortex / of oriental anxiety' mainly because, in view of all the border crossings, it would seem impossible to determine precisely who is who: 'Not Hanoi our enemy / Not China our enemy / The Viet Cong?' But the reader might just as readily encounter a similar conundrum besetting the poet's own identity . . . . In 'Wichita Vortex Sutra,' now we see him: 'I am the Universe tonite / riding in all my Power . . . thru my self'; now we don't: 'May I disappear / in magic Joy-smoke! Pouf!'" (83).

STOP DO NOT ENTER

Throughout *Me and My Brother*, Robert Frank emphasizes the disruptive "now you see him, now you don't" aspects of Ginsberg's poetics and the resulting critique of stable self that such a poetics entails. The film begins with an image of a blinking sign bearing the legend STOP DO NOT ENTER — the ideal of a viewer/reader's unmediated admission into a text is thus immediately threatened. (We might add that this sign is the polar opposite of Rudy Burckhardt's lightly demotic choice to linger on the sign "Come in We're OPEN" featured in his film *Wayward Glimpses*, which I discuss in detail in chapter 7.) As we look at the blinking sign, we hear a voiceover of the actor Seth Allen (who is playing the part of Peter Orlovsky) warning, "Watch out for the cars, Julius!" We are told not to go in (DO NOT ENTER) before the "narrative" of the film has been articulated. Compounding this resistance to narrativity, the voice that we hear is a mimic of the "original" Peter Orlovsky. The tacit messages that flow from such a cranky anti-welcome agitate against enjoyment, against relating to the subjects depicted herein, against losing ourselves in the pleasures of a story, against the contract between filmmaker and audience to suspend disbelief in favor of treating the film narrative as, well, *real*. Film will not present itself to us as an enactment of what the "real" world is, but instead is foregrounded as artifice, and a hostile one at that.

The "real" is interrogated throughout the film in various guises. As the "DO NOT ENTER" sign blinks, we hear Seth Allen begin a monologue that works immediately to point to Orlovsky's and Ginsberg's real-life sexual polymorphousness as it highlights the fluidity of sexual identity. Seth Allen/ Peter asks, "Where else but in 1968 could you get to do something like this. I mean, a *sex experiment*," adding, "*Sex*, right in front of a camera! . . . Hey Julius, come on . . . they're going to film us making love. I feel horny. I *feel horny*. The idea is this and it's a beautiful idea, to record the sex act. It's also a first. It's also a *gift to mankind*." A scene follows in what looks very much like a bedroom stage set. There, the two actors playing the parts of Ginsberg and Orlovsky prepare to make love as a psychiatrist peppers Julius Chaikin (playing the role of the catatonic Julius) with questions while a cameraman films the scene. Moments later, Actor/Ginsberg says to the Kinsey-like psychologist (John Coe), "What sort of people have you filmed here" and "you've been here quite a while I guess." Coe replies, "Oh yes, twelve years now. We get all sorts. Prostitutes, female and male homosexuals, heterosexuals, various combinations of each, masturbators, necrophiliacs, almost every variety of sexual experience known to exist has taken place in this room." Actor/ Peter than asks wonderingly, "*Animals*?" and the shrink firmly replies, "Yes, I once filmed two gibbon apes in the sexual act." After more of this banter, the Actor/Ginsberg announces, "Well I'll read my poem now, alright?" and begins to recite the first lines from the poem "Mescaline": "Rotting Ginsberg, I stared in the mirror naked today / I noticed the old skull, I'm getting balder / my pate gleams in the kitchen light under thin hair." As the poem is read, we can hear the whirr of the camera overwhelming the recitation, Actor/Peter insisting, "This is the *movies*, Julius! A little movie never hurt anybody," and the psychiatrist, leaning over the silent, seated Chaikin, says, "If you'd care to tell me anything at all about what you're feeling and what you're thinking, I'd be more than happy to listen." The actors then begin making love on a bed.

The exchanges between what is happening in the film and what is typical of Ginsberg's (and Orlovsky's) poetry are rich and complex. Of course, the totally uncritical take on the varieties of unrestrained sexual permutations finds a corollary throughout Ginsberg's and Orlovsky's work, where orgies, sex with either gender, and so on are evoked in various registers including the celebratory, the abject, and the lighthearted. I would argue more specifically that what we see during the sex scene seems informed not so much by Ginsberg's recitation of the poem "Mescaline," but by Ginsberg's poem "America." I say this because of one trenchant moment in this scene: as the two men nosh on each other's torsos and necks, the camera swings away from them, pans over to Julius, pans over to and lingers on an image of an American flag mounted on the wall, and then swings back to Julius and the sexual activity. Now, I saw this film four nights in a row when it was shown at Anthology Film Archives in New York in November 2006, and I noted that the audience laughed precisely at the moment when the flag appeared on the screen. Perhaps part of that laughter was a vague and guilty relief at the respite focusing on the flag offered us from viewing two men's erotic entanglement. And yet surely this laughter was based more on the profoundly dissident gesture of the moment, one predicated on aligning flag-waving Americana with exhibitionist homosexual sex.[24] Like Ginsberg's poem "America," in which Ginsberg states in part that his "national resources consist of two joints of marijuana millions of genitals an unpublishable private literature that jetplanes 1400 miles an hour and twentyfive-thousand mental institutions" and ends with the manifestly fey line, "America, I'm putting my queer shoulder to the wheel," the lovemaking-flag-lovemaking scene in *Me and My Brother* presents us with an alternative vision of what might constitute American freedom and liberty (*Collected Poems* 146, 148). Based as it is on polymorphous perversity and the critique of "mental institutions" embodied by the catatonic Julius and the sexually writhing bodies of actors playing Ginsberg (who himself was famously a patient at a mental institution) and Peter Orlovsky, this scene in *Me and My Brother* alludes to and enacts basic themes in the protagonists' poetry to radical effect.

Of course, as the fake Peter insisted earlier, "This is the *movies*, Julius." While certainly evoking Ginsberg's poetry, the fact that our introduction to Peter Orlovsky and Ginsberg is based not on the "real" Ginsberg and Orlovsky but on their mimics suggest Frank is using his film to extend his evaluation of what constitutes the genuine. While Frank has provided us with enough visual cues in the sexually charged scene described above to help us identify the various actors as their famous poetic counterparts, he nevertheless continues to warn us DO NOT ENTER by foregrounding the artificiality of his medium: following the bedroom episode, we next encounter a scene taking place in a movie theater. The perspective is from behind the audience settling down to watch the film, so that the backs of the audience's heads and the movie screen are visible. And what is the audience in this scene watching? What we were just watching previously. In other words, the movie we have been watching is now the movie the audience in the movie is watching. The autotelic aspects of the film take on an absurdist cast as the psychologist asks in an increasingly exasperated tone, "Can you tell me something Julius? Anything at all! Anything you want!" while members of the audience in the film begin to mutter and act out their frustration. A male member of the audience stands up suddenly, faces the camera, and, pointing to a newspaper headline announcing a Mets victory, shouts out triumphantly, "Hey you! See this! . . . That's real!" Pointing back at the screen, he yells, "That's imaginary. Yogi and Casey! Real!" Other voices are heard — a concerned, sensitive sounding woman implores, "Julius isn't replaceable. Why use an actor?" Another guy complains, "Julius bores me. The whole Orlovsky family bores me!" Other voices of protest are heard, and people begin to file out. One particularly winsome male character turns around in his seat, faces the camera, and enthuses, "This is a wonderful movie. It's great. I really like it," while, in the background, the psychologist can still be heard beseeching, "Can you tell me something, Julius?"

This movie theater within a movie theater reappears a number of times in *Me and My Brother*;[25] it serves to extend the warning "DO NOT ENTER," if by "entering" we mean approaching the film as an experience offering transparent access to a narrative along with "insight" or "understanding" of a character's essence. When a woman in the audience asks, "Julius isn't replaceable. Why use an actor?" we are encouraged to suspect that not just Julius but everyone is, to some extent, acting. The woman asking the question is, after all, an actor herself. We, watching her inside our own movie theater,

Me and My Brother © Robert Frank.

begin to feel that the line dividing us from the movie theater audience we see on the screen is becoming increasingly blurry. Frank has said, "The world of which I am a part includes Julius Orlovsky. Julius is a catatonic, a silent man: he is released from a state institution in the care of his brother Peter. Sounds and images pass him and no reaction comes from him. In the course of the film he becomes like all the other people in front my camera — an actor."[26] Shakespeare's epigrammatic "All the world's a stage / and all the men and women merely players" is updated by Frank when he presents Julius as a kind of cipher into which the fiction of a stable core self is absorbed. The distinctions between the "real" Julius, Peter, and Allen and their actor counterparts are permeable, to the extent that taking on another's mannerisms underscores the performativity of the "originals" themselves.

Subsequent scenes build on this theme — for example, Chaikin, looking out of an apartment window as a young woman stretches herself out provocatively on the bed behind him, admits, "I don't trust actors, you never know what they're doing or what they're really feeling. They're modifying the way they come out, the way they present themselves to people. But everybody does that in a way. I mean, everybody sort of edits what comes out. I mean, I'm doing it now." Later, we find the film photographer, Roscoe Lee Browne, admitting, "Sometimes I go off somewhere and I start to walk like Julius as though walking like him I'm where he is. . . . If you strip anybody of his style he'd be where Julius is." In one of the final scenes, Orlovsky discusses Julius's disappearance: "He was wearing gray shoes, uh, black pants, tan shirt and a grey raincoat, and he had an Uncle Sam's color hat with red and blue and white stripes. And uh, so the cop was filling out these forms. And the detective gets on the phone to call Missing Persons to find out if they'd report anything in. While he's speaking on the phone to the Missing Persons Bureau gives uh my brother's name and uh . . . does it like this. O as in Offense. R as in Robber. L as in Illegal. O as in Operation. V as in Violence. S as in Steal. K as in, uh, Killer, and Y as in Why Not. Y as in uh . . . Y as in uh . . . uh Y as in uh . . . why why." Ginsberg then asks, "But then how did we get this hat back if he got lost in the hat?" Putting on the "Uncle Sam's color hat with red and blue and white stripes," Ginsberg then smilingly announces, "I'm Julius. I'm Julius now. Ha ha ha I'm Julius now."

What does this have to do with Ginsberg's poetry, we might ask? The prophetic mode itself, so crucial to Ginsberg's reputation and sensibility, is severely interrogated by these moves and resonates with the shift Ginsberg made from a bardic persona in "Howl" and "Kaddish" to a poetics of dictation evident in many of the poems included in "The Fall of America" section of his *Collected Poems*. Frank appears to highlight this shift in Ginsberg's poetics by illustrating the performativity inherent in the projection of self and, specifically, how performative the very notion of Ginsberg-as-seer had become by the mid-1960s. In the scene following the "movie within a movie" episode just described, for example, we see Ginsberg and the two Orlovskys on a Kansas nightclub stage. The context for this performance is provided for us via voiceover: "In February of 1966 Allen Ginsberg and Peter Orlovsky were on a poetry reading tour in Kansas. They took Julius along." Allen and Peter are shown chanting mantras and ringing finger cymbals while a bearded Julius sits catatonically behind them. The environment is clearly raucous: members of the audience protest, yell, whoop, and shout at each other to shut up. The audience clearly came to see *Allen Ginsberg*, spokesman for the Beats, as opposed to a playful oddball freak smoking cigarettes and singing Hare Krishna.[27] Instead of giving a bravura performance of "Howl," however, Peter Orlovksy and Ginsberg instead lean over Julius and whisper, "say something Julius, say something." We barely hear Julius whisper "say something," after which Ginsberg reports to the audience, "Julius says

Me and My Brother © Robert Frank.

'say something.'" Peter Orlovsky then begins to inform the crowd of Julius's medical history, explaining that for the last thirteen years Julius has been in the hospital, and that he "used to be a *body*-builder with a fantastic *body*. And Robert Frank here is making a movie of him because Robert says you know when Julius looks at a statue or a Picasso ass Julius takes a look and walks around the whole statue, and that is his little thing. And he is very funny and very odd. You see in the mental hospital they give you *Thorazine*, and if anyone here has ever had Thorazine and I tried and sampled my brother's Thorazine . . . it knocks you out . . . it's worser than pot, it's worser than marijuana because it doesn't focus your *eyes*! And it doesn't focus your *bowels*! You see, and so he has a big bowel hang-up." Peter Orlovsky then shifts into reciting an actual poem about Julius. (Line breaks added to performance poetry to make it easier to read. Poems were read in draft form.)

Every day!
I would see him!
Half blind! With a palsy hand!
Dressed in gray state robes!

Almost morning I meet him!
He would say, *Come Peter, take me to the subway.*
Give me a nickel.
Come we go to my old barbershop in Brooklyn.
"One day," I said,
and led him down the hall,
letting him believe
I was going to take him to Brooklyn.

With no warning whatsoever, we hear a voiceover announce, "And there he is. Allen Ginsberg," and the film cuts moments later to another environment entirely, this time a university lecture hall where Ginsberg is reading a line from "Wichita Vortex Sutra" ("A giant dormitory brilliant on the evening plains"). This performance morphs into a draft of what was to become "Wichita Vortex Sutra":

crime prevention show sponsored by Wrigley's spearmint
Much delight in weeping! ecstasy
in singing, laughter rises that confounds
staring Idiot mayors
and stony politicians eyeing
Thy breast,
O Man of America, be born!

As Ginsberg chants these lines, Julius is shown sitting quietly in the background, every now and then blowing a note into a harmonica. There is a cut to a garage where we find Julius playing violin in the mechanic's pit. Superimposed aurally over this scene are sounds from the nightclub in which we hear Orlovsky and Ginsberg chanting mantras again. Then we see Julius wearing headphones, wandering around what looks like a museum as Ginsberg, heard in voiceover, recites more draft lines from "Wichita": "revolving my head to my breast like my mad mother, / chin abreast at Allah," then,

Truth breaks through!
How big is the prick of the President?
How big is Cardinal Vietnam?
How little the prince of the FBI, unmarried all these years!
How big are all the Public Figures?
What kind of hanging flesh have they, hidden behind their Images?"[28]

The distinction between daily speech and poetry, documentary and fiction, is here manically blurred. Frank provides us with a moving visual corollary of Ginsberg's shift from a poetics of messianic revelation ("I saw the best minds of my generation destroyed by madness," the iconic first line of "Howl") to a poetics of collage, notation, and dictation ("sponsored by Wrigley's spearmint"). Now, "truth" is not entirely thrown out the window: as Ginsberg insists in his filmed reading of "Wichita Vortex Sutra," "Truth breaks through!" What's different here is that Ginsberg arrives at his "truth" through a Burroughs-like cut-up, one that quotes from, chops up, and reassembles an endless stream of information. The "truth" that results tends to undermine all normative expectations of what constitutes an ordered self and society. Truth is unstable, fluid, and permeable. What Ginsberg and Frank show is that to "say something" leads not to a foundational conclusion and insight, but to reiteration and dispersal. Julius said "say something."

A SAINT, FULL OF POETRY

Subsequent scenes focus on Julius wandering around Ginsberg's apartment building in an Uncle Sam top hat; Peter Orlovsky reading a letter from Julius's hospital describing how Julius was dismissed from his job as a sanitation worker for masturbating on the job; Julius reenacting his job as a sanitation worker; Julius wandering around an aquarium, a beach, and the streets of the Upper West Side in the company of a young boy; Ginsberg's apartment, where Orlovsky continues reading from the hospital letter; and a dentist's office, where Julius examines his mouth in a hand mirror. We then are reintroduced to John Coe, Julius's psychiatrist, who is in the backseat of a cab driving out of what appears to be an upper-class apartment building. The camera focuses on a still photo mounted on the dashboard of Julius looking at his mouth in a hand mirror — an image that we have just witnessed acted out in the prior scene. Coe announces in voiceover, "My name is John Coe, I play the psychiatrist and Julius is one of my patients." He continues, "I think Julius has a new vision of today's world. He expresses something we all feel but we keep it inside us. To me he is like a saint, full of poetry. Only he doesn't sit in the woods and mountains of long time ago. It's difficult to be a saint here in our time." Harking back once again to Ginsberg's "Howl" and "Kaddish" (and pointing to Frank's original plan to create a parallel structure contrasting "the fears of Naomi and her final breakdown" with Julius's own experiences in mental institutions), Julius is positioned here as holy fool, crazy saint, one of the best minds destroyed by madness.

And yet the visual cues, combined with the practically pathetic exchanges between Julius and his psychiatrist thus far, generate a melancholy that runs counter to Ginsberg's generally progressive thrust. That a picture of Julius is mounted on the dashboard suggests the psychiatrist reads what he wants into whatever fragments of Julius he finds useful. Julius becomes, as Frank would have it, an "actor," who in this case is playing the role of modern-day saint for the spiritually hungry shrink. We find Coe in a sense stealing Julius: Coe's own bourgeois privilege, represented by the fancy building he lives in and the cab ride he can afford, is productively and magically complicated by the bohemian wand that is Julius's picture.

The very fluidity of the subject, a theme that is embodied in the still photo of Julius, takes on an increasingly disorienting cast in the next scene when we find Coe and Julius engaged in something approximating a conversation. Coe asks, "Did your brother bring you to my office? Are you going to talk to me today? Can you answer a simple question? Now I'm going to ask you a simple question. Does the name John F. Kennedy mean anything to you?" At this point, a male voiceover begins to repeat or extemporize on Coe's questions (repetitions are marked in brackets; Julius's responses are contained in double brackets):

> Does the name John F. Kennedy mean anything to you? [Does the name John F. Kennedy mean anything to you?] Are you reading David Copperfield? [Are you reading David Copperfield?] We want to discover if your trouble is subject to therapeutic help or if you require hospitalization. Where do you live? [[408 East 10th Street]]. Do you live with your brother? What is your brother's name? [[Peter]]. How long have you lived with your brother? How long? Julius, I want to help you express yourself. What is your name? [[Julius]]. What activities please you most? [Do you sleep well?] Do you still like to lift weights? [Do you like to walk around the neighborhood where you live?] Do you remember what you were like when you were young? [Do you walk by yourself in the neighborhood where you live?] You used to live in Long Island. Do you remember your mother? [Can you tell me where you go walking? Did you have breakfast this morning?] Can you tell me what you had for breakfast this morning? [[Coffee]] Can you make it yourself? Who made your breakfast this morning? You ought to take your pills. Two of each, twice a day. They'll make you feel less depressed. If you don't take them, does Peter give them to you? [[Sometimes]] No, you've got to take them every day. You'd be more relaxed, less afraid.

As this series of repetitions persists, the film cuts from Coe's office to an elevator where we see a clearly nervous Coe sharing the small space with an

African American male. Questions to Julius continue as voiceover as the African American becomes increasingly threatening by looming over Coe as Coe continues his anxious twitching: "[Do some people frighten you?] Do people sometimes frighten you? Do people sometimes frighten you? Do people sometimes frighten you? Do people sometimes frighten you?"

It seems that no sooner is a character established in Frank's film than he or she is immediately splintered into other voices, other people, other rooms, even, in Julius's case, from real human being to numinous photograph. Voices and images are used consistently throughout *Me and My Brother* to readministrate subject positions. No stentorian voice arrives that declares, as Ginsberg did in "Howl" and "Kaddish," respectively, that "everything is holy" or that madness will ultimately be reconciled as part of the "Visions of the Lord / Lord Lord Lord caw caw caw Lord Lord Lord caw caw caw Lord." Working against coherence, the only totalizing move Frank makes is to consistently enact the fact that identity is amorphous, authority borrowed and dependent on context. Merely by recontextualizing the question, "Do people sometimes frighten you?" so that it applies to the psychiatrist himself, we find that power — be it of the psychiatrist over the patient, the hipster over the square, the white over the black — is a fluctuating thing indeed.

Rethinking the shift in Ginsberg's poetics from inner-directed revelation to a more surface-oriented aesthetic helps us appreciate Frank's project all the more, as we find Ginsberg's efforts towards transcendence in the face of Moloch give way to a poetics of dictation and resistance to closure. We should note the very openness of Ginsberg's final lines in "Wichita Vortex Sutra," particularly as they contrast with the totalizing moves in "Howl" and "Kaddish": "The way is over now — *except* for the souls / held prisoner in Niggertown / still pining for love of your tender white bodies O children of Wichita!" (411; emphasis added).

This is a new Ginsberg, one who resists the temptation to reconcile opposites (seen in his attempted synthesis of the dark crow and the holy "Lord" at the end of "Kaddish") in favor of creating space for exceptions independent of the organizing chant of the bard.

Such gestures are repeatedly evoked throughout *Me and My Brother*, with Julius emphasizing the impossibility of universal consciousness and love that has informed so much of Ginsberg's poetry prior to *The Fall of America*. In a particularly poignant voiceover near the end of the film, Julius's answers to a series of questions serve (perhaps inadvertently) as a commentary on the characters in the film generally. More specifically, we find Julius addressing the problematic role someone like Ginsberg plays in his attempts to take on Whitman's capacious and totalizing mantle. As Bob Dylan's "Ballad in Plain D" plays in the background, we hear Julius offscreen quietly stating, "It's not good to be too holy, you know. It's bad. It's bad to overdo something. People tend to overdo things. Investigate too much. Or be too indifferent. Or they work too much. They give off poison you know. Or they're not able to seek." When Dylan sings the line "leaving all of love's ashes behind me," Frank asks Julius, "Have you ever loved somebody?" and Julius responds, "Not really. I'm not able to. Because there's so many people in the world, you know? You got to keep on going, you know?" As Ginsberg's poetry began increasingly to resist the urge toward closure evident in his earlier work, we find Frank's film allowing for the kinds of contingencies that arise when we acknowledge that "there are so many people in the world." We got to keep on going, you know?

OH, MY NAME IS JULIUS ORLOVSKY

The final scene in *Me and My Brother* finds Frank attempting to interview Julius Orlovsky. Frank maintains an offscreen presence as Julius is shown standing out on a porch in what was likely Allen Ginsberg's Cherry Valley farm in upstate New York. As the film ends here, I will finish by reproducing Julius's achingly sweet responses to Frank's questions about shock treatment, Allen Ginsberg and Peter Orlovsky, the role of the camera, and the nature of truth. Note specifically how Julius's discussion of his shock treatment unavoidably evokes Ginsberg's own "Kaddish," filled as it is with "remembrance of electrical shocks" (*Collected Poems* 212), "new shock for her — Electricity, following the 40 Insulin" (ibid. 217), and so on. Naomi has in this sense been transposed into Julius. This might remind us of Frank's original decision to parallel Julius's experiences with evocations of Naomi, and it fits in overall with Frank's decision in the final version of the film to consistently displace identity and blur the boundaries between bodies. Chaikin becomes Julius becomes Frank, Julius becomes Naomi, Ginsberg becomes Julius, and on and on. (As Julius says more succinctly to Frank, "I'm Peter.") This disorienting dispersal of identity rhymes generally with what has been a central concern in Ginsberg's "Wichita Vortex Sutra" — how truth is contingent on the way language and images are framed. As Julius himself suggests, truth is not a metaphysical verity but "an idea or theory" that "is all we can uh . . . we can uh . . . *arrive* at":

Me and My Brother © Robert Frank.

Frank: Now Julius, um . . . we want to know how you feel about the shock treatment.

Julius: I thought maybe I committed a crime against the state by taking shock treatment that wasn't uh . . . at all justifiable . . .

F: How?

J: . . . consider . . . well . . . considering, uh, any uh, experiential uh outcome or of . . . of . . . of being in shock treatment or around it or near it or . . . or . . . or . . . or *talking* about it.

F: What do you think of Allen?

J: What do I think of Allen? I consider Allen as being . . . just being . . . Allen. For what he is. I'm not too . . . I'm not too . . . uh . . . uh . . . uh . . . familiar with the man anymore than I am, actually. It's as clear as I can be on that matter.

F: And Peter?

J: Peter? Well, Peter's my brother. And he knows about my receiving shock treatment. For what reason I don't know. For what reason I received shock treatment I don't know. Nobody has ever uh . . . satisfied me . . . uh . . . uh . . . uh . . .

F: How do you feel about acting?

J: Acting? It's something beyond my uh, collaboration.

F: Tell it to the camera, what do you think about acting?

J: Acting is beyond my, my uh, thought processes sometimes. Sometimes . . . it may be a waste of time . . .

F: A little bit more over here, Julius. There, that's good. Say something to the camera . . .

J: Well the camera is a uh . . . it seems like a uh . . . a uh . . . a uh . . . a uh . . . a reflection of of disapproval or disgust or uh or disappointment or uh unhelpfulness ness . . . or uh unexplanation . . . unexplaining . . . unexplainability . . . abil . . . unexplainability . . . abil . . . ability . . . to uh, to uh to disclose any real real uh, *truth* that might uh, possibly exist.

F: Where does truth exist?

J: Inside and outside the world. Outside of the world is, well, I don't know. Maybe it's just a uh, a theory. An idea or theory is all we can uh . . . we can uh . . . *arrive* at . . . a uh, theory or a explanation . . . to the matter, whatever you concern yourself with.

F: Look into the camera. And say "My name is Peter," you know . . .

J: My name is Peter.

F: No, no.

J: Oh, oh. My name is Peter.

F: No. Your *name*! Tell us your name.

J: Oh, my name is Julius Orlovsky.

F: And where do you live?

J: 408 East 10th Street.

F: You going back to New York?

J: Uh, yeah, I think, uh on the . . . on the 17th, something like that Peter said. Taking me out to the Islands, to see my family out there. That's a . . . [Julius's teeth visibly chattering from the cold]

F: It's cold, huh . . .

J: It's chilly . . . it's chilly . . . well winter's cold, I don't know . . . but uh . . . [Julius walks inside and off-camera]

F: Cut!

six

The Conversations between
Andy Warhol, Gerard Malanga,
Allen Ginsberg, John Ashbery,
and Frank O'Hara

As I argued in the previous chapter, a central concern in Ginsberg's "Wichita Vortex Sutra" and Robert Frank's *Me and My Brother* was finding a way to enact visually and textually how "truth" is contingent on the way language and images are framed. The "self" itself is consistently performed in the two men's work as a construct of "language language," and various media forms— the radio, the tape recorder, and, ultimately, the film camera — are employed materially to reproduce, deflect, and disperse any essentializing moves that would seek to use the discourses of "truth" to impose normative readings of sexuality, family, power. Let us move on, then, to consider the work of Andy Warhol, as Warhol — an artist very much engaged with New York's poetic community — used technologies from the silkscreen to the film camera in order to undermine "essence" in all kinds of coolly thrilling and surprising ways.

SACRED WARHOL?

In her groundbreaking study of Warhol's art in relationship to poetic communities of the 1960s, Reva Wolf consistently characterizes Warhol's output as emanating out of a "conversation" with poets and assorted hangers-on in Warhol's Factory. "Warhol's interactions with poets do tend to have one thing in common: they function as pieces of conversations" (*Andy Warhol* 7). Wolf historicizes her argument by recovering those oft-forgotten if well-cataloged moments in Warhol's life that found him reading poetry, writing poetry, going to poetry readings, and enthusing over what he characterized as practically magical moments of poetic composition. We find that Warhol screened his films at Diane di Prima's and Alan Marlowe's American The-atre for Poets in New York; that he attended readings at the Gaslight Café in the 1950s and at the Café Le Metro in the mid-1960s;[1] that he hired poet Gerard Malanga as his assistant; that he produced covers for poetry journals, including Ted Berrigan's *C* and Ed Sanders's *Fuck You / a magazine of the arts*; that he included poets such as Ron Padgett, John Ashbery, Ted Berri-gan, and Allen Ginsberg as subjects for his "Screen Tests" series. Before we start protesting that Warhol's surface-oriented work was worlds away from the kinds of hippie-dippy spiritualism that so often characterized the culture of those elusive "Sixties," we learn that a poet like Allen Ginsberg, for one, found in Warhol's visual art and film an "analogue to his own concerns. [Ginsberg] once remarked, 'I was interested in [Warhol's] Zen aspect of the taking an object of ordinary consciousness or ordinary mind or ordinary use and enlarging it and focusing attention on it so that it became a sacred object or a totemic object, mythological. And that seemed very much paral-lel to the notion of a kind of attentiveness you get in Zen or Buddhist medita-tive attitude'" (ibid. 138).

Of course, most of us are not used to thinking of Warhol in the same breath as we think of Ginsberg's iconoclastic Buddhism. Neither were many of Warhol's own contemporaries in the New American Cinema, as Juan Suárez points out:

> The commercial interests subtending Warhol's films, together with his artis-tic persona, were initially at odds with the romantic ideologies of the under-ground. The underground film community fashioned itself as a bohemian group characterized by its unswerving dedication to marginal film produc-tion. Jonas Mekas often praised such devotion in such figures as Jack Smith, Stan Brakhage, Harry Smith, and Kenneth Anger, all of whom were close to the idealized image of the romantic artist, striving on their own with little or no financial support to materialize their artistic visions. . . . As gallery art-ist turned filmmaker, Warhol appeared close to such underground figures as Robert Frank, Bruce Conner, or Carmen D'Avino; however, the quick success of his pop art and the ambiguity of his imagery — was it critical or celebratory of consumer society? — corroborated the reservations some felt toward him. On a different level, his conceptualism and disregard for subjectivity were fur-ther grounds for mistrust in a milieu that favoured subjective expression and self-involvement. (Suárez 222)

And yet, Ginsberg was not alone in his readings of, variously, a latent religiosity, romanticism, and overall dissident aura into Warhol's practice. This is not to say that Ginsberg and others would necessarily deny Warhol's "conceptualism and disregard for subjectivity," as Suárez puts it. Rather, it is *within* those conceptual practices that poets and other filmmakers found aesthetic elements that rhymed surprisingly with "the romantic ideologies of the underground."

Even someone as wholly invested in the relationship between art and a kind of enchanted self-expression as Stan Brakhage found (albeit after some prodding) a visionary element in Warhol's practice: "On first exposure to Warhol's early films, Brakhage had disparaged them, only to retract his verdict after rescreening them at 16 frames per second. Mekas reports: 'Suddenly, he [Brakhage] said, when viewed at 16 frames per second, an entirely new vision of the world stood clear before his eyes. Here was an artist, he said, who was taking a completely opposite aesthetic direction from his, and was achieving as great and clear a transformation of reality, as drastic and total a new way of seeing reality as he, Stan, did in his own work'" (ibid. 224–25). As coldly monumental as, say, Warhol's eight-hour-long shot in *Empire* (1964) of the Empire State building was, or as demanding and boring as his loops in his film *Sleep* (1963) of the poet John Giorno sleeping might appear to be, poets and filmmakers like Mekas and Brakhage understood such work to be a real alternative to Hollywood values as they were celebrations of the quotidian.[2] Suárez states that "Warhol's films are eminently devoted to real-time recordings of his performers doing such banal tasks as applying makeup, making coffee, talking on the phone, gossiping, having casual sex, drinking, arguing, kissing, sleeping, and eating. Capturing ordinary, everyday occurrences that seemed too small for Hollywood pictures was a central interest of the underground, an interest that Mekas most consistently articulated in his criticism and films" (ibid. 223).

In a letter from Gerard Malanga to James Broughton (November 24, 1963), Malanga links the relatively Romantic, erotic, and ludic films of Broughton's with the comparatively procedural experiments of Warhol's films:

> Tomorrow night I plan to see all your films at the Pocket Theatre in NYC. The young lady whom I will be accompanying is my new co-star in the longest kiss movie ever made. Andy Warhol has entered filmdom with an eight hour movie of someone sleeping for eight hours. The film is entitled "8". He is doing a series of "kiss" films in order to break all censorship on two people kissing on the screen. The best part about it is that I have a choice with whom I kiss.

I've already performed in one 3 minute spectacular which was printed 5 times and spliced to make a fifteen minute featurette. . . . I would also like to use "The Aspicked Lovers" for a new magazine which Andy will be publishing in February and I will be editing. It's called *Andy's Magazine* with an original silk screen painting on the cover and will probably sell for 25 c or 50 c. The first issue due in February will contain poems by Barbara Guest, Kenward Elmslie, Arnold Weinstein, Howard Moss, Horace Gregory, Richard Eberhart, Willard Maas, and a lot of younger people.

Here, Malanga positions a variety of practices as one overall project — from Warhol's film work to Broughton's poetry to Malanga's own role as editor of a poetry magazine that, not insignificantly, featured work by poet/filmmakers including Maas and Broughton. Given the interrelated nature of these various scenes, it is no wonder that by around 1968, "Malanga envisioned [the magazine] *Interview* as an organ focusing on film and poetry; he copyrighted the magazine in the name of 'Poetry on Film, Inc'" (Wolf, *Andy Warhol* 51). It is also not surprising that a number of Malanga's contemporaries began writing poetry directly influenced by Warhol's aesthetics.

As I have written previously, Andy Warhol's impact on poets, including Ted Berrigan and Ron Padgett, became more evident as the abstract expressionist painting of De Kooning, Jackson Pollock, and others favored by the first generation New York School and championed in the 1950s made room for the Pop aesthetic developed by Warhol and advocated by poets of the second generation. Berrigan published poems in his *C* magazine, including Padgett's "SONNET to Andy Warhol," which Reva Wolf has already linked to Warhol's film *Sleep. Sleep*, in which the camera simply trained its eye on the sleeping figure of poet John Giorno, was echoed in poetry by Padgett:

SONNET to Andy Warhol
Zzzzzzzzzzzzzzzzzzzzzzzzzzzz
zzzzzzzzzzzzzzzzzzzzzzzzzzzz
zzzzzzzzzzzzzzzzzzzzzzzzzzzz
zzzzzzzzzzzzzzzzzzzzzzzzzzzz
zzzzzzzzzzzzzzzzzzzzzzzzzzzz
zzzzzzzzzzzzzzzzzzzzzzzzzzzz
zzzzzzzzzzzzzzzzzzzzzzzzzzzz
zzzzzzzzzzzzzzzzzzzzzzzzzzzz
zzzzzzzzzzzzzzzzzzzzzzzzzzzz
zzzzzzzzzzzzzzzzzzzzzzzzzzzz

zzzzzzzzzzzzzzzzzzzzzzzzzzz
zzzzzzzzzzzzzzzzzzzzzzzzzzz
zzzzzzzzzzzzzzzzzzzzzzzzzzz
zzzzzzzzzzzzzzzzzzzzzzzzzzz

Padgett's "SONNET to Andy Warhol" presents a series of "zzz"s as a sonnet, having some fun at the expense of poetry traditionalists — more significantly, the poet as a biographical "I" representing the poem is comically
extinguished by the surfeit of "z"s, as the *visual* effect of the "zzz"s march-
ing along the line recalls the cellular structure of the filmstrip (Kane, *All
Poets Welcome* 116–17). Yes, this is a "conceptual" poem. But, like so much of
Warhol's purportedly "conceptual" or "non-subjective" work, we sense that
Padgett's poem urges us charmingly to pay attention to that which we would
otherwise ignore or pass over quickly. Revel in the "zzz"s, the poem advises,
giggle at the "zzz"s, see the "zzz"s as if for the first time.

SUPERSTARS AND POETS TAKING SCREEN
TESTS IN THE UNDERGROUND

To be fair, it would be ludicrous to present Warhol's films as wholly opposed
to or outside Hollywood conventions. Andy Warhol's consistent engagement
with commercial and popular culture in his artwork and through his realign-
ment of the "superstar" economy from one based on Hollywood creations to
one based on an alternative economy of street hustlers (Joey D'Allesandro),
femmes fatales (Nico), wounded trust-fund babies (Edie Sedgwick), Chaplinesque prancing homosexuals (Taylor Mead), and many others certainly
depends on Hollywood models for its efficacy.[3] I want to emphasize here that
Warhol, like Smith and Anger, does not simply evoke Hollywood for parodic
effect. Rather, Warhol's film world is one that is more camp than parody.
Dissident elements already seeded into "mainstream" film itself are highlighted, enacted, and exaggerated. The vivid effeminacy evident in some of
Chaplin's roles, for example, is widely recognized. Chaplin's dancing in films
including *The Floorwalker* (1916) and *The Gold Rush* (1925) was presented "as
effeminate, unmanly, socially marginalized, and queer" (Franklin 63). We
can certainly see this as early as Chaplin's *The Masquerader* (1914), where
Chaplin dresses so convincingly in drag that he ends up fighting off several
men's sexual advances, and in *Behind the Screen* (1916), where Chaplin, after
discovering a stagehand is really a woman in male drag, ends up kissing

her. (Caught in the act by another *male* stagehand who naturally assumes Chaplin is kissing another man, the viewer is treated to the male stagehand mocking Chaplin by acting in an exaggeratedly feminine manner.)

The barely coded and potentially liberating effeminacy in Chaplin's character is allowed in Warhol's films to find full expression via Taylor Mead's exaggerated skipping, dancing, whirling, and fluttering. Establishing himself as a kind of "out" Chaplin in Ron Rice's *The Flower Thief* (1960), where he wandered beatifically around San Francisco, Mead was encouraged by Warhol to further establish this persona in films including *Tarzan and Jane Regained . . . Sort of* (1963) and *Lonesome Cowboys* (1967).[4] As David E. James points out, "Both [Jack Smith and Andy Warhol] were centrally concerned with sexual ambiguity, but where Smith was interested mainly in transvestism, [in *Lonesome Cowboys* and *Tarzan and Jane Regained . . . Sort of*] Warhol cavorts with male effeminacy. . . . Mead's musculature and his sexual response to Jane are equally undeveloped, and he becomes comic as his mincing puniness parodies Tarzanic virility" (88–89). James's distinction is useful, though we might take issue with his assertion that Mead is merely parodying "Tarzanic virility." The very excess of machismo in traditional representations of Tarzan, particularly as those representations are queered via the "beefcake" look of such former Tarzans as Johnny Weismuller and Gordon Scott, invites subsequent filmmakers like Warhol to further elaborate on the recognizably queer qualities inherent in a character who, after all, runs around in the jungle in an itsy-bitsy teeny-weeny loincloth flexing his muscles. (Frank O'Hara, of course, had already highlighted the inherently queer nature of the early Tarzan films in his poem "To the Film Industry in Crisis," in which he exclaimed breathily: "the Tarzans, each and every one of you [I cannot bring myself to prefer / Johnny Weissmuller to Lex Barker, I cannot!]") (*Collected Poems* 232).

Again, the point here is that Warhol looked towards so-called majority culture as a source for liberatory representations of gender and sexuality, representations that he could then extend in his own work. (In a similar vein, one could argue that the restrained chaos inherent in the cinematic cocktail hour epitomized by Frank Sinatra and others is let loose in films including Warhol's *Chelsea Girls* (1966), where Ondine and Brigid Polk shoot methedrine, in Polk's case by simply poking the needle through her jeans.) Gender trouble, social deviancy, chemical dependency, and sexual transgression were always partly visible in Hollywood films—Warhol appeared determined in his films to make such behaviors fully and hilariously visible.

Warhol's "Screen Tests" are perhaps the pithiest expression of how some avant-garde cinema looks to Hollywood sources to perform a complex blend of parody and what might be called cultural archaeology, mining mainstream sources for their latently transgressive elements.[5] Named comically after that typical Hollywood practice of "testing" a potential actor by giving her a small scene to act out, Warhol's screen tests featured his subjects seated in front of a mounted camera. Asked in the early *Screen Tests* to sit as still as possible — in fact, to even avoid blinking — Warhol's subjects embodied the distinct and comical possibility that stardom is predicated to a great extent on the mechanisms that surround and promote it rather than on the inherent skills of the actors themselves. Granted the glamor embodied by the very phrase "screen test," a motley assortment of figures — including poets Allen Ginsberg, Ted Berrigan, Ron Padgett, John Giorno, and John Ashbery; filmmakers Barbara Rubin, Harry Smith, Jack Smith, and Jonas Mekas; folk/rock stars Bob Dylan, Donovan, and Mama Cass Elliot; critics Susan Sontag, Barbara Rose, and Andrew Sarris; Warhol "superstars" Edie Sedgwick and Ingrid Superstar; and relative unknowns including "Archie," "Steve America," and "Betty Lou"[6] — became, at least temporarily, equal in fabulousness and glamorous potential. As these various figures sat — or, as Callie Angell points out, demonstrated modeling moves (Donyale Luna), made Eskimo string figures (Harry Smith), spun around on a chair (James Rosenquist), and more — the lines between people whose cultural work covered a wide variety of social and artistic communities (say, Ginsberg, Sontag, Dylan) and people whose contributions were predicated almost entirely on Warhol's machinations (Sedgwick, Superstar, and more marginal figures, including methamphetamine addicts and teenage runaways) were violated via what Reva Wolf recognizes as the dynamic created by flattery and vanity:

The very act of producing screen tests, as well as their subsequent inclusion in *Screen Tests*/A Diary, was, like Malanga's use of appropriation in some of the poems in this book, a form of flattery, on the giving end, and vanity, on the receiving end (two components of portraiture that the essayist William Hazlitt, for one, had already acknowledged in the early nineteenth century). This flattery-vanity dialogue is apparent in the description by the art critic Robert Pincus-Witten of his experience of sitting for his screen test: "I remember, Gerry Malanga and Andy were there, and Andy would say things like, 'Isn't this wonderful! Isn't he terrific! He's doing it!' As if one is really doing something wonderful by simply remaining static and unmoving before the lens, but the hype was very, very exciting." The power of flattery largely explains why

Warhol and his associates succeeded in getting several hundred individuals to sit for screen-test films. ("Collaboration as Social Exchange" 61)

Warhol was guaranteeing his subjects a kind of immortality predicated on the idea that acceptance into a cultural field marked "film" ceded transcendent import to their names and faces. This was achieved by usurping the mechanisms and language of Hollywood — literally speaking, the film camera and the glamorous significations engendered by the very phrase "screen test" — and applying those mechanisms to the already famous and not famous, conventionally attractive or just plain pimply. The screen test *captured* Warhol's subjects and elevated them into the realm of cinema history, whether they actually did anything culturally significant or not.

THE ASHBERY SCREEN TEST

What did some of the poets considered here look like in the "Screen Tests"? John Ashbery's performance (1966) is worth noting briefly. Callie Angell reports that "Ashbery first met Andy Warhol in the fall of 1963, when Ashbery visited New York and gave a poetry reading at the Living Theater. As Ashbery recalled, Gerard Malanga, who was a poet as well as Warhol's assistant, took him to the artist's studio for an introduction. . . . When Ashbery moved back to New York at the end of 1965, Warhol threw a big party for him at the Factory. Ashbery maintained his interest in Warhol's work after his return to New York. . . . Ashbery recalled that his *Screen Test* was shot one day when he had dropped by the Factory from his job as executive editor of *Art News* magazine: 'I found it kind of intimidating,' he confessed, 'because there were all these people doing their strange tasks' " (33). Ashbery's intimidation is visible on the screen. We first find Ashbery, dressed neatly in suit jacket and tie, his face situated just to the left hand side of the screen. We then notice his eyes moving around a little bit from side to side, and then up. A touch of aggression is evident in his overall composure, which is accentuated further when Ashbery turns to face the camera directly. The confrontational aura, however, is quickly undermined by a rather rapid back-and-forth movement of his eyeballs. Ashbery then looks down at one point as if he's uncomfortable (maybe because of the light shining so brightly on his face). He moves his head slightly, and then the screen test ends with one of Warhol's characteristic light flares.

While not referring specifically to Ashbery's screen test, Jack Sargeant's discussion of Warhol's work is certainly relevant to the discussion we're having here. Sargeant emphasizes how the screen tests do not so much embody as perform the self, and he rightly focuses on the way in which subjectivity in film is always a kind of immanent spectacle: "When their image collapses and the person [sic] underneath emerges in minute flickers of anxiety, then the self-designed spectacle collapses and a new form of spectacle emerges. This is not the emergence of an essence, but a manifestation of immanence. Nothing is revealed; certainly any truth of the subject remains under erasure. The brief displays of nervousness . . . enables the subject to re-immerse themselves in the spectacle, thereby allowing the viewer to catch a glimpse of the constructed nature of the spectacle of the public self" ("Voyeurism" 90). Given Sargeant's reading, we should address the fact that Ashbery's notorious *The Tennis Court Oath* (1962) — Ashbery's most radical interrogation to this day of what constitutes originality, subjectivity, and "essence" — was attracting a new wave of interest in downtown New York around 1965–1966, thanks in part to poet Ted Berrigan's trumpeting its value to the denizens of the Lower East Side. Warhol was surely familiar with *The Tennis Court Oath*. Warhol was friendly with Ted Berrigan and had produced cover art for Berrigan's poetry journal *C*. Berrigan and Gerard Malanga recycled some of the book's lines for their own work, in Berrigan's case by knitting them into his legendary *The Sonnets* (1964). Warhol attended an Ashbery reading at the Washington Square Art Gallery in 1964 at which Ashbery recited a number of poems from *The Tennis Court Oath*. More generally, "Warhol was fond of Ashbery's poetry. In an interview several years [after the Washington Square reading], when asked whether he had a favorite poet, Warhol replied, 'John Ashbery, and Gerard Malanga. Do you know him?' . . . The fact that Warhol mentioned Malanga in the same breath as Ashbery suggests he was aware that Malanga's poetry drew heavily on that of Ashbery" (Wolf, *Andy Warhol* 90).[7]

In *The Tennis Court Oath*, Ashbery negotiates consistently between the fractured nature of the texts, his commitment to expressing sexual and national identity, and his more amorphous desire to liberate language from stable referentiality. The poem "America," for instance, suggests an almost apprehensive resistance to the artificiality of film and an arguably ironic cry for national coherence: "And I am proud / of these stars in our flag we don't want / the flag of film / waving over the sky / toward us — citizens of some future state" (69). That resistance toward "the flag of film" is, in Ashbery's own screen test, embodied directly by the poet's glower at the camera. Forget about notions of self, of citizenship, of belonging naturally to a specific geographical space called "America" — Ashbery in his screen test is practically a free-floating signifier. Even the backdrop (what looks like a slab of grey stone wall) that Ashbery is foregrounded against could be pretty much anywhere, anytime. And, in case we don't get the point, the very performativity of Ashbery's role is further highlighted at the end of the film through the light flare that at first flickers and then wholly subsumes the image on the screen with its great wash of bright light. Like the consistently constructed and deconstructed poetic persona visible throughout *The Tennis Court Oath*, Ashbery in Warhol's screen test is at first annunciated only to be wiped out.

ANDY IS CERTAINLY ONE: O'HARA AND WARHOL

And what of Ashbery's New York School colleague, Frank O'Hara? O'Hara, after all, was a poet whose work Warhol read devotedly; in whose social world, as Reva Wolf shows us, Warhol so much wanted to be a player; and who was filmed by Warhol giving a poetry reading either in late July 1963 or one of the following years. ("The footage, two or three 100-foot reels of silent black-and-white film, was never screened [and according to Malanga, it 'disappeared into Andy's apartment. . . . Frank didn't take Andy seriously, so this was Andy's way of getting back at Frank'])" (Wolf, *Andy Warhol* 21). O'Hara, I would argue, conceived of the cultural field of poetry in a fashion similar to the way Warhol approached filmmaking, particularly in his *Screen Tests*. What other poet of the twentieth century besides O'Hara at once democratized and exalted a wide variety of historically real, named individuals simply by placing them in texts we call poems? How many of us now feel we know Bill, Norman, Joe, Ashes, Joan, Mike, Kenny, Johnny, and Alvin? It is important, however (particularly given Warhol's inclusion of anonymous dropouts, marginal social figures, and the like), that we recognize one doesn't need to be a poet or painter to look good in O'Hara's poems. We recall "Ashes" perhaps as well as we recall Miss Stillwagon (first name Linda, I once heard), or that "blonde chorus girl" who "clicks," or that "sissy truck driver." As Brad Gooch recognizes, in O'Hara's poetry "even construction workers — staples of the midtown [Manhattan] terrain — are made to seem mysterious and glamorous and tropically sexual" (289). O'Hara inscribes elements of grace, pulchritude, style, camp, and sophistication consistently in people affiliated with working-class, art world, music, and poetry communities.

Can we not see O'Hara's poems, particularly in their "I do this, I do that" mode, as textual anticipations of Warhol's "Screen Tests," radical usurpations of who is supposed to be taken seriously and look good within a given

genre? Correspondingly, is it so far-fetched to imagine that Warhol's cinematic practice at least partly resonated with O'Hara? After all, O'Hara wrote
the film script "Love on the Hoof" in collaboration with Frank Lima specifically for a Warhol film. (The film, unfortunately, was never produced. The
"script" came complete with disaffected Warholian lines including "I never
jack off unless I *know* nothing's going to happen. . . ." [175]). Beyond this
concrete evidence that O'Hara wanted to be a part of the Underground film
scene typified most glamorously by Warhol, we might remind ourselves that
O'Hara's friends, students, and admirers, including Edwin Denby, Ginsberg,
Ashbery, John Wieners, Ron Padgett, Joe Brainard, and Ted Berrigan sat for
Warhol's screen tests, and that O'Hara was on record as praising Warhol's
work.

O'Hara's response in a 1965 interview to Edward Lucie-Smith's question
asking him what he thought about "'Underground' movies for example.
Warhol. This kind of thing," is certainly telling:

> Well, it's an acknowledgment. . . . I think actually that in many cases it's an
> acknowledgment of the best work of a lot of other people. And not to be mis-
> understood or to have a misunderstanding. If so much really marvelous work
> hadn't been done in the twentieth century by artists of a great many nationali-
> ties, there would be no . . . Wait, let's put it — I was going to say there would be
> no necessity for Andy Warhol to decide to devote himself to films. I'll put it
> more positively — he would not feel that it was OK for him to devote himself
> to films. But if he does so, then it must mean that he as an artist assumes that
> a great deal of pictorial and sculptural imagery has been dealt with adequately
> *in* painting and sculpture but *not* in films. I think most artists take the, most
> responsible artists, and Andy certainly is one — no matter what set of rumors
> go around about him — improve the medium they choose. (7–8)

We should pause for a moment and consider that this interview took place in
1965, the midpoint of Warhol's "Screen Tests" project, which began in early
1964 and ended in November 1966. It is probable, particularly given O'Hara's
reference to "pictorial and sculptural imagery," that O'Hara is referring specifically to the *Screen Tests*. The tests were "conceptualized and shot as direct
approximations or imitations of still photography . . . . The camera should
not move; the background should be as plain as possible; subjects must be
well lit and centered in the frame; each poser should face forward, hold as
still as possible, refrain from talking or smiling, and try not to blink" (Angell
13–14). Parodying stasis by asking the subjects to remain as still as possible,
the tests — by showing, however slightly, that subjects are in a constant state

of flux — worked as a kind of death knell for the effort of sculpture, painting, and photography to capture essence. Such an approach extends the theme captured in O'Hara's cry in "To Hell With It": "How I hate subject matter!," which continues "all things that don't change, / photographs, / monuments" (275). While O'Hara did not go so far as to include painting in his list, what's important to focus on here is the overall critique of art that does not reflect the fact of its subjects' will to change.

By May 1965 Warhol also appeared to resist creating things "that don't change" by announcing, "I was going to retire from painting. Art just wasn't fun for me anymore; it was people who were fascinating and I wanted to spend all my time being around them, listening to them, and making movies of them" (*Popism* 113). By rejecting painting in favor of "making movies," Warhol in his *Screen Tests* was aligning himself with the increasingly favored tendency, beginning in the early to mid-6os, to create artworks that manifested their own and their subject's contingency. "The canvas was no longer sufficient. It was during the 1959–1960 season that painters began to stage 'happenings,' screen 'underground movies,' and sell plaster-of-Paris pie slices in Lower East Side storefronts" (Hoberman, "The Forest and *The Trees*" 108). Allen Kaprow's Happenings, Jackson Mac Low's "simultaneities," the nascent Earthworks movement, and other related phenomena all resonate with Warhol's shift from static art to moving art, as do those movements' tendencies to impose arbitrary time limits on their performances. The very fact that Warhol asked his subject not to move, knowing such a thing was simply impossible (the inadvertent blink of an eye, the shift of a shoulder, or Bob Dylan's far more insurrectionary refusal to sit still for his test) suggests Warhol was taking a practically minimalist approach to manifesting the failure of static art to embody presence.

SCREEN TESTS / A DIARY: PART OF A CONVERSATION
BETWEEN GINSBERG AND MALANGA

As I have been suggesting, the screen tests presented the "self" as a kind of performance. Given our earlier discussion of Allen Ginsberg's work in film and poetry, we should turn to Ginsberg's own role in the series. In Ginsberg's screen test, we find the histrionic Ginsberg replaced by someone wholly in tune with Warhol's laissez-faire vision. Though he is obviously Allen Ginsberg, there are none of the performative madcap hijinks one might associate with this figure in 1966. Instead, there are the head and shoulders of the bearded figure looking straight ahead at the camera with a little wry smile on his face. Ginsberg, aiming to follow Warhol's injunction to be as still as possible, blinks only occasionally at first through his thick-rimmed glasses, though a little while into the film he scrunches his eyes up completely (perhaps because he is experiencing a bit of pain over Warhol's caveat not to blink). As Callie Angell reads it, Ginsberg "holds so still throughout the film that his features — his large forehead, bushy hair and beard, white skin, and thick glasses — seem to freeze into an emblematic, high-contrast graphic" (82).

This performative shift from wailing Bard to an almost cartoon-like, cool graphic is in contrast to Warhol's earlier representation of Ginsberg in his film *Couch* (1964). "*Couch*, which was made at the Factory in July 1964, opens showing the poet Piero Heliczer lying on a couch, as if either asleep or dead, and Malanga, who wears a black leather jacket, looking at him while lying on the back of the couch. One of the Flower paintings is behind the couch and serves as a backdrop for the scene. Heliczer's deathly appearance corresponds to the connotation of death embedded in the Flower image. Malanga, his head resting on his hand, seems to be in a reverie prompted by the deathly image of Heliczer. The scene — indeed, the entire film — has a dreamlike, otherworldly feel and brings to mind the protagonist's fantasies about convicts, some of whom are already dead, in [Jean Genet's] *Our Lady of the Flowers*" (Wolf, *Andy Warhol* 115).

Elements of mysticism and trance seed *Couch*, particularly (as Reva Wolf has recognized) as the film is informed by homoerotic ur-texts like Genet's book and Kenneth Anger's *Scorpio Rising* (1964). (In homage to Anger's film, Warhol includes a number of scenes featuring a man astride or sensuously examining a motorcycle while various erotic scenarios play themselves out on the eponymous couch. I would add that, like Anger's film, Warhol's *Couch* is divided up into thirteen distinct sections, thus lending a funnily daemonic element to the film overall.) Ginsberg shows up in the third section of *Couch*, and his persona here is instantly recognizable — he is an echo of the Ginsberg that appeared five years earlier in Alfred Leslie and Robert Frank's *Pull My Daisy* (1959). "In [*Pull My Daisy*], Leslie's couch is a central locus of activity. At distinct moments, different groupings of people sit on this couch — for example, Ginsberg, Corso, and Orlovsky . . . or the bishop's mother (played by the painter Alice Neel), Ginsberg, and the bishop's sister (played by Sally Gross)" (Wolf, *Andy Warhol* 134). As Corso, Ginsberg, Kerouac, and Orlovsky appeared in *Pull My Daisy*, so Warhol featured them in *Couch*. We first see Kerouac sitting on a couch reading a book, with Corso sitting next to him — both men are bopping around animatedly with a kind of wild energy reminiscent of the performed goofiness in *Pull My Daisy*. Ginsberg is shown kneeling in front of them drinking a beer, dressed in one of his at the time prototypical white cotton guru-type getups. Corso every now and then reaches over and touches Ginsberg. Corso takes out a cigarette, everyone starts drinking cans of beer, Orlovsky sits in front of Kerouac as Kerouac drinks, Ginsberg enters the frame again, sits down and attaches something to the couch, Kerouac stares at the camera in a practically hostile manner, Corso curls up against the corner of the couch, more (silent) conversation is had as cigarettes are passed around, there are a couple of light flares, and the section comes to an end. Beer, cigarettes, male bonding, goofing around — these guys are acting Beat.

Not so, however, two years later when it came to Ginsberg's test. The Beat persona is here frozen, practically evacuated. Ginsberg in his screen test becomes a kind of cipher on which the viewer imposes her own reading of what constitutes the barely blinking, barely moving apparition.

Ginsberg's screen test would end up being recycled by Gerard Malanga, a filmmaker in his own right who created such appreciated if rarely seen works as *In Search of the Miraculous* (1967), *Pre-Raphaelite Dream* (1968), and *The Recording Zone Operator* (1968). Malanga's *Screen Tests / A Diary* (1964) further distributed and diffused Allen Ginsberg's Beat/prophet persona into some surprising and complicated inter-genre spaces. The book featured "double-frame (actually two-and-a-half-frame) images taken from fifty-four "Screen Tests" of fifty-four different people, numbered one through fifty-four and arranged in alphabetical order by last name. Each person received a two-page spread: the enlarged frames from each *Screen Test* appeared on the right-hand page opposite a poem, on the left-hand page, written by Malanga about that person. After the book was published in April 1967, ads for *Screen Tests / A Diary* described it as 'poems plus film strips'" (Angell 288). In terms of the Ginsberg image and Malanga poem included in *Screen Tests / A Diary* specifically, we find that the pages as a whole, composed of stills from Ginsberg's screen test placed to the right of Malanga's poem, cause an interesting kind of genre trouble. The pages resemble not so much a text one reads that reflects Allen Ginsberg's influence on Malanga's life, but a diptych that one initially sees. The effect is such that Malanga's attempt to make the filmic subservient to the textual is compromised.

Because of the poem's proximity to the strip of celluloid, we end up having some difficulty administrating between the two genres. Is the poem a series of subtitles for the film fragment embalmed to its right, we might ask? Should we look at the stills first and then read the poem, or would it be

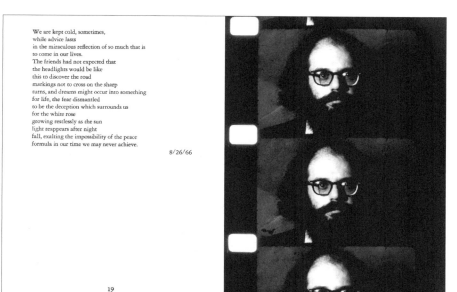

We are kept cold, sometimes,
while advice lasts
in the miraculous reflection of so much that is
to come in our lives.
The friends had not expected that
the headlights would be like
this to discover the road
markings not to cross on the sharp
turns, and dreams might occur into something
for life, the fear dismantled
to be the deception which surrounds us
for the white rose
growing restlessly as the sun
light reappears after night
fall, exalting the impossibility of the peace
formula in our time we may never achieve.

8/26/66

19

Reproduction of Allen Ginsberg Screen Test (1966), by Gerard Malanga
and Andy Warhol, and accompanying poem by Gerard Malanga,
from *Screen Tests / A Diary* © Gerard Malanga.

better the other way around? Shouldn't the poem "speak for itself"? Does
the image complement the poem, or are the two genres perhaps uninten-
tionally autonomous? Is there a hierarchy evident in the two media, given
that the visual effect dominates initially, even though we are bound to focus
on the meaning of the text following the optic shock? The diction and tone
of Malanga's poem is at the far end of Ginsberg's often grandiose stance —
indeed, the poem reads like an improvisation off of something Ashbery
might write[8] — and generally serves to emphasize a disconnect between
text and image. Such disconnect is further established when we realize that
Malanga makes no direct reference to the Beat bard. The two pages do not
seem to communicate a clear-cut narrative or theme. The connection between poem and screen test subject is tenuous throughout the book. (I would
argue, if gently, against Callie Angell's assertion that the poems are "about"
the filmed subject. Out of the fifty-four poems/images included here, only
seven refer by name to their subject.[9] Out of those seven poems, none uses
the subject's last name, and the content of the poems is such that any connection between text and image is purely associative and intuitive, as opposed to solidly biographical.)

Malanga's Ginsberg poem presents itself to us as a total product — it ends with a period, and the "8/26/66" quite clearly marks when it was composed and/or completed. (The date might serve to recall both a date of birth and an obituary date.) Compare such relative unity with the fragmentation visible in the stills. The way that Ginsberg's face is cropped in the first and third frames suggests subjectivity in flux. But then again, the fact that the three frames are published as a photograph on the page makes us question the aura of instantism we generally associate with "film." The stills, after all, were originally designed to be invisible facets of a Warhol "Screen Test," streaming through a projector onto a screen. Ripped away from their original function and made static on the page, the stills become a single photograph that practically announces film as a series of motionless pictures. We sense in dealing with these pages that we are experiencing a new kind of genre, one that is predicated on destabilizing the narrative and lyric functions of poetry and the representational, real time enactments of cinema.

Ginsberg and Malanga maintained a correspondence for a number of years that focused often on the connections between film and poetry.[10] Malanga wrote in one letter (January 8, 1968), "What I want to bring back with me is what my eyes have seen daily walking around Rome, waking up each morning with sunlight reflected on the bedroom wall: a film." I hear echoes within these sentences of Allen Ginsberg's and Frank O'Hara's poetry — O'Hara's flâneur "walking around" the great city alongside hints of the final section of Ginsberg's "Kaddish," in which Ginsberg writes a series of lines beginning with the phrase "with your eyes": "with your eyes of Russia / with your eyes of no money / with your eyes of false China / with your eyes of Aunt Eleanor" (226–27) and so on.

Perhaps these echoes were in the letter because during his stay in Rome, Malanga was rereading Donald Allen's anthology *The New American Poetry*, in which part of Ginsberg's "Kaddish" and a great deal of O'Hara's poetry played starring roles. Malanga was in Italy working on his film *Pre-Raphaelite Dream*. As Malanga remembers it, he "arrived in Rome in September 1967 as a guest of the composer/poet/playwright, Peter Hartman. Peter had a copy of the Don Allen anthology which I started re-reading in a kind of voracious way. My daily walks around Rome at that time seemed to correspond directly with what Frank was expressing and this sensibility started seeping into my own work. So it was actually Frank's 'walking around' poems in the Don Allen anthology which informed my letter to Allen" (e-mail).

In one particularly interesting letter (November 29, 1967), we find Malanga bringing O'Hara's "I do this, I do that" manner into the world of New

American Cinema. Similar to the conflation of Beat- and New York School–affiliated poetry noted above, Malanga's reference to Jonas Mekas serves to temper the privileged cosmopolitanism inherent in much of O'Hara's writing with a recognizably "Beat" valuation of voluntary poverty: "It's approximately 2:00 pm, a Wednesday, three days after the beginning of my mother's sixtieth year. It's been raining for three days, also. Rome afternoon solitude. Antonioni grey sky. . . . A few days ago finished reading Gregory Battcock's book, *The New American Cinema*, from cover to cover. The only sincere piece in the entire book was Jonas Mekas's humble writing where he describes 'people who were walking like one thousand painful pieces' (after the war) and he felt that there was nothing to lose any more, suddenly seeing the broken pieces of himself coming together. And the only way out for all of us he could see for himself also was to 'eliminate our egos, our bad faith, our mistrust, our sense of competition, of personal profit. . . .'"

Film and poetry naturally intertwine — there is a tacit faith on Malanga's part that Ginsberg will automatically accept the relationship between the two genres and recognize that Malanga was making an effort to beatify the New American Cinema scene that he participated in. That Malanga consistently fused O'Hara's "I do this, I do that" style with recognizably Beat values serves to productively complicate any facile attempts at establishing clear boundaries between Beat and New York School modes.

Malanga's letter certainly resonates with Ginsberg's and O'Hara's own synthesis of purportedly competing styles in poems including Ginsberg's "My Sad Self" (dedicated to O'Hara, and beginning with the manifestly O'Haraesque lines "Sometimes when my eyes are red / I go up on top of the RCA Building" [Ginsberg, *Collected Poems* 201]) and O'Hara's "For the Chinese New Year and for Bill Berkson" (with its elegiac, high-rhetorical lines, including "whither Lumumba whither oh whither Gauguin" [O'Hara, *Collected Poems* 30]). Importantly for this study, this synthesis is extended more generally by Andy Warhol and the Factory scene into the worlds of the New American Cinema. Beat, New York School, film, poetry, Pop Art — all in a conversation that served to question and complicate (if not entirely break from) the visionary tradition of Brakhage and Anger. By the late 1960s, the way forward seemed to be an ever more playful, sexually polymorphous, and decentered aesthetic.

seven

The Conversation between
John Ashbery and Rudy Burckhardt

As we have seen, the idea of a core stable self was intuited to some extent by filmmakers like Anger and Brakhage as a potentially heroic, even rhapsodic fact even as that sense of self was perhaps inadvertently problematized by the filmmakers' engagement with an increasingly language-centered poetics. That said, such an intuition on the part of some of the filmmakers and poets affiliated with the "New American" scene was interrogated in the mid-1960s by people including O'Hara and Leslie, Ginsberg and Frank, and the Warhol scene generally. This is not to say that these artists had given up entirely on positioning their work as a projection of their particular experiences in the world. In particular, artists like Ginsberg, O'Hara, Frank, and Leslie saw in the decentered model of self both a form of resistance to the terrifying politics unfolding in their backyards and abroad and a way of theorizing a queer aesthetic liberated from essentialist understandings of sexual "norms." Even Warhol, as inscrutable as he insisted his public face be, and as apparently divested from the antiwar movement raging south of his Factory, cultivated many of the main players in the counterculture as subjects for his films and participated symbolically in the antiwar activities typical of the era. Wolf has recalled that "in the mid-1960s flower imagery became for the population at large a trademark of pacifism. Warhol grafted this signification onto the flower-poetry association by placing his flower images in a bookstore owned by a poet [Ed Sanders] and called Peace Eye. . . . Warhol's Peace Eye banner is but one indicator that he contributed (like virtually everyone around him) to the antiwar activities of the time, a point that tends to be overlooked" (*Andy Warhol* 57).

What then happens, decades later, to the players affiliated with the New

American Cinema and Poetry communities? What is their take on the relationship between self and society, gender and sexuality, contingency and
truth, private life and global politics "in a period of American avant-garde
cinema in which the tradition of contemplative subjectivity has perhaps run
its (often glorious) course" (Gunning, "Cinema of Attractions" 61)? While
Tom Gunning was certainly correct in implying that many of the artists
associated with Underground cinema had by the late 1980s lost a measure of
their favor and had moved on (if not died off), it behooves us to at least look
at some of the work that continued to be produced into the 1980s and 1990s
by artists who were there at the inception of experimental cinema in the
United States. Let us go then to revisit some of the later work of filmmaker
Rudy Burckhardt and poet John Ashbery who, as early as 1950, began working with each other. These two figures are particularly significant in terms
of the way they straddle that always-contested divide between modernism
and postmodernism. (Burckhardt produced his early films toward the end
of the 1930s and, due in part to his Swiss nationality and love for travel, was
very much engaged with the European avant-garde. Ashbery's personal and
poetic relationship with Auden, to give one example, lightly if interestingly
complicates any reading of his work that frames his more radical formal
breaks within the context of a more recognizable avant-garde tradition). I
will pay particular attention to Burckhardt's *Ostensibly* (1989), a film/poetry
hybrid that in many ways reflects and extends the main ideas discussed in
this book thus far.

RUDY BURCKHARDT AND THE NEW YORK SCHOOL

While perhaps better known as a photographer, particularly for his now-
iconic images of the Flatiron Building in Manhattan, Rudy Burckhardt was
an accomplished and prolific filmmaker whose work influenced generations
of writers. As his friend and one-time lover Edwin Denby recalled, "Well,
I learned a lot from Rudy Burckhardt's photographs and movies. I got very
interested in them, the way that you can study them, and learn what the texture of light and air is all about. I wanted that in my poetry. Nobody really
understood the films of Rudy Burckhardt because he was trying to capture
that, to make you feel as if you might be able to touch the air and light" (qtd.
in Pettet *Conversations* n.p.). Burckhardt's circle included poets Kenneth
Koch, James Schuyler, John Ashbery, and Frank O'Hara, as well as a wider
group of painters, musicians, dancers, and theater people affiliated with the
New York scene. Many of these individuals participated in Burckhardt's

films. Dancers like Dana Reitz, Yoshiko Chuma, Douglas Dunn, and Paul
Taylor, and artists such as Trevor Winkfield, Nell Welliver, and Alex Katz all
made appearances in Burckhardt productions. "In 1950, having come into
contact with a younger generation of poets and painters, Burckhardt made
Mounting Tension, with John Ashbery, Jane Freilicher, and Larry Rivers,
when they were all in their mid-twenties. . . . A little later, Burckhardt met
Red and Mimi Grooms, embarking on another collaborative friendship.
Their first joint effort was *Shoot the Moon* (1962), a takeoff on Georges Méliès's *Voyage à La Lune*" (Katz 191). Like Stan Brakhage, Burckhardt worked
in collaboration with Joseph Cornell on a number of films, including *The
Aviary* (1955), *What Mozart Saw on Mulberry Street* (1956), and *Nymphlight*
(1957).[1] Burckhardt's friendships with New York School poets extended to
"second generation" writers, "particularly Ron Padgett and Anne Waldman"
(Katz 187),[2] and he would spend the next four decades working with poets
from Edwin Denby to Kenneth Koch to David Shapiro to Taylor Mead to
Alice Notley to Wang Ping. As visual artist Yvonne Jacquette (Burckhardt's
second wife) recalls,

> Edwin Denby influenced Rudy a great deal. Rudy was making films shortly
> after meeting Edwin, and they went to Haiti together. As soon as they came
> back Rudy did this little film called "145 West 21st" where a lot of friends of
> Edwin's including Virgil Thompson and Aaron Copeland and DeKooning and
> Paul Bowles and John LaTouche participated. So here's an early instance of
> interaction with these poets and the scene generally, pretty soon after Rudy
> got to New York. As soon as Edwin started connecting with those poets, then
> Rudy got involved, taking part in discussions, looking at the poetry. . . . I
> remember when John Ashbery's first book "Some Trees" came out, Rudy was
> just amazed . . . so after that he followed everything Ashbery did . . . he met
> John through Jane Freilicher when Rudy was shooting "Mounting Tension."
> Jane brought along John and asked "can he be in this film."

While always on the periphery of the various subcultures that called New
York home, Burckhardt nevertheless found increasing recognition as his career developed. He explained:

> In the 1950s, 16-millimeter films were called experimental, independent or cre-
> ative. Maya Deren was showing her surreal, slow-motion films, and Stan Bra-
> khage followed with his hand-held camera and inspired, fluent editing. Amos
> Vogel's "Cinema 16" presented cultural films with elaborate program notes on
> Sunday mornings, instead of church. I was around, but my films did not quite

fit in. Then came the hippie, anti-Hollywood, pro-sex, revolution, of which I became a fellow traveler and beneficiary. My films were shown more often, and I received a good review from Jonas Mekas in the *Village Voice*, while he was struggling against censorship and promoting far-out, uninhibited films like Jack Smith's *Flaming Creatures*. . . . Kenneth Anger's *Scorpio Rising* became a big hit. Soon, Hollywood was stealing their freewheeling camera movements and editing. (qtd. in Katz 195)

Burckhardt understood that there was a correspondence between the surreal, whimsical, and immediate nature of much poetry associated with the New York School and the ability in film to represent "real time," the use of montage to create startling juxtapositions, and so on. Particularly in watching Burckhardt's collage and diary films, we get the sense that the kind of free association rooted in cosmopolitanism and urbanity that we associate with Ashbery's and Frank O'Hara's poetry is being enacted visually. Burckhardt's 1975 film *City Pasture*, for example, features a "narrative" that in the "Program Notes" is broken down into a series of scenes beginning with "A snow storm — Disney World — self important New York — ox-pull in Maine — a special old man — strip tease — an ant in the woods — wild 14th street — a mugging survived — the end." These discrete scenes, despite at first seeming a little arbitrary, are nevertheless linked by qualities we associate with the lyric. Repetition of spoken poetic lines, images, and musical motifs, the presence of poets and painters including Trevor Winkfield (as well as Kenneth Koch, Edwin Denby, Ron Padgett, and Lucille Nickens, all of whom are credited with providing "Poems and Images"), serve as connecting threads between the otherwise disparate incidents included in the film.

At points, however, we could be forgiven for thinking that the film is a wholly self-referential exercise. Burckhardt shoots several scenes at high speed and uses Ron Padgett's line, "Here the film speed increases" (spoken flatly as voiceover by Yvonne Jacquette). And yet Burckhardt takes great care to insist that such self-reflexivity does not proscribe an affective response. Lines that are repeated throughout the film, including Edwin Denby's "Daily life is a wonderful thing to see" (from his essay, "Dancers, Buildings and People in the Street") and Ron Padgett's "An ant is crawling up a wall" are revelatory in the same sense that Frank O'Hara's famous cri de coeur "ah lunch!" is. The casual celebration of the quotidian, long acknowledged as a primary gesture in much of the poetry affiliated with the New York School and extended in the New American Cinema scene by artists as disparate as Brakhage and Warhol, is expressed in Burckhardt's case visually — the filmmaker lightly and happily connects those objects, people, and places we would ordinarily not link together, including an eighty-seven-year-old loner living in a shack near a chicken factory in Maine,[3] a carnival drag performer, women shopping, beggars, the painter Trevor Winkfield describing being mugged, Burckhardt himself acting out a role as mugging victim, snow falling around the Flatiron Building. This is not social realism or pedagogy, but rather a kind of tallying designed to help us have a feeling for the wonder of "daily life."[4]

Vincent Katz makes much the same point when he links Burckhardt's project to a James Schuyler poem: "Ultimately, it is not the randomness of existence that is Burckhardt's subject, but rather the significance of it all, as in the James Schuyler lines, 'I can't get over / how it all works in together'" (193). What is especially interesting here, however, is how Ashbery and Burckhardt manage actually to enact Schuyler's idea formally rather than going right out and saying it as Schuyler does. Phillip Lopate's essay on Burckhardt is revealing on this point: "I once asked Rudy why he never used the poems of James Schuyler [in his films]. He said he didn't like Schuyler as much; he had tried to put some on a sound track once but 'they were too — tragic or something. Whereas Ashbery's poems always work: because his lines are like dreams, and when you put them over a film image it helps the viewer to see the image in a dreamlike way'" (42).

Burckhardt was not limited to making diarist films or hybrid city/country landscapes, however. Indeed, the variousness of his films is analogous to the variousness of forms his fellow poets tried on for size in an effort to expand the possibilities of the ostensibly normal or traditional. Experiment, as Burckhardt shows us, occurs both within and outside traditional genres and forms. As Ashbery, Koch, Padgett, Berrigan, and others experimented with the possibilities inherent in the sonnet, pantoum, canzone and sestina, so Burckhardt produced diary and collage films, screwball comedies,[5] parodic adventure films,[6] parodic monster films, and so on.

Burckhardt's *Lurk* (1964) is an instance of his working within a recognizable genre while at the same time imploding it.[7] Anticipating Mel Brooks's *Young Frankenstein* (1974), *Lurk* stars Edwin Denby as Professor Borealis, Mimi Grooms as Aurora Borealis, Red Grooms as Lester Slabs and the Frankenstein-like Creature, and Burckhardt's son Jacob as Jake Slabs. The narrative retells several of the key scenes in the Frankenstein myth, though to utterly comic effect. The acting is ham-handed at best, opening with a scene of Denby (Professor Borealis), dressed in full "mad scientist" regalia, dancing crazily around in an old house. Subsequent scenes find Aurora

Borealis and Professor Borealis wandering around in a meadow; Jake and Lester Slabs walking through a field carrying Bergmanesque scythes; Professor Borealis, clearly up to no good, examining a frog in his lab only to be interrupted by his wife, who comes down with a sandwich; Aurora Borealis and Lester Slabs fooling around in a field while Jake cheers them on from the sidelines; Professor Borealis injecting Lester Slabs with a hypodermic, then hypnotizing Jake Slabs who becomes a kind of assistant zombie; Jake Slabs and Professor Borealis sawing open Lester's skull to use the brain for the soon-to-be animated Creature; and the requisite scene where Denby shows the creature to an assembled group of notables, only to have the Creature lose control and attack everyone.

Lurk can be read as a typically parodic (if willfully amateurish) example of the subversive possibilities inherent in playing *within* genre conventions to highlight the frail, permeable, and fundamentally constructed nature of those genres. That such play in Burckhardt's case occurred in the context of a New York School–populated cast and crew is something we need to consider if we are to understand why the purportedly avant-garde work of Burckhardt and poets like Ashbery and Kenneth Koch included a marked affection for traditional forms and genres. Burckhardt's parodic films are as challenging to our notions of what constitutes genre as Ashbery's widely anthologized sestina, "Farm Implements and Rutabagas in a Landscape," which circulates around cartoon characters including Popeye, Wimpy, and Olive Oyl. Dating from the twelfth century, the sestina has traditionally been employed for serious effect.[8] Ashbery's sestina, however, which begins with the line, "The first of the undecoded messages read: ' 'Popeye sits in thunder' '" (260), emphasizes and foregrounds the inherent artificiality of the form in which the content is contained. Ashbery's poem suggests all order is artificial and subject to fun — a tacitly political gesture that finds a cinematic partner in Burckhardt's own usurpations of the various filmic genres in which he participates.[9]

A LAUNCHING PAD FOR FREE ASSOCIATIONS

In an interview, Ashbery defined his working method as "just free associating, which is basically what I'm doing when I write. I use the poem as a sort of launching pad for free associations" (Interview 34).[10] While this assertion might appear simplistic, Ashbery's — and Burckhardt's — approach toward composition resonates with the Beat fetishization of unmediated naturalness. This is an important point to make, if for nothing else than to question once again the lines that so often distinguish Beat and New York School poetry from each other, despite the social, literary, and aesthetic connections between the two groups. Consider, as Yvonne Jacquette reminds us, that

> Rudy was interested in being wide-angled . . . he was totally involved in the Beat world . . . definitely Kerouac . . . he was interested in them. . . . Anne Waldman . . . through her the whole Naropa thing connected to his work . . . he read most of what he could find around him . . . certainly Ginsberg, Kerouac . . . Ginsberg sent him a copy of his Collected Poems . . . the inscription on the inside was "For Rudy's 80th birthday. . . . I should live so long." We'd go to readings featuring Ginsberg, Corso. . . . Rudy loved the idea of underground film . . . that came out maybe through the Beats. . . . When he started getting showings in University film societies with titles like "The Latest Underground Films," he was delighted . . . finally a label that didn't sound snooty to him. . . . It was all downtown, all in the neighborhood. . . . He loved Jack Smith, he loved *Flaming Creatures*, he said "Wow! this is really breakthrough! I wouldn't have the nerve! This is terrific!" It was interacting between the poets and St. Mark's and Anthology Film Archives. . . . It was all one world in those days. (personal interview)

The poetics behind Ashbery's "free associating" and Burckhardt's unscripted, undirected films certainly echo Jack Kerouac's "first thought, best thought" and Allen Ginsberg's "spontaneous mind" slogans, and they further trouble any firm academic distinction between the poetics of Beat and New York School–affiliated writers. Given Burckhardt's love for the Beat scene, we should examine more closely how film's ability to represent real time informs what Daniel Belgrad has called the Beat and New York School's "culture of spontaneity."[11]

Hannes Schüpbach's comparison of Burckhardt's "The Climate of New York" to Paul Strand's and Charles Sheeler's film *Manhatta* (1921) illustrates this point. "The Climate of New York" "makes it clear with what directness Burckhardt could photograph people. In the small number of takes including people in *Manhatta* they are shown as a crowd or distributed across the scene, from slightly above, or on Wall Street in front of a powerful, gloomy façade. . . . Burckhardt, on the other hand, mixes easily among the people as he looks" (124). Where Sheeler and Strand cite the secular epic poetry of Walt Whitman, Burckhardt instead cites "short lines from Edwin Denby's volume of poems *In Public, In Private*" (ibid. 124). Anything privileging the vatic and monumental cedes to the particularity of the "direct," of actual people, places, and things that Burckhardt, camera in hand, is able to represent. If not

literally spontaneous, the effect or semblance of spontaneity in Burckhardt's
—and Ashbery's, Kerouac's, and Ginsberg's—writing is crucial for these
artists' projects. "Spontaneity posed intersubjectivity, in which 'reality' was
understood to emerge through a conversational dynamic" (Belgrad 5). Burckhardt's place among the people suggests a participatory democratic ethics
that his filmic predecessors were as yet unwilling to display in their own
celebratory, if ultimately formally grandiose, city symphonies.

This commitment to lightness and spontaneity and, consequently, openness in form and content is extended and expressed visually throughout
Burckhardt's work. His use of New York School–affiliated poetry serves to
emphasize his social world and invite cross-disciplinary dialogue. In his film
Wayward Glimpses (1992), Burckhardt uses lines from a poem by Alice Notley beginning "I work in a whorehouse, I seem to like it / it is dark like a cave,
with pink light" as subtitles for a series of shots of New York City. The way
Burckhardt combines this lighthearted appreciation of brothels in tandem
with quotidian urban scenes is framed in such a manner as to undermine
authority, be it the authority that argues one should not "like" working in
whorehouses, the authority that insists an enchanted Nature holds prece-
dence over the worldly city, or the formal authority that insists a monumental building is more worthy of attention than a commercial sign.

One particular sequence of scenes from *Wayward Glimpses* (divided up
into eight discrete shots) illustrates how Burckhardt presents the natural
and urban worlds in no particular hierarchical order. The first shot shows
people standing still and walking in New York. The subsequent five shots
are composed entirely of images of flowering trees and petals on boughs.
On the sixth shot, the camera lingers on a flowering tree and then cuts to
a shot of the Empire State Building. This is followed up by a shot of a store
sign: "*Come in* We're OPEN." Burckhardt's petals are presented lightly and
casually alongside the cityscapes, lingering on one or the other shot for no
apparent purpose other than to concentrate, perhaps, on a particularly interesting rustle of branch or brightness of sign. Burckhardt dallies from
blossom to person, from iconic Manhattan building to a funny expression,
reveling in surface delights and unarticulated connections. (I might add that
the music in this film, characterized in this sequence by a composition of
Elliott Carter's in which clusters of bright, quick outbursts of flute and oboe
suggest sparrows darting about, adds to the viewer's sense of the film as a
playful enterprise.)

That he focuses so consistently on flowering branches alongside urban
scenes suggests Burckhardt might very well be responding in some sense to

"Come in, We're Open," from *Wayward Glimpses* © Rudy Burckhardt.
Courtesy of the Estate of Rudy Burckhardt.

Ezra Pound's iconic juxtaposition of "faces in the crowd" alongside "petals on a wet black bough." And yet, while Burckhardt seems to be aware of the fact that his juxtapositions might point back to a literary tradition, he works to resist such absorption. Anything that even begins to seem too "serious" in the sequence is immediately undercut with an image that emphasizes surface and wit and resists paraphrase. The rather impressive shot of the Empire State Building as it is framed against two smaller buildings is followed up with the gleefully goofy sign, "*Come in* We're OPEN," which immediately and wittily undermines the gravitas inherent in the monolithic building. "*Come in* We're OPEN" is particularly significant as a declaration of aesthetics. It can be read as a momentary definition of the form and content of *Wayward Glimpses* itself, whose form is "open" in the sense that it does not follow a linear narrative and includes genres such as collage and dance within its frames, and whose demotic dallying on flowers, trees, and people of all types and sizes is in and of itself an invitation to the viewer to imaginatively *come in* to the film. This resistance to seriousness and narrative coherence is something poets including John Ashbery have remarked on appreciatively:

What appealed to me so much about Rudy was his total lack of pretension and his doing whatever he felt amused by doing, like "Mounting Tension" for instance. This was sort of the opposite pole of someone like Maya Deren, who was supposed to be profound and "meaningful"—it was certainly very unfashionable; no one took notice of Rudy for a long time. The things and people that amused him were things I could go along with. He seemed so much more of a genuine artist that I naturally gravitated towards. What we used to call "deep Chelsea" when no one wanted to live here, a rough neighborhood, there were these people like Rudy, Nell Blaine, Elaine DeKooning, Helen De-Mott—she's the woman in *Mounting Tension* who chases Larry Rivers with an umbrella—these were all people who were resolutely opposed to doing anything that the world at large would consider important or fashionable . . . they seemed to be the good guys as far as I could tell. (personal interview)

This "lack of pretension" and daring to be "amused" as opposed to being possessed, enthralled, oracular, or what have you is perfectly embodied by the sign "*Come in* We're OPEN." The phrase is perhaps the pithiest description yet of the poetics of sociability typical of much New York School–affiliated writing, as it suggests how far New American Poetry and Cinema cultures had moved away from the spirit-and-self saturated aesthetic of Brakhage, Anger, and others.

Consider Ashbery's *Three Poems*. The book announces itself as "open" immediately, in that genre definitions are threatened by the fact that the vast majority of *Three Poems* is composed in prose chunks. Encouraged by the sight of page after page of prose framed as poetry, the reader is invited to question rigid definitions of kinds from the outset. Significantly, moments throughout the book emphasize a cinematic seeing linked to an articulation of the sociability ("*Come in*") inherent in group activity:

I seem to hear you and see you wishing me well, your eyes taking in some rapid lateral development

reading without comprehension

and always taken up on the reel of what is happening in the wings. Which becomes a medium through which we address one another, the independent life we were hoping to create. This is your eyes noting the passing of telephone poles and the tops of trees. (*Three Poems* 13)

This passage is interesting for the emphasis it places on cinematic tropes in relationship to breaking down the boundary between scriptor and reader.

"I seem to hear you and see you wishing me well" evokes the multi-sensory possibilities of film, where soundtrack and image combine. One might argue that we can "see and hear" in other genres — theater, dance, and so on. Ashbery appears to anticipate such a reading by making sure to focus our interpretation of the phrase as predicated on film: "always taken up on the reel" suggests film itself being threaded into or "taken up on" the reel. The "wings" included in the phrase "what is happening in the wings" adds to our sense of the filmic suggested by the "reel," bringing to mind as it does the "wings" of a theater.

Finally, the line, "This is your eyes noting the passing of telephone poles and the tops of trees" is allusively cinematic, suggesting any number of moving camera takes of telephone poles and trees throughout cinema history and especially in early avant-garde film. We should perhaps acknowledge here how ingrained that sense of looking at telephone poles or trees as we drive past them has become practically a trope for the film experience. We can certainly refer, for example, to Eisenstein and G. V. Alexandroff's *Romance Sentimentale* (1930), a film that opens with images of "tops of trees" shot from a moving car juxtaposed against images of waves crashing against rocks; René Clair's and Francis Picabia's *Entr'acte* (1924), where we see repeated shots of trees, telephone wires, and poles as the camera tracks the adventures of an out-of-control funeral procession; and scenes of trees, telephone wires, and poles shot from a moving car in Jean Epstein's *La Glace à Trois Faces* (1927). Tracking the tops of trees and telephone poles from a moving vehicle is particularly useful for exploiting the rhythmic possibilities inherent in manipulated static lines, and it illustrates how early avant-garde filmmakers understood how film offered synaesthetic potential for transforming images into lyric pulses. (Such images even helped solved the "problem of flicker": "Albert E. Smith, founder with J. Stuart Blackton of Vitagraph, is said to have solved the problem of flicker in film images while riding a train. Peering out the window while riding through the New Jersey landscape, Smith saw an analogy to screen flicker in the repetition of telegraph poles the train swept past. He remarked a similar effect in that produced by looking through a picket fence as the train passed through a station. This gave him the notion of dividing up the flicker of the motion picture by adding blades to the then single-bladed shutter. He tried this out and found that by multiplying the flicker he in fact eliminated it in effect. The resulting betterment of projection was extraordinary'" [Kirby, *Parallel Tracks* 47]).

Poles and trees are objects that the eye can fix on, objects that can make movement visible by allowing the viewer to trace the spaces between the lines the objects provide when shown as a moving sequence. Filmmakers delight in such objects because of how they can illustrate the way light falls through leaves to become abstraction, suggest movement occurring horizontally and vertically, and illustrate the way the repetition of lines serve as a kind of mimetic representation of spooling film frames.

Ashbery evokes similar responses from his readers, particularly when we consider how overt references to filmmaking coincide with Ashbery's decision to mimetically represent the movement of eyes through the *vers concrete*–like positioning of the line "reading without comprehension" on the flush right margin of the page. This visually provoked interruption may make more than one reader feel suddenly jolted awake from the reverie induced by the text's Byzantine philosophical patter. We are suddenly launched into abstraction — "reading without comprehension" — as our eyes follow the "rapid lateral development" of the line. It is perhaps significant that "lateral" means "relating to, or situated at or on the side" of something, as well as being a term specific to linguistics, where "lateral" relates to or is a sound produced by breath passing along the tongue. The lateral movement of frame following frame here combines with allusions to orality and voice, emphasizing the inherently social nature of Ashbery's project. "This is *your* eyes noting" (emphasis added) cedes authority from the writer to the reader, an idea that is emphasized in a subsequent line of the prose stanza: "In you I fall apart, and outwardly am a single fragment, a puzzle to itself. But we must learn to live in others, no matter how abortive or unfriendly their cold, piecemeal renderings of us: they create us" (*Three Poems* 13). This poem moves toward a social model of readership, one in which meaning is multiply determined not by the producer but by the crowd of "you's" engaging with the poem.

The pronominal shifts from "you" to "I" to "we" tend to blur even further the distinctions between who is being addressed, who is writing the text, who is making meaning, and what the interrelationships are between the pronouns as they play out in the "wings" of the theater. That this wild sociability is evoked partly via filmic representations is clearly of great import to Ashbery. Near the end of "The System" (the second section of *Three Poems*), Ashbery writes, "We are both alive and free," adding in the next prose stanza, "If you could see a movie of yourself you would realize that this is true. Movies show us ourselves as we had not yet learned to recognize us — something in the nature of daily being or happening that quickly gets folded over into ancient history like yesterday's newspaper, but in so doing a new face has been revealed, a surface on which a new phrase may be written before it rejoins history, or it may remain blank and do so anyway: it doesn't matter because each thing is coming up in its time and receding into the past, and this is what we all expect and want" (ibid. 102). The "movies" offer us a model of freedom where "we" are able to take comfort in the *recordability* of the present as it represents the past and winds into the future. As chaotic and unanchored the present, secular moment must seem, nevertheless movies are able to show us materially that, in James Schuyler's words, "it all works in together" anyway. As Ashbery adds later in the stanza, "one must treasure each moment of the past, get the same thrill from it that one gets from watching each moment of an old movie. These windows on the past enable us to see enough to stay on an even keel in the razor's-edge present which is really a no-time, continually straying over the border into the positive past and the negative future whose movements alone define it" (ibid. 102–3). Film, being a window "on the past" even as it enacts the present through projection, offers what Ashbery in a subsequent line calls a "signpost" that helps secure us from the tyranny of not knowing what's going to come next.

In a fascinating passage of the stanza, Ashbery positions the text itself as film: "But only focus on the past through the clear movie-theater dark and you are a changed person, and can begin to live again. That is why we, snatched from sudden freedom, are able to communicate only through this celluloid vehicle that has immortalized and given a definitive shape to our formless gestures; we can live as though we had caught up with time and avoid the sickness of the present, a shapeless blur as meaningless as a carelessly exposed roll of film" (ibid. 103). Whereas much of *Three Poems* (and Ashbery's work generally) emphasizes the materiality of the *book* in relationship to the addressed "you" and "we," Ashbery here pushes his text resolutely into another genre ("this celluloid vehicle") in order to more convincingly assert the possibilities for art to give shape "to our formless gestures." We find Ashbery agitating against the restrictions inherent in a text-bound medium, displaying, if not precisely anxiety, at least a sense of belatedness over the fact that his words are trapped on the page rather than projected as light. Indeed, the still photographic image is critically aligned to bound text ("as meaningless as a carelessly exposed roll of film"). Like Burckhardt's film sequence described above, Ashbery's writing serves as an implicit critique of the static juxtaposition of images. The instantism and movement of film, which paradoxically serves as both a record of the past and an enactment of the present, is here hierarchically placed above the stasis of word and still image.

BURKHARDT OSTENSIBLY ASHBERY

The friendship between Burckhardt and Ashbery lasted for decades and found the two collaborating through the 70s and 80s as Burckhardt included poets of the second and third generation New York School into his evolving projects. On the process of making Rudy Burckhardt's film *Ostensibly* (1989), Ashbery recalls, "Rudy came to my apartment and he just filmed me reading my poem 'Ostensibly,' and then he made the movie on his own. It was a collage of images, different things happening. I liked the sort of collage-like thing of images that he had chosen. It seemed — you know — to reflect my writing" (personal interview). How might we then read the ways in which Burckhardt's film reflects Ashbery's poem? How might Ashbery's poem itself be a way into reading significance and pleasure into Burckhardt's film? How does the film *Ostensibly* exhibit qualities we associate with poetry, and, conversely, how does Ashbery's poem display those filmic strategies that are key to its composition? Beginning with an analysis of Ashbery's poem, we will consider these questions in order to explore the ways in which the two artists' work helps extend the conversation between film and poetry into the 1980s.

Given that "ostensibly" refers to something that seems to be the case but is probably not, Ashbery's poem "Ostensibly" places us immediately in the realm of appearances, a typically Ashberian place to be. In light of the title, the first line, "One might like to rest or read," encourages a reader to respond with some doubt. *Might* we really like to rest or read? This *might* appear to be the case, particularly given the fact that we are reading the poem itself — a self-reflexive move that draws our attention to the materiality of the text — but doubt has already been planted by the title. Such doubt is further established by the oddly stilted, formal manner evoked by the use of the word "one." This outmoded politesse suggests the pronoun is being used here generically to mean "anyone." Subsequent lines invite *us* to imagine playing the subject-position in the poem — and we find ourselves shunted from scene to scene:

> One might like to rest or read,
> Take walks, celebrate the kitchen table,
> Pat the dog absentmindedly, meanwhile
> Thinking gloomy thoughts — so many separate
> Ways of doing, one is uncertain
> How the future is going to handle this. (55)

Rest, read, take walks, "celebrate the kitchen table," pat a dog, ruminate gloomily . . . these are indeed "so many separate / Ways of doing." The tangible melancholy in the lines, tempered by a kind of avuncular humor, is typical Ashbery — "one" wants to break through limitations imposed on him by the physical world, somehow manage to experience "so many separate / Ways of doing" simultaneously, but one cannot. Ashbery seems in part to be channeling Robert Frost, if elliptically, particularly the Robert Frost of "The Road Not Taken," whose speaker famously struggled over which path to take. (I might add here that Ashbery more directly misprisioned Frost's poem in "The System" section of *Three Poems*.)[12] Significantly, Frost's speaker was "sorry I could not travel both / And be one traveler" (1). Both Frost and Ashbery express a marked frustration over their inability to surmount their hidebound place in the world, and look to poetry to in part reach for simultaneity.

"One is uncertain / How the future is going to handle this" ("Ostensibly" 55), Ashbery continues, and ends the opening stanza with a question:

> Will it reveal itself again,
> Or only in the artificial calm
> Of one person's resolve to do better
> Yet strike a harder bargain,
> Next time? (ibid.)

What does the "it" refer to? There is certainly no clear answer to this question, though syntactically speaking, Ashbery might want us to consider "it" as that "future" mentioned in the preceding line. Where, though, can the future — by definition unknown, unwritten — reveal itself? "Only in the artificial calm," Ashbery writes. Ashbery mournfully acknowledges the inability of the poem to fulfill its Blakean role as prophecy and authentic harbinger of change. The possibility of taking both roads at once, of breaking through the boundaries the physical and rational world imposes on us, is the dream of poetry, yet poetry's "artificial" nature means one will never be able to achieve such a state outside the imagination. That said, while Frost wrote "Oh, I kept the first for another day! / Yet knowing how way leads on to way, / I doubted if I should ever come back" (1), Ashbery is not ready to give up. One person can "resolve to do better / Yet strike a harder bargain, / Next time."

As if to emphasize that this task will never be achieved through the Frostian pastoral, Ashbery continues in the second stanza by suggesting that it is only through "artificial" means that one might "make the world":

> Gardeners cannot make the world
> Nor witches undo it, yet
> The mad doctor is secure
> In his thick-walled laboratory,
> Behind evergreen borders black now
> Against the snow, precise as stocking seams
> Pulled straight again. There is never
> Any news from that side. ("Ostensibly" 55)

"Ostensibly" works increasingly hard here to free itself from the pagan elements revealed throughout Frost's poetry. Consider, for example, Frost's repeated evocations of witchcraft and the supernatural in combination with the pastoral in poems like "Design," "The Witch of Coos," and "Mending Wall." If gardeners and witches cannot make or undo the world, who then has power? "The mad doctor," the only "secure" character so far, who mixes any number of artificial ingredients together to make his monsters or redeemers.

It is hard not to hear the phrase "mad doctor" without thinking of any number of Frankenstein films. (In terms of Burckhardt specifically, we might even think about that "mad doctor" in reference to *Lurk*, Burckhardt's own take on the Frankenstein genre discussed above.) The sense of a more purely literary tradition evoked by "gardeners" and "witches" is here undermined by the artificial and hokey "mad doctor," who amusingly is more able to "make the world" than his literary predecessors. And yet, as Ashbery maintains throughout much of his work, we are still not allowed full communion with the seer. "There is never / Any news from that side." The cinematic mad doctor is shuttered out of the poem as soon as he is identified.

As if to mock the disappearance of the only character thus far who offered us any chance of reconciling "so many separate / ways of doing," Ashbery continues in the third stanza with the lines "A rigidity that may well be permanent / Seems to have taken over. The pendulum / Is stilled; the rush / Of season into season ostensibly incomplete" (ibid.). Movement — of time, lyric, season — has here apparently ceased forever. Stasis is akin to apocalypse. The movement of the lyric falters via occasional enjambment as the stanza creaks slowly but surely into a kind of freeze-frame:

> A perverse order has been laid
> There at the joint where the year branches
> Into artifice one way, into a votive
> Lassitude the other way, but that is stalled:

An old discolored snapshot
That soon fades away (ibid.)

As the movement of the seasons ceases, Ashbery provides us with a practically crystalline tree where "a perverse order" has its foundation. "The year" not only branches "into artifice one way" and into a paradoxically wishful and religiously inflected weariness and listlessness the other way, but is itself stalled. The branches here have grown as far they are going to — all is still. Emphasizing pictorially the connection between an apocalyptic "perverse order" with motionlessness, the stanza ends on "an old discolored snapshot," a move that may remind us of Burckhardt's rueful claim that "a picture . . . becomes like a fact," something which he compares negatively to a film which is "fleeting, things come and go" (Lopate 27). When things stop being fleeting — when dreaminess and movement are stalled by the hard fact of a concrete, unmoving image — "a perverse order" is sure to take hold.

Indeed, the first two lines of the next stanza mourn, "And so there is no spectator / And no agent to cry Enough" ("Ostensibly" 55). A spectator by definition is someone who watches things unfold as they happen in time — he is an observer of an event. Again, the loss of movement is tacitly lamented here when the spectator is frozen out of the poem. Succeeding lines of the penultimate stanza are practically opaque (perhaps a perfectly reasonable move given the fact that the "perverse order has been laid" and we are frozen, as if in amber, in "a rigidity that may well be permanent"). However, allusive characterizations of a "stilled" "battle chime," a "defeated memory gracious as flowers" that is "permanent in its way," and a "fortified dose of the solid, / Livable adventure" point (if ever so elusively) to the general theme of movement verses stasis.

The final stanza finds Ashbery trying to extricate us out of the freeze-frame created thus far by once again encouraging us to start moving:

And from growing dim, the coals
Fall alight. There are two ways to be.
You must try getting up from the table
And sitting down relaxed in another country
Wearing red suspenders
Towards one's own space and time. (ibid. 56)

The still photograph has faded, and apparently the coals were growing dim as well, but once they are impelled to move they light up again. The love-light, however flickeringly, is beginning to shine once more. "There are two ways to be," Ashbery adds, taking us right back to his evocation and revision of Frost in the first stanza. While Frost intoned "two roads diverged in a yellow wood" and admitted his desire and inability to take both at the same time, Ashbery injects a surprisingly sweet optimism into this relatively gloomy poem by insisting we can swing both ways, as it were. We must try "getting up from the table" and magically cut ourselves into an entirely new scene, "sitting down relaxed in another country." For good measure, we should also consider wearing a practically cartoon-like set of "red suspenders" as we explore the ways we can locate and traverse our own "space and time."

Ashbery's consistent references to movement, particularly as they are situated hierarchically over stasis; his characteristic pronominal shifts; his ceding authority to the reader over the writer; his negotiation between auto-telic materiality and stable signification; his quiet critique of a stable literary history; his revisioning of the "artificial" as potentially liberatory; and his use of juxtaposition to suggest freedom and progress all find a corollary in Burckhardt's film, *Ostensibly.* This is not to say that *Ostensibly* is merely an MTV-style music video, in which images work in slavish adherence to the given narrative of the lyric. What Burckhardt does in the film is to open up the door between two genres — film and poetry — in order to illuminate how they inform and enhance each other. Poem becomes film becomes poem, to the extent that the viewer's sense of what constitutes genre is drastically, if wholly pleasurably, altered.

The mood is set immediately in *Ostensibly* with Alvin Curran's solo piece for piano, *For Cornelius.*[13] A small number of notes are played rapidly and repeatedly in the minor key as the first scene in the film — a shot of a rural highway filmed from a moving car — fills the screen. A series of shots of signs follows. The first one we see is a classically American road sign for the Blue Ridge Motor Lodge with a message board proclaiming "Welcome Peking Acrobats" directly underneath it. Burckhardt's choice to feature this particular image as the first one in the series is significant. The global con-sciousness (if not outright cosmopolitanism) implicit in the welcome mes-sage impels viewers to immediately widen any conventional notion of what constitutes homespun Americana. That "Peking acrobats" have made it to this seemingly rather desolate environment (a desolation underscored by the "Vacancy" notice) resonates quite clearly with Ashbery's poetry of mixed discourses, one in which we find a vast and often amusing number of refer-ences in his work (Giorgio de Chirico, Daffy Duck, the French Revolution, the Bobinski Brothers).

Other signs follow — McDonald's, Firestone, Gulf — and the camera lingers on their gaudy colors lovingly. The way in which Burckhardt focuses his camera eye not just uncritically but admiringly on these capitalist emblems at once distinguishes him from the social critique of fellow filmmakers and photographers like Robert Frank and Brakhage as it aligns him with the gleeful gusto found in O'Hara's and Ted Berrigan's writing. (After all, both these poets treat Pepsi, cheeseburgers, and other less-than-stellar contributions to American cuisine and culture in a whimsically celebratory manner.)

As if to emphasize this aspect of the New York School, Burckhardt then cuts to an image of the Manhattan skyline, followed by a series of close-ups on city signs, including one of an old Automat, a liquor store, and a Korean nail salon, again evoking the urbanity and cheerful entrepreneurship of any number of O'Hara's "I do this, I do that" peripatetic journeys around Manhattan. These images are then interspersed with shots of people entering and exiting a subway from the street level, shots of water towers, tracking shots and pans of various famous and not-so-famous New York City buildings, including the former Twin Towers and Bank Street College, and shots of New Yorkers walking near City Hall, street musicians, workers eating on their lunch hour, tourists looking through telescopes at the Statue of Liberty, and so on.

Following these outdoor scenes, Burckhardt takes us indoors to a light-filled apartment where Kia Heath, an attractive young blonde woman, proceeds to disrobe. Once fully naked, Heath sits in lotus position on a desk. All these images, richly demonstrating themes we can associate variously with Jack Kerouac's road trips and Kama Sutra–type fantasies as well as the New York School flâneur, have thus far been a kind of warm-up or appetizer for the main course, which is John Ashbery's actual reading of the poem "Ostensibly."

Ashbery is shown sitting on a couch with a manuscript in his hands. With Curran's melancholy music playing in the background, Ashbery begins to read "Ostensibly" in his characteristically flat voice. At the line "so many separate ways of doing," there is a cut to the Statue of Liberty, and the camera then pans down to the Hudson River, which shimmers and reflects the sun. "One is uncertain how the future is going to handle this," Ashbery says, as the screen is taken up entirely with a gorgeous image of light shining in the water. Burckhardt appears to be stretching the interpretive possibilities of the poem here. As I discussed above, Ashbery's use of the pronoun "one" is used generically as a plural "anyone." The "one" is us, and we are a crowd. Burckhardt's alignment of this implicitly plural pronoun with images of the Statue of Liberty, followed by the multitude of sparkles glancing off of the water, serves to situate Ashbery's poem firmly within that Whitmanic tradition that simultaneously individuates and collectivizes the mass of individuals that make up the urban crowds of Manhattan. After all, a crowd is precisely a model of "So many separate / Ways of doing" — Burckhardt's decision to frame these lines within a clearly celebratory Americanist context does much to direct our attention to the possibility that Ashbery's poem can be read, despite its at times admitted gloominess, as an extension of a democratic poetics. The film uses the poem to celebrate the individual and a cosmopolitan American diversity. This is not, however, an example of mindless patriotism on Burckhardt's part. The uncertainty in Ashbery's poem is included within these frames as well as the Whitmanic "so many separate ways of doing," thus lending an implicitly critical aura to the symbols of American freedom.

At the end of the first stanza, there is a cut and we return to Ashbery, this time appearing in a tightly framed Warhol-style head shot in front of a bare white wall.[14] As Curran's minimalist composition plays in the background, Ashbery continues his reading of the stanza, every now and then looking slightly so nervously up at the camera as if attempting to connect with the eyes of the audience. The sight of Ashbery all alone against a bare background adds a visual and aural corollary to the underlying melancholy that pulses so discreetly throughout the poem itself.

At the phrase "precise as stocking seams / Pulled straight again," the film cuts to the shots of tops of trees filmed from a moving car. Burckhardt — as he does in so much of his work, and as so many poets affiliated with the New York School do — consistently yokes images of the urban with the pastoral and rural. (I discuss this aspect in more detail below.) The "gardeners" and "witches" representative of the English literary tradition in Ashbery's poem are here lightly alluded to in the images of the classical forest, as the cinematic modernity implicit in "the mad doctor" and wholly contemporary-sounding phrases like "There is never / Any news from that side" is evidenced in the obvious technology of the tracking shot taken from a moving vehicle. Additionally, the disappearance of the "mad doctor" himself is further emphasized by Ashbery's absence from the screen — there is no more news "from that side."

The third stanza is then heard as voiceover — "A rigidity that may well be permanent / Seems to have taken over" — as the camera continues to track the trees. As Ashbery reaches the line "A perverse order has been laid," there is a cut to a scene focusing on Kia Heath sitting naked on the desk. This is perhaps a somewhat obvious little joke on Burckhardt's part, in that he aligns sexually suggestive phrases including "a rigidity" that is "permanent," "perverse order," and "has been laid" to Heath's body. Obvious or not, such a free representation of Ashbery's lines certainly illustrates the very freedom of interpretation that Ashbery consistently invites from his readers. Ashbery has rather casually asserted, "It's OK to interpret poetry in a variety of ways. In fact, that's the only way poetry is read, I think. We all interpret poetry according to what we've experienced, therefore everybody's interpretation is going to differ from everybody else's" (Ashbery, "Interview with Daniel Kane" 35). Burckhardt has taken Ashbery at his word by reframing sexually suggestive lines and phrases in a wholly heterosexual context. Once again, viewers are reminded that there are "so many separate / Ways of doing." This move on Burckhardt's part certainly runs counter to the recent and increasingly dominating readings of Ashbery's work as grounded in a queer aesthetic. John Shoptaw's understanding of Ashbery's "homotextuality" and John Vincent's discussion of Ashbery's "queer lyrics," Mark Silverberg's "Laughter and Uncertainty: John Ashbery's Low-Key Camp," Catherine Imbriglio's "The Rhetoric of the Closet in John Ashbery's *Some Trees*," and recent shorter review pieces by critics including Alfred Corn tend to position Ashbery as representative of a specifically homosexual textuality. Burckhardt appears to flout the gay chic of much Ashbery interpretation by rather blithely misreading the poem for its heterosexualized implications, perhaps intentionally and comically illustrating the fact that, as Ashbery puts it in the final stanza of the poem, "There are two ways to be."

Subsequent lines are used as voice-over until we reach "but that is stalled"; the film then cuts to an image of a television set that is turned on to a show featuring two newscasters — the self-important puffery of a daytime news show, evident in the faux-serious, faux-concerned visages of the presenters, is aligned by Burckhardt to the final lines of the third stanza, "An old discolored snapshot / That soon fades away." The fourth stanza is heard as voiceover for a montage of street scenes, close-ups on a flickering television, a close-up of Heath's breasts, and roller skaters in Central Park. "And so there is no spectator / And no agent to cry Enough" is literalized by the seemingly endless play of possibilities available to the camera. Burckhardt, like Ashbery, appears here to want to enact the loss of authorial/directorial control by cutting in an apparently random way through a series of scenes and subjects. Ending, however, on an exciting scene of a roller skater in Central Park wending his way rapidly between a series of cans, the optimism that begins to shine through in the final stanza is here visually anticipated. Such a reading is emphasized when Burckhardt continues to show us the roller-skating scene as Ashbery begins to read the final stanza. "There are two ways to be," we hear, and then Burckhardt cuts from the roller skater and takes us back to the "mad doctor," Ashbery himself. As if to emphasize the relative jolliness of this tonal and visual shift, Ashbery is now shown wearing a pair of red suspenders to coincide with the "red suspenders" in the poem's penultimate line.

As Curran's repetitive notes play in the background, the viewer is treated to another scene of Kia Heath, this time getting off the table and putting her clothes back on, followed by another scene where Ashbery gets off the couch, shakes hands with two of the filmmakers, and generally looks genial and pleased. The self-reflexive aspects of the poem, embodied most clearly in its first line ("One might like to rest or read") are here comically and surprisingly extended to film. The suspension of disbelief crucial to so viewing so much mainstream film — one that relies on the viewer's decision to forget she is watching a constructed, edited narrative in favor of treating the succession of images as a transparent record of natural events — is here wholly upended by the sudden appearance of the camera and sound guys (Christopher Sweet on the left and Jacob Burckhardt [Rudy Burkhardt's son] on the right).

As Ashbery consistently reminds us that we are reading and interpreting text rather than receiving vatic wisdom from a Parnassian height, so Burckhardt creates a visual takeoff on textual self-reflexity. Here, the poet and filmmakers show themselves: the "mad scientist" who is editing the film reveals his movie-making laboratory at the same time as Ashbery reveals himself in his "own space and time" by acknowledging his physical place in the filmic reconstruction of the poem.

And yet, even though the poem is over, the film continues. What follows is a succession of New York City streets — one extended scene features a particularly animated conversation between two men, one of whom is of apparently Italian American extraction, adding another funny counterbalance to the melancholy strain of Curran's music. The next scene focuses on the billboard of an adult film theater. Burckhardt himself then appears, playing the role of a cranky, perhaps mentally ill old man meandering through the Times Square district. He stares and mutters at pornographic movie posters and pokes garbage around with his walking stick while the camera cuts occasionally to marquee signs and local traffic.

Subsequent scenes show snow falling on city streets, a woman walking through the city winterscape confusedly in a red sweater (perhaps to rhyme

John Ashbery, Christopher Sweet, and Jacob Burckhardt, from *Ostensibly*
© Rudy Burckhardt. Courtesy of the Estate of Rudy Burckhardt.

with Ashbery's own red suspenders and to further extend the subject position of the speaker of the poem), clouds (filmed in fast-forward) floating in a
beautiful sunny sky, more street scenes (including a scene of a family filmed
in reverse walking back up some stairs, which works as a visual rhyme with
the fast-forward clouds), stop-time animation of a vase with flowers in it,
and a scene of Burkhardt and friends posing against a large rock. Burckhardt
here is wearing a blue and white checkered shirt that, while not necessarily
identical to Ashbery's shirt, certainly looks like the same item.

What follows after the shot of Burckhardt in Ashbery's clothing is familiar to anyone conversant with Burckhardt's oeuvre — scenes from a rural
fair, complete with spinning Ferris wheels, log-throwing competitions, and
the like. After a minute or so of this, the camera pans back up to the tops of a
group of trees and the sky, filmed at high speed, and a woman begins to read
the poem "Ostensibly" as voice-over. Once again, Burckhardt seems to be
distributing authorship of the poem merrily to a variety of unlikely subjects.
Moving away from a model of the poetry reading as one centered on the authority of the scriptor — and certainly liberating himself from the essentially
organic tie-in that Brakhage, for example, made between Creeley's work as a

poet and Creeley's own image in film — Burckhardt here gives the last word
to a female speaking voice, one who is unidentified in the credits and is, by
virtue of her gender, offering us the clearest example yet of "two ways to be."
The authority we invest in the "true" voice of the author is here undermined
lightly by an unidentified woman reading Ashbery's lines.

Individual lines and phrases in the first stanza continue to be illustrated
compellingly and complexly. "So many separate / Ways of doing" serves as
voice-over for a young couple about to get married. As Burckhardt did with
his images of the naked Kia Heath, the implicit homotextuality of Ashbery's
poetry generally is here countered by an assertive, if not overbearing, het-
erosexuality. As discussed above, Ashbery's "A rigidity that may well be
permanent," once it becomes soundtrack to images of Heath's naked body,
becomes metaphor for a raging heterosexual hard-on. In this case, Ashbery's
lines, "so many separate / Ways of doing," continue to work in service of
creating a nonessentialist queer space, where the fey, mannered voice of Ashbery becomes literally feminine and works in service of propelling images
of the most conventional of unions. Queer and "straight" images, tones, and
themes all find a place within the space of the film.

As the lines progress, there is a cut to a close-up of leaves shadowing a
tree trunk. The film continues by cutting back and forth from a table with
leaves, photographs, and apples on it to scenes of the developing wedding.
What then follows is an extended sequence in the Maine woods, where the
camera treats natural objects rather abstractly as the poem is read via voice-
over. Making Ashbery's line "A perverse order has been laid / There at the
joint where the year branches / Into artifice one way" literal, Burckhardt provides the viewer with dramatic shots of branches shot from below. When
the woman reading the poem recites "but that is stalled: / An old discolored snapshot," the accompanying images consist of three freeze-frames of
a pond — the illusion of movement in film is here "stalled" and shown for
what it truly is: a series of static frames or snapshots that will fade, as all
things do, with time. The line "And so there is no spectator" is accompanied
visually by a shot of a young man jogging up a dirt road toward the camera.
As the stanza progresses, the scene shifts from the jogging man to cars on
a city street — as they are driving towards the camera, a visual rhyme is attained where the mechanical resonates with the human.

At the beginning of the final stanza, Burckhardt uses some images to
closely reflect the content of the poem. "And from growing dim, the coals /
Fall alight," for example, is illustrated by a shot of a burning fireplace, while
the final lines, beginning with "You must try getting up from the table / And

Rudy Burckhardt pushes down a tree, from *Ostensibly* © Rudy Burckhardt.
Courtesy of the Estate of Rudy Burckhardt.

sitting relaxed in another country," are read against the image of the edge of
a large apartment building framed in front of a Constable-like, cloud-filled
twilight sky.

While the poem, read once by Ashbery and once by a woman, is not repeated again, the film is not quite over. The "narrative" as such continues
with a scene of a raucous costume party, followed by an extended sequence
of Burckhardt in the woods. Burckhardt is again wearing the flannel shirt
resembling Ashbery's. Amusingly, the shirt is put to good use in terms of
the function many of us might associate with it. While Burckhardt is at
first shown sitting in meditation position in a forest, a position that rhymes
comically with the prior image of Kia Heath sitting in naked lotus position
on a desk, subsequent shots find Burckhardt playing around in the forest
by sawing into a small tree, play-fighting with a tree, acting cranky, pushing rotten trees down to the ground, grooming himself, and the like. The
film then continues with an elegant rhythmic montage of shots of ferns and
mushrooms; a shot of a jet plane and jet exhaust; an extended shot of daisies
in a field; water tanks on building roofs; a taxicab on a rain-slicked street;
a woman in a red raincoat walking up a street (again reminding us of Ash-

bery's "red suspenders" and extending the theme that there are "so many separate ways of doing"); close-ups of tree bark; the reflection of pond water against a tree; a city avenue; the city sky framing water towers; city buildings at dusk; more water towers; more sky; rain-slicked streets; cars waiting at red lights; and, finally, speeded-up clouds moving against twilight sky.

With *Ostensibly*, Burckhardt creates a universe that informs and is parallel to Ashbery's universe. And yet, the film does not propose itself as a decisive interpretation of the poem "Ostensibly." By literalizing images that Ashbery appears to present as opaque, by effecting a sense of visual stream-of-consciousness analogous to (as opposed to specifically imitative of) Ashbery's textual stream-of-consciousness, and by normalizing Ashbery's queerness via practically traditional heterosexual strategies, *Ostensibly* enacts the possibilities offered by the poem while further diffusing it through film. The conversation between film and poem takes us further out "Toward one's own space and time," where both the poem and film urge us to confront our responsibility as interpreters and encourage us to enjoy the process of imagining "so many separate ways of doing."

conclusion

Lisa Jarnot and Jennifer Reeves
in Conversation

On July 13, 2007, I sat down for an interview with filmmaker Jennifer Reeves and poet Lisa Jarnot to discuss Reeves's film, *The Time We Killed* (2004). The film is centered on a character named Robyn, who is played by Jarnot. Robyn is a bisexual, borderline agoraphobic writer who only ventures out of her Brooklyn apartment in the wake of the attacks of September 11, 2001 and the "Shock and Awe" campaign.

DK: What made you want to work with each other for Jennifer's film, *The Time We Killed*?

JR: For a little background, I've always worked with nonactors in my narrative films. Oftentimes I've played the main part of my films. In that context I was looking for a friend, someone that I'm close to or have some kind of personal relationship to, but I was also wanting to work with someone who shared a lot with me in terms of our ideas about politics, aesthetic tendencies in our own work. . . . We were actually introduced to each other by Stan Brakhage and Robert Kelly. . . . The first time I was really getting to know Brakhage and Kelly they both told me *"You have to meet Lisa Jarnot. You have to read her work."*

LJ: And I was teaching at University of Colorado and Stan showed Jenn's work in one of the salons. When I first saw Jenn's early film *Chronic* [1996] in one of Brakhage's salons, I was more than delighted — it felt familiar, and really exhilarating in the motion from past to present and from present to past. On another level, the textures that arrived out of layers of film and painting on the film and complex sound compositions were inspiring to me in the same way that Brakhage's films were inspiring to me — it was what I always sought out in poetry — a work that was so richly textured that it never came to an end. In some ways it was spooky — seeing *Chronic* was like seeing my own process and psyche on the screen. I felt really blessed when I told Brakhage I was moving back to New York and he gave me Jenn's phone number.

DK: How did you two meet Stan Brakhage?

JR: I first met Stan very briefly in 1996 on my first tour to the West Coast with my films. Stan came to the screening and just before it started he came up to me and said, "It's wonderful to meet you. I'm sorry I won't be able to stay for all your films. I have a previous engagement, but thank you for being here." It was something to that effect, as if he was giving himself an early exit. Maybe he really did have plans, but anyway he ended up staying through the entire ninety-minute presentation of my films, and at the end of it he stood and clapped. During the show I could hear his bellowing laughter at the right moments. . . . These were my earlier short films. . . . I was utterly thrilled that he was staying and clapping. . . . If he left I wouldn't have known whether he didn't like the work or if he really had an appointment, but the fact that he stayed really said something. A bit later he curated three of my short films in a series at Anthology Film Archives. It was a three-screening event, something like "Stan Brakhage Curates New Avant-Garde Films" or "What's Being Made Today." I was included, and another young and barely known filmmaker at the time, David Gatten, was included. . . . We were both pretty blown away by the honor.

LJ: I'd been aware of Brakhage's work early on, having studied in the English Department at the University of Buffalo, where Charles Olson's influence was still very much felt during the 1980s. Later, when I began research toward a biography of the San Francisco poet Robert Duncan, I interviewed Stan and we became friends. When I lived in Boulder briefly in 1998 and 2000, I spent a good deal of time at Stan's Sunday night salons. He'd always show a handful of experimental films from his archives (some of his work, but primarily work by others). For me, Stan's films did what I wanted poetry to do — to create a world that is free from the strictures of traditional form and content while at the same time insisting on a storytelling of sorts. I guess you could say that Brakhage was an inspiration for me in continuing my

Lisa Jarnot in *The Time We Killed* by Jennifer Reeves © Sparky Pictures, Inc.
Courtesy of Jennifer Reeves and Lisa Jarnot.

work in an "open field" poetics, but more importantly, he simply confirmed for me that one's creative work is always deeply integrated into the rest of one's life. Stan was never not working.

DK: Jennifer, can you tell me what about Lisa's work seems to rhyme with your filmmaking?

JR: On the one hand it's the associations and layers in the work, and . . . I find her work is very visual. . . . When I read her work there are such strong images, whether they are animals or the place she's in, it's not narrative or conventional in any sense, yet it gives you this real sense of place and presence.

DK: That's interesting. That sense of presence or even simultaneity . . . that sense of everything happening at the same time is analogous to film's ability to enact presence, to show us that everything works together all at the same time.

JR: Yes, and I never have a film that's about one thing. I'm always making a lot of different connections. Most films really simplify things, to make a nice and tight ninety-minute experience where the viewer is never unsure what to think about. Both her work and my work sort of spin you out into different associations. Things are presented in this complex layered way, but then what is offered is essentially meant for viewers or readers to make their own associations and images in their mind. The other part of our work that's important to note is our mutual sense of *rhythm*. Obviously, with her work there's a certain amount of repetition of words and phrases. One of her poems will start in the present but then refer back (to itself) so that it's in the past, and then suddenly the register will shift into the future. In my work, also, and in particular with *The Time We Killed*, there's a lot of emphasis on memory that's signified in montage with visual tropes, composition and forms repeating or echoing. I guess I'm making two points here. Through the repetition you have this rhythm in time . . . but then there's the vocal and phrase repetition in Lisa's poems that creates rhythm. In my film, it may be a theme or a thing repeating (trees, birds, bodies of water, or dogs), or it is form and movement from cut to cut that create a nonrepresentational visual rhythm. I think of music.

DK: Lisa, when I heard you describe Jenn's work earlier it made me think that you might as well be describing your own poetry. . . . I think of your work as a verbal equivalent of a kaleidoscope, where you have a certain range of visual and verbal tropes that are repeated in different variations so that the experience of reading is akin to watching something shift subtly and beautifully over time. Jennifer, do you see what I mean here? Is this something you attempt to represent visually in your film?

JR: I repeat scenes in the whole body of my work. What is shown as the main material in one film will be repeated in another film as a glimpse. This happens with Lisa's work as well. My body of work is something connected with images and themes in the same way that I think Lisa's poems work within themselves and throughout her work generally.

LJ: In some ways I'd say that's an inevitable part of creating a body of work, or one's "life's work" so-called. There are signature themes and images that bubble up out of the autobiographical.

DK: Well, it seems that both of you are suggesting that your artistic production is conceived as a serial process. This reminds me of Robert Duncan's work, particularly in his *Passages* series, where you'll go through three or four books and, because of his use of repetition — repetition of actual words and phrases as well as repetition of specific themes — you'll sense all of a sudden that you're reading something that is part of an ongoing process, not something that is presented to you as completed product.

LJ: It happens in Duncan, and I'd say it happens even more consistently and clearly in Jack Spicer's work. My sense of seriality is certainly influenced by both Duncan and Spicer. And of course there are several instances of seriality in Brakhage's longer projects, where he was looking for a sustained narrative through several films.

JR: That's what can happen when art is coming from as personal a place as my work or Lisa's work. It's an extension of us. People have themes in their lives, images that stick and return. Work that's more conceptual or less immediate doesn't quite have that sense to it. In *The Time We Killed*, Lisa wrote these poems while I was shooting. Basically, there were scenes in the film where her character is writing fiction, but Lisa — just herself — started composing poems in front of me, on camera.

LJ: That was one of the nice things about working with Jenn. I think we really trusted each other. When she asked me to be in one of her films I immediately said yes. When she told me I was going to star in it I think I was a little shocked, delightfully so. I wanted to be there just to see how she worked, and at every step along the way it was a real treat. She was fiercely independent in all of the aspects of the shooting and production, so a lot of times it was just the two of us. When I got over my initial awe of watching all the setup and technical aspects of the shoot, I began to settle into character by writing on the set. We workshopped the character of Robyn in some ways. Jenn would have an idea about how Robyn felt or what Robyn was thinking about and I would push forward from there.

DK: I had no idea it was that intimate! The composition of the poems came out of a dialogue then between the writing of poetry and making of film.

JR: Yes, and Lisa did that entirely spontaneously. I did not ask her to do that. I actually edited the film to the poetry, using her cadences to sequence the images.

DK: So, in the section where Lisa is reading a poem about dogs and sand-pipers, were you initially listening to a recording of Lisa reading as you were editing the film in the studio?

JR: Yes. Basically, she wrote that during a kind of bland scene of Robyn in her apartment typing. She wrote it while I was setting up the lights, after we had discussed the scene, and while we were shooting. Afterwards, I recorded her reading the poem, and then I took that recording, put it into my com-puter where I was editing the film, and then I edited the image *to* the poem. So *The Time We Killed* is a real collaboration in that the film inspired her to write the poems, and then I took the poems as inspiration and backbone to edit certain scenes.

DK: Lisa, did the process of working with Jennifer as intimately as you did in *The Time We Killed* inform your own writing practice?

LJ: I'm not sure that it informed my own writing practice so much as it granted me the space of a really useful collaboration. It was especially free-ing to collaborate across genres. I knew that Jenn was going to do something spectacular with the visual composition. That made it easy for me to do my own thing as a writer.

DK: The way the two of you describe the process almost makes it sound like jazz improvisation, where you're working off a riff, feeding off of each other.

JR: When we were shooting, it was just me and Lisa in my apartment, which maybe made it a safer place for her to write that spontaneously. But she did not edit those poems. She basically just tossed off these perfect poems. They were completely direct and spontaneous.

LJ: I think partly that happened because we had already arrived at some parts of the dialogue in the film. I knew basically who Robyn was and what was on her mind. I also spent a lot of time on the set working myself up into a dissociative state, getting into that lonely angry obsessive state of mind. The repetitions in the poems were partly a by-product of that.

DK: Jennifer, you said a little bit earlier that your work was "personal," that you see it as emanating out of your personal experience. One of the things that I've been thinking about a lot in my own work for this book is how work like Brakhage's has at this point in time been somewhat marginalized precisely because it doesn't fit into the ideologies we associate with postmodern theory.

JR: Right, Stan's work is considered as somehow modernist, stuck in another time.

DK: Yes, a retrograde symbolist. . . . This to a somewhat lesser extent applies to a filmmaker like Kenneth Anger, who in all sincerity believed his films worked in part as occult spells.

LJ: This really brings up an issue that's important to me as a writer . . . that one does one's work away from the labels that critics and academics later apply to it. . . . What Jenn talks about as the "personal" experience doesn't necessarily mean "confessional" or "romantic." . . . It means simply that the life and the work are feeding off each other. It's not part of the creative work to think about modernism or postmodernism. And certainly Brakhage is a key example of an artist who had very little use for that kind of talk around the work.

DK: Jenn, I'm curious as to how you see your own work, particularly as it comes chronologically after the structural film movement we associate with filmmakers like Michael Snow.

JR: It's interesting because in graduate school a well-known theorist and conceptual video and computer artist, Lev Manovich, was on one of my panels in graduate school and he asked me, "How is this significant for the late 1990s, what's different about your work from Brakhage?" It was basically a less-than-tacit accusation that I'm stuck in a period that is no longer important, that's no longer relevant.

DK: Well, Brakhage after all was accused of being a male chauvinist and reactionary. . . . Amy Taubin wrote of his "Arabic Numeral Series" [1980–1982] and "Roman Numeral Series" [1979–1980], "Brakhage's antifeminist position has never been so clear"! Do *you* feel old-fashioned in terms of your working procedures? Here you are hand-painting films like Brakhage and Len Lye did earlier, and vocally framing your work in the context of the "personal." Many people might argue that any art that purports to be innovative or avant-garde should resist or at least problematize the very concept of the "personal," of the stable "I."

JR: Well, galleries don't seem to want to show my work even though my work is tactile, "painterly," and visually stunning according to some people. A lot of contemporary video art is pretty anti-beauty, lacking the cinematic. Well, visual pleasure is not enough of course, but it seems unnecessarily problematic these days. Is a work Romantic and without cultural value if there isn't a pun or an obvious social critique incorporated into it? But there are things that take patience and perhaps a dark screening room to appreciate. When I was first embraced by Stan and the filmmaker Phil Solomon, Phil said something like, "What's great about your work is that you've embraced and updated the avant-garde film tradition, you're making feminist work that's beautiful, it's work that combines the personal with the political." And I was happy to hear this. . . . Was I, as Barbara Hammer said at one of my first public screenings, "carrying the torch"? I could only see this as an honor, not something irrelevant!

But I do feel a bit out of another time . . . as I make work that isn't derived from a conceptual place. My intellect is always there making the work, I make conscious decisions about all the details underlying and on the screen. But I also care a lot about nonverbal, personal, emotional communication and experience, and I think an approach like that has been marginalized. Some people respond like I'm a "woman filmmaker," because my work comes off as more personal than conceptual. This sometimes irks me because I think the "emotional" is unfairly marginalized and associated with femininity. Emotions and physicality, as the feminine realm, are valued less than intellect or the rational (male) mind in our society. But the physical and the mental should be equal as opposed to separate. We get sick otherwise.

DK: Given this question of what the phrase "woman filmmaker" means, it strikes me that most of the filmmakers we've been discussing so far are considered part of the independent cinema of the 1960s, and most of them are male. What about the women filmmakers of that era? I'm thinking about Shirley Clarke, for instance, or Barbara Rubin. Do you feel any desire to recuperate their work, particularly given the place you find yourself being put in as a "woman filmmaker"?

JR: Shirley Clarke is a great filmmaker and Rubin made one work that stands out for me, *Christmas on Earth*. I DJ'd to that film in a New York community garden a few years ago, and it was a wonderful feeling of time travel, thanks to M. M. Serra, who does a lot to recover that early work. A lot of other great work has really fallen through the cracks, like Joyce Wieland's *Rat Life and Diet in North America* [1968] and *Barbara's Blindness* [1967]. I was exposed to feminist film criticism in college, and that was very influential to me. Mulvey's essay, "Visual Pleasure and Narrative Cinema," was eye-opening and remains fundamental. But, yes, many of my first big influences were part of that male-dominated 60s scene. I was certainly influenced by Maya Deren's work, of course, in fact it is such a given that I forgot to mention her, . . . how terrible. But remember how literally formative her work was to the whole New American Cinema movement.

DK: Yes, and of course she was particularly important to Brakhage. Indeed, the way you talked earlier about emotion being somehow beyond language reminds me immediately of Brakhage's chestnut, "How many colors are there in a field of grass to the crawling baby unaware of 'Green'?" Brakhage seemed to want to evoke what it might be like to experience the world in a preliterate or preverbal way, what he called the "primordial mind." What's curious to me about Brakhage's and your work is that you're both drawn to poetry, which, at the risk of making a generalization, is perhaps *the* genre most committed to exploring the intense possibilities in and of language.

JR: You know, I should point out that my first finished film, *Elations in Negative* [1990; silent], was based on a William Carlos Williams poem.

> *What are these elations I have*
> *At my own underwear*
> *I touch it*
> *And it is strange*
> *Upon a strange thigh*

The text is in the film (each line gets one title card, I think), with a counterpoint of dark imagery. This has shown publicly, and I rather like it. It scares people — there's blood.

But anyway, it's interesting because about half of my films are nonverbal, and then the other half is heavily verbal. I use voice-over in *The Time We Killed* . . . the nonverbal films are more universal and less specific, they transcend time. I can watch them for many years because they still seem current; they're not limited by the language. When I make a film with a voice-over, I feel it becomes locked into the time that I made it, even on the most basic level of how your perspective changes as you grow. But constructing meaning through speech can be the most powerful thing because it takes more risk. You are committing to the meaning you make through language.

DK: Although at the same time look at Lisa's poetry and look at Brakhage's love for Gertrude Stein's poetry. This is a poetry that resists paraphrase, narrative, the basic structure of beginning, middle, and end.

LJ: I think there are different ways of looking at narrative. Brakhage helped me to see something interesting about my own work when he described it as creating stories out of the relationships between individual words. When I look at his work, I'm immediately drawn into the "stories," which may simply be formed out of two shapes rubbing up against each other.

JR: Obviously, film and poetry are linear — you read it from beginning to end, you watch it from beginning to end, but the experience doesn't feel linear because work like Jarnot's, Stein's, Brakhage's, and my own is so associative. My experience watching Stan's direct-on-film or single-frame work, or of hearing Lisa's poetry, is one that makes me feel as if I'm living entirely in the moment. I want my film to be like that. It will mix memory with the present and fantasy . . . in that way it becomes nonlinear.

LJ: I'd also introduce here the idea of process versus progress. With traditional linear narrative we think of a progress towards an end. But in the real world things are much more complicated than that. Events occur simultaneously. This is very much the idea that is spawned by the Black Mountain School and Charles Olson during the 1950s. You see it in abstract expressionist art, which was also very important to Brakhage. There is a field of activity or energy, for example, the field of the canvas or the field of the poem or the field of a frame of film. Many things can happen in that field at the same time.

DK: Yes, simultaneity is something that doesn't necessarily freeze out a story, if we understand "story" to be an audience member's identification with or apprehension of feelings and events outside his or her own immediate physiology.

Now, both you and Jennifer have talked a bit about the associative gesture, which you suggest resists linearity. There's an interesting tension in *The Time We Killed* between narrative and a more expressionistic, practically interiorized aesthetic. The film goes back and forth between story and vision. There's a murder mystery with two bodies in the neighbors' apartment, intimations of Ground Zero, 9/11, and so on. These stories and allusions agitate against practically spectacular, almost abstract gestures. Jennifer, can you discuss how you imagined this back and forth?

JR: I'm always interested in parallels. In *The Time We Killed* there is a woman living in her apartment, not leaving the house, very afraid of the outside world, trying to create a safety zone. But it's also very boring, she's depressed . . . this is not a life to love. She's escaping into her imagination, mixing fantasy with memory, nostalgia, and sometimes the memories are frightening, like the 9/11 stuff, her childhood, suicide attempts, amnesia. So, the structure of her in the apartment is basically a more traditional representation of the present, a constant that's slowly changing. . . . She ends up leaving in the end. But the montage sequences, the parallel to this outer reality, which are essentially internal thoughts and fantasies, are utilizing traditional principles of montage . . . early Eisenstein and Kuleschov . . . connecting many different memories, many different places, using form, light, white and black form, and camera movement to cut from the waterfall scene in New Zealand to a beach scene in California to a mountain scene in Utah. Then there'll be a montage of different people she knew in different times and places. I wanted to show memory and thoughts in a more "true" way, in that when you're thinking you will jump from one idea or image to the next and have a memory that connects them, then your attention cuts to present where your body is right now.

DK: The way you're talking about your aesthetic evokes Charles Olson's "field" method of composition, and reminds me of Lisa's earlier comments regarding Black Mountain and the abstract expressionist canvas. . . . I'm imagining synapses crackling, apparently unlinked phenomena meeting each other in an open space.

JR: Yes, and that's what makes the work associative. . . . You know, another thing that Lisa and I have in common is an interest and experience in psychoanalysis . . . so when I talk about "associative" I'm referring to the practice of free association on a psychoanalytic couch.

LJ: This was another place where Jenn and I were really tuned into each other during the work on *The Time We Killed*. We'd both been in analysis. When the film played at the Tribeca Film Festival, someone during the question and answer session described Robyn as "primitive," using psychoanalytic jargon to diagnose the character. I thought sure, that's fine, but actually Robyn is quite inventive and adaptive in her responses to the world. What's happening in the world around her is much crazier than she is.

DK: Lisa, have you thought about your work in terms of montage? I'm wondering about this particularly in the context of your book *Some Other Kind of Mission* [1996], which I've always read as a kind of fractured road-trip narrative in the lineage of Kerouac's *On the Road* and Ginsberg's "Wichita Vortex Sutra" — I've always felt these two works suggest a practically cinematic poetics.

LJ: I hadn't thought of it but there is some Beat influence in that book. And yes, to pick up on the cinematic: that's entirely where it's at. I was making super-eight films at the same time that I was writing the book, and I was very much trying to pull the poems up off the page and animate them. There are a few places in the collages where you will see strips of film pasted in. I knew that something spectacular was going to happen in working with Jenn. I handed the work over to her with a complete confidence that she would tune into the deadpan and satire and wit and tenderness. She was really able to maintain the integrity of the work.

JR: Well, thanks! I think that a lot of the way the montage works in the poem/film sequences is there'll be some connection, certain themes between the poem and the image that connect, but it's not imagery to illustrate the poem. Both work independently, but meet. It's actually the way great sound-tracks work in film, where the sound isn't constantly reinforcing the visual. They have their own independence. . . . The sound gives information that you don't *see*, and the visual gives you information that you don't *hear*. The two combine together and make a new strong experience.

DK: What about your use of actual text in the film? There are moments in *The Time We Killed* when you use subtitles — for example, "Is she in there" followed by "It's not going to do you any good to stand here and be upset." You foreground the text against a black screen . . . and the text itself looks like old typeface. Can you talk about the way you envision the relationship between text and image in this film?

JR: It's there to point out a moment that's real rather than fictional. The murder-suicide in the plot of the film is actually based on an actual murder-suicide that happened in my apartment complex, and that's the actual audio of my neighbors finding the bodies.

DK: Really?! The real-life moment, real-life neighbors finding real-life dead bodies.

JR: Well, I'm a filmmaker, and I have a microphone in my house, and I will set up my microphone in my apartment if I hear something through the walls or through the windows. It's a kind of belief that if sound enters my home it's part of my experience too and its part of my material, in the same way that I'll shoot film in and of my own life. This kind of diary footage makes up most of the montages in *The Time We Killed*.

LJ: That actually really resonates with the way in which I go about writing my poems. I've never been able to separate the composition of poems from the physical activities of the world. I write whenever and wherever a phrase in my head starts to turn into a series of phrases. It's like hearing a tune and jotting it down and letting the composition emerge from there.

DK: But getting back to my initial question. . . . Why have actual text in the film? I mean, you have the aural recording of the poem, and you have the visual experience of the film, so why inscribe language onto the screen using typeface?

JR: The black screen, with text inscribed, is a place for the viewer's imagination. It is meant to stop the film and give the viewer a direct experience. And the "murder-suicide" scene is the only sequence in the film where I use text in this way, to echo what we hear on the soundtrack. The scene's a turning point . . . the text is an old typewriter Courier font. . . . It's kind of like the writing on a tombstone . . . text embalms an idea, so I'm giving weight to the scene that's taking place, the death scene. . . . The black screen gives the viewer space to imagine what the bodies look like, to really *hear* the emotion in the neighbors' voices and words.

I also use text in the mise-en-scène. Robyn the character is often at work writing, and so there are shots of the text she's typing. That's all very literal, but as a viewer you can read suggestive bits, like the fragment "when I jumped off the bridge in Ohio." Again this is meant to spur the imagination of the viewer. I use text in a simple, functional way too . . . to state the month and year of the upcoming section of the film, with letters burned over the picture.

DK: The times in which you date events in the film lent the work a conventional aura, which I found interesting in terms of the way that agitated against the more abstract and impressionistic elements.

JR: For me the dates are important because of the political situation. I wanted to contextualize it. We were after all filming in the six months leading up to the invasion of Iraq.

LJ: We were doing that work at a time when it was still a little bit taboo to bring September 11th issues into art, especially in New York where people were very much traumatized. Obviously that moment has passed, but at the time it felt really edgy and liberating to present this character who said, "Fuck terrorism, I'm afraid of my own government."

DK: So the film was a kind of collaborative diary, then, of the way the two of you responded to the beating of the war drums. Now, of course there's a tradition of diaristic film in much of the work affiliated with the New American Cinema — Brakhage's *15 Song Traits* [1965], Jonas Mekas's *Walden* [1969], Warren Sonbert's *Carriage Trade* [1971], and the films Rudy Burckhardt produced in the 1970s come immediately to mind. Who might you point to as direct influences?

JR: The filmmakers I was exposed to when I first started making films were very formative to my process: Stan Brakhage, Bruce Baillie, Ken Jacobs, Su Friedrich, Jack Chambers, Peggy Ahwesh, Bruce Conner . . . Baillie's *Quick Billy* [1967–1970] and *Mass of the Dakota Sioux* [1963–1964] combine personal and political concerns; they're layered and beautiful visually and on the soundtrack. *Mass* is critical of society, it's a mourning . . . and has been a strong inspiration. Jane Campion's *Angel at My Table* [1990] influenced me in its structuring of narrative, but also because it is one of the most thoughtful and intelligent films I know that deals with a character with psychological difficulties and psychiatric hospitalization. Tsai Ming-Liang's slower-paced work is entirely different than mine, but inspired my work quite a lot the last few years. . . . One of his films pays special attention to a hole in the wall between two apartments and has a great parallel structure using fantasy and reality.

DK: You know, one of the things that strikes me in terms of the names and films you mention is that the formal techniques evident in work associated with these artists, Lisa's approach to her own poetry, and the conceptual framework you've been providing for us here, all suggest that what might be read as anti-essentialist disruptive practice is actually designed to evoke a kind of holistic realism, a more "natural" way of seeing how we act and think in the world. The way Jennifer's talked about how memory consistently interrupts one's desire to move as if in a rational, step-by-step sequence, and how Lisa tacitly links the form of the film to the underlying political message, is particularly pertinent here.

JR: And if you think about just how you experience the world . . . you're walking through the world doing your thing and then suddenly you're in your head not really aware of your body or where you are. . . . I'm representing that split in the film, which is more interesting to me than what conventional narrative films do. They don't generally go inside characters, they're more akin to theater, and I'd say I'm more influenced by poetry where there's more freedom to be internal *and* external, which opens up more layers of meaning. Most film will show memory or fantasy as a coherent, very clinical, realistic scene . . . like a "flashback" . . . there's some artificial clue to indicate the past, like a wash on a filter . . . or a title reading "5 years ago." I was much more interested in getting inside a character, particularly a character who is struggling with a sort of mental illness. If you watch any conventional film about someone struggling with this (especially as part of the plot) they seem crazy, weird, mysterious. I think of Ed Harris in *Pollock* [2000], or Jessica Lange in *Frances* [1982] or even *The Virgin Suicides* [1999]. . . . You don't go into their minds. It's rare that you get to know them to realize that what they do is connected to all of us. Their actions seem irrational; they are of another mold so in a sense less threatening.

But I'm saying behavior that may come off as crazy can be an expression of survival or some other natural instinct. For me in this film it was very important to get into the mind of this particular character: the dysfunctional but also the positive, the power of her imagination. And Lisa's poetry that she wrote for the film embodied this imaginative leap, the associative and free mind, and that's why her poems inspired me in editing the memory and fantasy montage sequences that were also free of boundaries.

NOTES

INTRODUCTION

1. I'm going to use the terms "Underground Film," "experimental film," and "New American Cinema" interchangeably, given the lack of one fixed term that is applicable to the wide-ranging film scenes in New York and San Francisco during the 1960s. Some of the many definitions of the film communities in question include, "The underground film is a certain kind of film. It is a film conceived and made essentially by one person and is a personal statement by that person. It is a film that dissents radically in form, or in technique, or in content, or perhaps in all three. It is usually made for very little money, frequently under a thousand dollars, and its exhibition is outside commercial film channels" (Renan 17); "The history of the Experimental (Avantgarde or Poetic) Film is a curious one that even possesses its Hollywood phase, when professional workers with serious, as opposed to commercial, ideas decided on their own, and on very small budgets, to do imaginative work that used the camera the way a poet uses his pen: as an instrument of invention; it is significant that these professional workers were typically camera specialists, for the first step in visualizing the Experimental Film as a distinct reality is to conceive the proper role of the camera as a visual medium (Tyler, "A Preface" 5); "One of the essential characteristics of so-called personal film (whether you call it avant garde or experimental) is that the maker has complete responsibility for each gesture that makes it to the theater. Each synchronization of sound and picture, each framing, each foot of image is an aesthetic fact, as intricately brute as any printed or intoned word from a writer. This intimate relation of individual process to the material result, articulated at the precise scale of thinking, is what makes film and poetry natural allies" (Steiner 1); and "The Cinema. Still in the Dark Ages. Again the same story. Man is afraid of the Dark, the New, the Different. Always clinging to his old hats. . . . The New American Cinema is just the first crack in the ice. What is going to be made and seen in the next ten years would cause your grandfather to leap from the grave. . . . And the beautiful part about it all is that you can, my dear critics, scream in protest to the skies. You're too late. The Musicians, Painters, Writers, Poets and Film-Makers all fly in the same sky, and know exactly where It's 'At'" (Rice 39).

2. See Alan Golding's "'The New American Poetry' Revisited, Again" for an assessment of the impact Allen's anthology had on the reception of postwar innovative American poetry along with a cultural history of the anthology's construction.

3. J. Hoberman lists John Wieners as one of the many "uncredited participants"

in Smith's film. See Hoberman, *On Jack Smith's Flaming Creatures* (8). Diane di Prima appears as the "Pregnant Cutie" in Smith's *Normal Love*.

4. See Turim's chapter on Child for an overview of Child's work.

5. Seventeen of Reeves's film works screen on 16mm only. Just two of her films — *Shadows Choose Their Horrors* and *Light Work 1*, which were shot mostly on film, screen digitally.

6. See Marcus's *Close Up 1927–1933* (edited with Ann Friedberg and James Donald) and *The Tenth Muse* for an excellent overview and analysis of the relationship between modernist film and literature.

7. Goldstein's *The American Poet at the Movies* is a groundbreaking study of twentieth-century American poetry's consistent fascination with cinema from the early modernist period through the contemporary.

8. Richard Abel provides readers with excellent histories of the exchanges between American and French surrealist literary and film cultures.

9. Susan McCabe's *Cinematic Modernism* is in many ways a model for my own work, in that each chapter in her book provides extended analyses of individual poets' works as they engaged with film.

10. Kadlec discusses modernist poetry and poetics from early modernism through the objectivist nexus, arguing cogently for a connection between the developments in filmic technique and the increasing use of collage and quotation in poetry.

11. As North asks rhetorically regarding his analysis of the seminal modernist journal *transition*: in "what sense might *transition* itself, and perhaps even the general modernist project behind it, be considered a kind of 'logocinema,' a revolution of the word accomplished quite literally by bringing to language the physical dynamism and energy associated with film?" (206).

12. Perloff locates Blaise Cendrars's work, among others, as influenced to a great extent by the mechanisms of cinema. As she writes regarding Cendrars's "La Prose du Transsibérien," "There is no transition between this scene set in the heart of Manchuria and the unanticipated and unexplained 'O Paris' that introduces what we may call the poem's coda. As in film montage, the two shots are simply juxtaposed, the return to the left margin and the setting-off of the words 'O Paris' in a separate line in heavy red type . . . providing the only signal" (Perloff, *Futurist Moment* 22).

13. Fleming goes far in problematizing the notion that Ezra Pound was wholeheartedly hostile to the cinema, in part by drawing connections between Imagism and Eisenstein's subsequent development of montage.

SOME EARLY CONVERSATIONS

1. See Scott MacDonald's "Poetry and Avant-Garde Film: Three Recent Contributions," 1–11, for an informative reading of this and other events surrounding poetry and film in the 1940s and 1950s, as well as a brief and illuminating encapsulation of the valences between film and poetry in the 1920s and 1930s.

2. While Tyler, Maas, and Deren were aware that the panel was designed around the topic of the lyrical or poetic film, Miller and Thomas rather obtusely continued throughout the event to wholly misunderstand the context of the conversation — Miller especially seemed to believe that his fellow panelists were talking about making films about or illustrative of a given poem, rather than film that was influenced by lyric practice.

3. The film opens with titles that read TOU HOLOU OUN TEI EPITHUMIAI KAI DIOXEI EROS ONOMA. As Tom Gunning points out in a different context, "There is . . . a primal story that narrates the relation between these two views of love, as wholeness and as lack: the tale Plato puts in Aristophanes' mouth in the *Symposium*. According to this satirical tale, human beings once consisted of three sexes — male, female, and hermaphrodite — and they possessed spherical bodies with four legs and arms, two heads, and two sets of genitals. Fearing this powerfully endowed mankind, Zeus divided them in two, weakening their strength by half. Each separate being now yearned for its complement. Aristophanes proposed love as the result of — and compensation for — this primal separation, declaring: *Tou holou oun tei epitumai kai dioxiei eros onoma* . . . 'The Desire and Pursuit of the Whole is called Love' " ("Love at the Movies" 7).

4. Discussing Deren's film *A Study in Choreography for the Camera*, P. Adams Sitney also connects Deren's work to Pound's imagism and extends his definition to moments in other filmmakers' works: "Maya Deren introduced the possibility of isolating a single gesture as a complete film form. In its concentrated distillation of both the narrative and the thematic principles, this form comes to resemble the movement in poetry called imagism, and for this reason I have elsewhere called a film using this device an imagist film. There I concentrated on pure examples and described the inevitable inflation of the simple gesture to contain more and more aesthetic matter. Kenneth Anger's *Eaux d'Artifice*, Charles Boultenhouse's *Handwritten*, and Stan Brakhage's *Dog Star Man: Part One* provided the examples. . . . In Anger's film it is the walk of a heroine through a baroque maze of fountains in pursuit of a flickering moth . . . and Brakhage's describes a man climbing a mountain" (*Visionary Film* 22).

5. Miller insisted "There is no separation in my mind between a horizontal story and the plumbing of its meaning in depth" (62).

6. See Sitney, *Visionary Film*, 3rd ed., 44–54, for more detailed information regarding Peterson's role as filmmaker and teacher.

7. Grove Press would end up re-releasing Maas's *Geography of the Body* (discussed above) to a wider audience. Maas's alliance with Grove must surely have resonated with the avant-garde poetry culture at the time, as the opening titles in *Geography* included "*Presented* by GROVE PRESS," followed by the legend "AN EVERGREEN FILM." By 1959, the *Evergreen Review* and Grove Press generally were strongly associated with most of the poets included in *The New American Poetry* (itself a Grove Press book) and the international literary counterculture overall. Grove Press became notorious for publishing previously censored works by D. H. Lawrence, James Joyce, and Henry Miller, and the *Evergreen Review* regularly fea-

tured the often scandalous writings of Jean Genet, Ginsberg, Burroughs, and so on. As independent scholar James Birmingham puts it, Barney Rosset, publisher and editor at Grove, certainly had a vision of "establishing a multi-media empire based on the underground. There was Grove, Evergreen Magazine, Black Cat as well as the unsuccessful Evergreen Records (Ten San Francisco Poets) and an Evergreen Films distribution company" (e-mail). In an article on Rosset published in 1968, readers discovered that "Rosset is convinced that other publishers will eventually follow his lead—into movie distribution at least. Apart from his own feeling that movies are 'what's happening' in the arts today, [Rosset] says that his authors are becoming increasingly film-conscious themselves" (Jonas 50). That Maas was so materially associated by the late 1960s with one of the main distributors of avant-garde poetry, literature, and film itself must surely have assisted in situating his film specifically and Underground cinema more generally as a natural part of an overall innovative arts community in which poetry and film played central roles.

8. See Ragona, 35–37, for an informative discussion of this particular film.

9. In David E. James's introduction to his edited collection, *To Free the Cinema*, James discusses Deren's role in the arts communities and provides a history of Jonas Mekas's arrival in the United States from Lithuania, along with a description of his film activities and the general underground scene—Deren's screenings at the Provincetown Playhouse in Greenwich Village, and particularly Amos and Marcia Vogel's Cinema 16—from the late 40s through the 60s. Paul Arthur's essay in the same volume is also very good on this score, particularly in its focus on Mekas's development into a countercultural and film icon/renegade. Arthur provides us with a good institutional history of the various organizations Mekas spearheaded, focusing especially on the Film-maker's Cooperative. For more on Vogel's Cinema 16, see Scott MacDonald's "Cinema 16: Documents toward a History of the Film Society."

10. Symphony Sid was a renowned disc jockey of the 40s, 50s, and 60s whose hipster lingo and encyclopedic knowledge of jazz music was an inspiration to writers affiliated with the Beat generation.

11. Given the relative lack of association between the New American and European art cinema communities, it's worth noting that Seyrig would go on to achieve a measure of fame in films including Alain Resnais's *Last Year at Marienbad*.

12. Sterritt's chapter, "Revision, Prevision, and the Aura of Improvisatory Art" (*Screening the Beats*, 57–76), considers spontaneity and improvisation in the work of Kerouac, Ginsberg, Burroughs, and others, and it frames the Beat valuation of spontaneity through jazz and film contexts, including the works of Warhol, Jack Smith, Godard, and John Cassavetes. Blaine Allan's excellent "The Making (and Unmaking) of Pull My Daisy" productively complicates and questions the myth of the improvisatory nature of the film.

13. Sterritt's discussion of the Beats and film certainly resonates with the analogy between teletype roll and film: "In a 1958 essay, Beat fellow traveller John Clellon Holmes imagined Kerouac in one of his trance-like writing sessions, 'recording the movie unreeling in his mind.' Not surprisingly, all the leading Beats were movie fans, and each dreamed occasionally of making his own films, creating Hollywood magic

that would somehow be unencumbered by Hollywood's money-minded motives. They shared a taste for Saturday-night entertainment, moreover: Kerouac saw Walt Disney's whimsy-filled *Fantasia* a whopping fifteen times, for instance, and Burroughs thought *The Wild Bunch* was terrific. But what they dreamed most ardently of finding were what Kerouac called 'eyeball kicks,' the jolts of cosmic energy that separate everyday diversions from visionary art" (*Screening the Beats* xiii–xiv).

14. See MacDonald's *Canyon Cinema: The Life and Times of an Independent Film Distributor* for a comprehensive and engaging archival history of Canyon Cinema.

15. David James's edited collection, *To Free the Cinema*, is a good place to start understanding Mekas's major role in creating poetic film culture in New York. Essays in the book include Vyt Bakaitis's "Notes on Displacement: The Poems and Diary Films of Jonas Mekas," which discusses Mekas's own poetry as it appears in his films and books. David Curtis's "A Tale of Two Co-ops" provides us with a good history of the Filmmaker's Co-op and Vogel's secession from the overall scene due to Mekas's rise, and it also discusses the development of the London Co-op, modeled in part after Mekas's project. Also, see Mekas's own essay, "A Few Notes on My Life on the Lower East Side and Cinema" in *Captured*.

16. See Aldo Tambellini's personal history of the Gate Theater, where he makes clear how it was a crucial site for the avant-garde scene beginning in the fall of 1966.

17. Ruth Galm's "The Millennium Film Workshop in Love" is a good mini introduction to this particular institution. As Galm points out, "Since 1966, the Millennium Film Workshop has offered this type of haven for 'personal cinema' on the Lower East Side" (101).

18. The Invisible Cinema, opened in 1970 and located at Joseph Papp's Public Theatre on Lafayette Street in New York City, was designed by filmmaker Peter Kubelka, constructed by Giorgio Cavaglieri, and funded by the art patron and filmmaker Jerome Hill. Its story is a fascinating one that traces the transformation of the Filmmakers Cinematheque on 41st Street in Manhattan to the specially designed space. See Sky Sitney's "The Search for the Invisible Cinema" and Robert Haller's *Perspectives on Jerome Hill and Anthology Film Archives* for a series of personal and historically informed essays on these institutions. Contemporary reactions to the space included the article "Pure Film" from *Newsweek* magazine: "The perfect movie theater has opened in New York. Called the Invisible Cinema, it is the headquarters of Anthology Film Archives, which under co-directors Jonas Mekas and P. Adams Sitney will provide a continuous cycle of classic and avant-garde films for scholars, students, and just plain film nuts. The ninety-seat theater, conceived by Peter Kubelka and built by Giorgio Cavaglieri, is the embodiment of the pure cinema sensibility of Mekas, the Lithuanian-born poet, filmmaker, critic, and saint-at-large to the film avant-garde. Seated on black velvet cushions, cut off from coughs and wheezes by black blinder partitions, the Invisible viewer sees silent and sound films in their true proportions and speeds. Watching such marvels as Georges Méliès's 1905, hand-colored *Voyage into the Impossible* on the brilliant screen, he recaptures the primal magic of the movie experience — and he can even sneak his hand under the partition to cuddle his girl.

19. See Alan Golding's *From Outlaw to Classic* and his essay, "'The New American Poetry' Revisited, Again," for excellent accounts of the work that resulted in Donald Allen's *The New American Poetry*. My own *All Poets Welcome: The Lower East Side Poetry Scene in the 1960s* and Michael Davidson's *The San Francisco Renaissance* provide cultural/literary/historical surveys of reading communities in New York and San Francisco.

20. While Markopolous's films are essentially out of circulation, excerpts from *Galaxie* and the film *Ming Green* are available to view through the Museum of Modern Art's film library. *Galaxie* is particularly interesting in that the "screen test" style Markopoulos employs suggests Andy Warhol's screen test series, though Markopoulos's aesthetic is such that Warhol's flat, disaffected method is ameliorated through overtly spiritual (if visually and aurally disorienting) techniques, including the pinging of Hindu bells and the presence of angel statuettes. Markopoulos's section on the subject Ben Weber, for example, begins with an unsettling focus in on Weber's red, bloated face. Weber is wearing a kind of crown or tiara and is singing (albeit silently). This scene is interrupted with unadorned head shots of Weber, followed by a series of rapid cuts between costumed and unadorned versions. Occasionally, leaves and plaster cast angels are superimposed over Weber's face. The pinging of the Hindu bells occurs a couple of minutes into film as the images increase in variety and speed. This particular section comes to a sudden stop, ending with a still of a jewel-encrusted box.

21. Jacobs edited footage originally shot by Fleischner and is generally credited as being the director or "composer" of *Blonde Cobra*.

22. While the focus in this project is on poetry and film, we should nevertheless note that William Burroughs's work seems especially predisposed to an analysis linking his "cut-up" aesthetic in many of his novels to the mechanisms and practices associated with avant-garde film. As David Sterritt notes, "The cut-up and fold-in have clear parallels with cinematic montage, which similarly involves the elision and recombination of semiotic material, and effects in Burroughs's writing have been duly likened to effects of cinema. Burroughs himself found the results of fold-in composition to be 'analogous to the flashback in film,' and critic John Tytell has attributed the entropic fastidiousness of Burroughs's literary vision to his presentation of 'precise, clinically observed and unemotionally rendered details . . . presented cinematically, with all the speed of the motion-picture lens'. . . . Cinematic variants of the cut-up method have also been used successfully in avant-garde film, most notably in Antony Balch's films (*Towers Open Fire* [1963] and *The Cut-Ups* [1966]), with Burroughs as actor or narrator or both" (*Screening the Beats* 79–80).

THE CONVERSATION BETWEEN KENNETH ANGER AND ROBERT DUNCAN

1. Duncan also began decades-long friendships with filmmakers, including James Broughton, and film critics, including Pauline Kael, when he was a young student at Berkeley.

2. The first indication of film's presence in Duncan's *Bending the Bow* is found in "Structure of Rime XXII (for Dean Stockwell)." There are a variety of historical reasons for Duncan's reference to Stockwell. First, it is possible that Stockwell — a quintessential child actor of the 1940s adored for his cupid-like features — may have reminded Duncan of Anger's own role as a child actor in Max Reinhardt's 1935 feature film, *A Midsummer Night's Dream*. According to Duncan biographer Lisa Jarnot, "Duncan and Jess were hanging out with Stockwell and someone named Tony (boyfriend?) quite a bit around the Topanga Canyon scene, 1970s" (Jarnot, "Duncan Essay"). Additionally, Stockwell was close friends with Marjorie Cameron, an actress who in 1954 appeared as the Scarlet Woman and as Lady Kali in Kenneth Anger's *Inauguration of the Pleasure Dome*. The final "Sacred Mushroom Edition" of *Inauguration of the Pleasure Dome* appeared in 1966. As the correspondence between Anger and Duncan makes clear, Duncan was interested in and approved of the film from its very inception. In a letter to Duncan dated 1954, Anger wrote "Thanks for your words and thoughts on Pleasure Dome. I'm touched, I'm glad to have some partisans. I myself have wanted to put it to sleep for a while, so I could gain a perspective; except for a showing for Cocteau at St. Jean some months ago, I haven't shown it; I'm waiting. Cocteau said of it: "Cette riche folie figée des etres Presque vivants.'" Cameron also played the part of the Water Witch in Curtis Harrington's film *Night Tide* (1963), acting alongside Stockwell and Dennis Hopper. It is no coincidence that Cameron was chosen to play this part, as by this point she was well-known in Hollywood for her participation in Anger's films and in occult circles generally.

Further references to film content and form appear in later poems by Duncan. In "At the Loom," images both of a literal loom and of a film projector weave in and out of given lines. The thread spooling through the loom is consistently granted qualities of light: "luminous soft threads" suggests film itself, as the images embossed on the celluloid are latently incandescent. The line "the fire, the images, the voice" combines the "fire" that is the light of the projector, the "images" projected onto the screen, and the soundtrack or "voice." "Let there be the clack of the shuttle flying / forward and back, forward and / back" (*Bending the Bow*, 11–12) refers to the shuttle of the weaver's loom as it implies the shuttle of a film projector, which can fast forward and reverse film according to the wishes of the projectionist.

In the poem "Where It Appears," we find the speaker of the poem composing "in the air," as if images are being projected not onto the material space of the blank page but into the unbounded atmosphere itself. Duncan asserts, "let image perish in image, / leave writer and reader / up in the air / to draw / momentous / inconclusions" (ibid. 15), and so "writer and reader" are left watching images as they appear and extinguish sequentially.

"The Currents (Passages 16)" refers to Jean Genet's film *Un Chant d'Amour* (a cause célèbre in 1964–1965 due to the fact that Jonas Mekas was charged with obscenity for showing the film at the Bridge Theater); "Then Jean Genet's *Un Chant d'Amour* / where we witness the continual song that runs thru the walls" (ibid. 58–

59). As if to emphasize the connection to film, "Passages 16" is followed by the poem "Moving the Moving Image."

"Structure of Rime XXV" refers to a "Fire Master" whose "rimes *flicker* and would blaze forth and take over" (ibid. 37; emphasis added). Employing the poetic equivalent of cinematic dissolve, Duncan writes in the final lines "the lion's face passing into / the man's face, flare into / flare, // the bright tongues of two / languages // dance in the one light" (ibid. 37). The poem ends as if aching to escape the boundaries of the page in order to appear as light.

In "Passages 30 (Stage Directions)" there is a clear reference to Stan Brakhage's oeuvre in the line "Behind the lids / an after-image burns." (Brakhage is often quoted defining his films as attempts to illustrate hypnagogic vision, what people see through closed eyes). Duncan's poem continues by making direct references to filmmaking: "He brings the camera in upon the gaping neck / which now is an eye of bloody meat glaring / from the womb of whose pupil sight // springs to see, two children of adversity." References to film reappear in the poem in the lines "thunderous hooves, striking // flashes of light from unbright matter" (ibid. 128–32). It is tempting to read these lines as suggesting the very materiality of the "unbright" filmstrip emanating "flashes of light," particularly in the context of the book's repeated references to New American Cinema and film technology.

We should also note that the spacing of the words and lines on the page in Duncan's poetry owes a clear debt to Charles Olson's essay, "Projective Verse." The use of dramatically empty space between words, the placement of slashes within lines, the blend of prosaic blocks of text and purely lyrical gestures, all hearken back to Olson's desire to, as Michael Davidson puts it succinctly in his essay, " 'Skewed by Design,' " "defeat Cartesianism by restoring the physiology of the poet's breath, musculature, movement — in the composition process" (71). What is interesting in light of Duncan's references to the technology of cinema is that Olson believed such a humanistic conflation of the poet's verse with the poet's body can (if ironically) be reenacted thanks to the technology of the modern typewriter. The typewriter "can, for a poet, indicate exactly the breath, the pauses, the suspensions even of syllables, the juxtapositions even of parts of phrases, which he intends" (*Bending the Bow* 23). Thus, Olson is a model for Duncan in terms of understanding how developing technology can help revive a shamanic conception of the poet's body as transmitting and projecting a literally magic series of chants/lines. The title of Olson's essay is itself instructive, in that it relies on the language of cinema itself. Like the film projector, Olson's typewriter assists the poet in his attempts to liberate language from the page, to project words *out*.

3. See Sitney, *Visionary Film*, 86–91, for a good narrative description of *Fireworks*.

4. "At fourteen [Anger] read Frazer's *The Golden Bough*, and later the writings of Aleister Crowley taught him, 'Love is the law, love under Will. Do what thy Will shall be the whole of the law.' And for Anger, it was" (Hardy 30).

5. Greg Hewett helpfully points out, "The madrone is a tree native to the west-

ern United States, and the eucalyptus, while originally imported from Australia, is abundant in California, as is the yew" (537).

6. In Anger's case, "Transubstantiation is one of [his] favourite themes. Frequently this takes the form of a reverse Eucharist where essence is converted into substance; this process can be discovered in *Fireworks . . .* , *Puce Moment, Rabbit's Moon, Scorpio,* and *Lucifer.* These films summon personifications of forces and spirits whose dynamic powers appear to 'break though' and turn against the character and/or structure" (Rowe 24).

7. I suspect that the lover who "pierces my side" is meant to evoke Longinus, the Roman soldier who pierced Jesus's sides as he hung from the cross: "But one of the soldiers with a spear pierced his side, and forthwith came there out blood and water" (See John 19: 34–35 in the King James version).

THE CONVERSATION BETWEEN STAN BRAKHAGE AND ROBERT CREELEY

1. Brakhage's resistance to standard language practices manifested itself in all aspects of his life, including the most purportedly mundane day-to-day exchanges. In a letter written in 1981 to Shirley B. Wendell, a "Supervisory Copyright Examiner" in the Performing Arts Section of the Library of Congress, Brakhage explained his refusal to provide written descriptions for his films "V" and "VII" — descriptions the copyright office insisted were necessary to copyright his work: "Why do I balk at sending you more descriptive material, as I have often and again in the past? Well, it is because the very act of making these little films, the reason they are given roman numerals (rather than some more easily remembered name) is to remove them from language as far as possible — that there be some films on earth that are not tied down to words. Intrinsic to the act of making them has been this drive to create out of the purely non-verbal areas of the mind."

2. See Prevallet's "Notes on *Daydream of Darkness*" and Killian's and Erlingham's *Poet Be Like God* for more detailed information on Adam's filmmaking activities. As Prevallet describes it, "*Daydream of Darkness* demonstrates Helen Adam's talent for drawing her friends into an imaginative world where they are transformed into ephemeral creatures who play out cosmic dramas. Going on extensive excursions through San Francisco's parks and beaches with the painter Bill McNeill, Adam wrote the poem/script spontaneously while McNeill shot the film. McNeill, who had never made a film before, must have been under a bit of pressure to find scenes in reality to correspond to Adam's wild, imaginative vision" ("Jack Spicer's Hell").

3. "The Romantic character of *Dog Star Man* is evident, too, in the shots that animate the mountainside, by shooting it either with a moving camera or with an anamorphic lens that Brakhage twisted while filming; such shots make it seem that a life force animates the mountain. . . . The Dog Star Man appears at the beginning of *The Prelude* with a moon superimposed on his forehead. The trope suggests that the Dog Star Man creates the universe in his imagination. The same suggestion appears elsewhere in the film, and it reveals that *Dog Star Man* rests on the Romantic

myth of cosmogenesis, according to which the human imagination is identical with a creative force immanent in nature" (Elder 144–45).

4. We can locate Brakhage's *The Dark Tower* in relationship to Byron's "Childe Harold's Pilgrimage," Robert Browning's "Childe Roland to the Dark Tower Came," and Yeats's many references to the iconography of the Tower, for example. Brakhage's program notes are included in *By Brakhage: An Anthology*.

5. I don't want to imply that Bernstein would agree with my relatively conservative, quasi-biographical reading of Creeley's textual breaks and performance style. Bernstein is careful to point out that any semblance of "personal expression" is, in his opinion, a kind of artifice or play. As he says to Creeley later, "Your work often *plays off* the lyric poem, the solitary self-expressing. It/his/your/my failings. But overpowering this expressive individual is a sense of company" (9; emphasis added).

6. Amy Taubin's critique of Brakhage's work is exemplary of the hostility Brakhage's own self-packaging met with in the late 1970s and 1980s — a hostility informed by the nascence of French poststructuralism and feminism in American cultural and academic circles: "Stan Brakhage . . . is one of the only filmmakers who does not regard the personal appearance as trauma and imposition. . . . What was most troubling in the recent series of screenings is that Brakhage produced a series of films, *Arabic* and *Roman Numeral Series*, that functioned to illustrate his most reactionary pronouncements. Obsessively pushing the beginning of vision and formal perception back up into the womb, he opted for an ideal vision outside and predating language, history, and ideology. His ahistorical position paradoxically placed him in perfect sync with the dominant reactionary bias that is currently attempting to fix the moment of the beginning of life at the expense of women's control of their own bodies. I would suggest that Brakhage's 'form in the womb' line and its corollary — the *Arabic* and *Roman Numeral* films, which through their amorphous forms attempt to evoke 'the underpinnings of all sight' — would make perfect ammunition for the Right to Life movement. Brakhage's antifeminist position has never been so clear."

7. In a letter dated May 5, 1962, from Brakhage to Broughton, Brakhage made repeated references to Creeley's *For Love*, and at times combined his references with allusions to Jack Kerouac's *On the Road*: "Joys! Joys! Joys! Jane and I and three children are coming to Albuquerque together, all driving down in car on or about the 15th. What an amazing day. Beginning with a long long-distance call from James Broughton (too long to go into here), followed by a cancellation of Los Angeles plus the enclosed letter (which I dutifully copied for friends, James, and the both of you), and then a mad wonderful car trip into Denver, reading from 'For Love' aloud all the way (with wondrous spells cast for both of us)." In a letter from Brakhage to Creeley dated May 25, 1962, Brakhage extended his references to Kerouac's iconic work by alluding to the oft-quoted section from Kerouac's *On the Road* where protagonist Sal Paradise relates, "The only people for me are the mad ones, the ones who are mad to live, mad to talk, mad to be saved, desirous of everything at the same time, the ones

who never yawn or say a commonplace thing, but burn, burn, burn, like fabulous yellow Roman candles exploding like spiders across the stars." Brakhage riffs off this passage as follows: "And when we got to the end of that tortured road, there was Max [Feinstein], like the most delightful demonic-flaming force in the world (like Guinness playing Fagin only burning, burning) smiling and revealing his beautiful fangs and taking us into his house full of children and all of living reaching out into the dream landscape thru his front window. And we managed to dig up a projector and showed him and friends some films, and heard him read from new poems, and had most wonderful time, all."

8. Paul Sharits's application for a grant for his film "N:O:T:H:I:N:G" illustrates the structuralist aesthetic that Brakhage resisted, particularly in terms of Sharits's qualified rejection of the "mystical": "The film will strip away anything (all present definitions of 'something') standing in the way of the film being its own reality. . . . The theme of the work, if it can be called a theme, is to deal with the non-understandable, the impossible, in a tightly and precisely structured way. The film will not 'mean' *some*thing — it will 'mean,' in a very concrete way, *nothing*." While Sharits describes the colors of his films as based "on the Tibetan Mandala of the Five Dhyani Buddhas which is used in meditation to reach the highest level of inner consciousness" he adds later, "I am not at all interested in the mystical symbolism of Buddhism, only in its strong, intuitively developed imagistic power" (15). With its essay "Structural Film," by P. Adams Sitney, along with articles on and interviews with filmmakers, including George Landow and Paul Sharits, *Film Culture* 47 (Summer 1969) is an excellent source overall for anyone interested in getting a sense of the contemporary reception to the nascence of structural film.

9. Brakhage told McClure that he was heading to New Mexico, adding, "I had never taken any images of him. I had, oh, maybe 50 feet in the camera. And I said let me get some pictures of you, and instantly I took the first little bit I suddenly knew that I wanted more than just some pictures of him. That whole section on Michael McClure has no editing — I knew suddenly I had to do something and it took all morning. He very graciously sat down and I got out the image of him with the lion make-up on *Ghost Tantras* — with the hair all over his face — and interspersed images of that with images of him sitting there in his chair, and he meantime was doing certain things as he sat and I was waiting and we were also talking, about Milton, as I recall" ("Poetry and Film" 222). Responding later to the question, "Well, then you say this film is a portrait; what does it have to do with Robert Creeley or Michael McClure?" Brakhage explained, "Michael McClure when he reads his poetry, he often reads especially softly the capitalized letters. Now he may have changed his act these days, but in the past that was a shock to people because Michael uses a lot of capitalized whole lines. Everyone expects when you see capitalized, that means headlines, that means *WAR IS DECLARED!* No — he reads them softer than the rest. He reads slowly, and he moves slowly. But his section in the film is the flashy one with a lot of single framing and quick movements, and there is quite a variety of rhythms in there. Unless you're really up to looking at rhythms fast right off,

it just looks like all flickering and burning, whereas Michael tends to move very stately. But I saw him as a man containing electricity that is just terrifying. It can be deceptive" (ibid. 226). Brakhage characterized his portrait of McClure as follows: "In Michael's case it would appear to be very stately and very composed. But right under the skin surface ripple constantly impulses that are visible if you choose to look for them, however hard he builds his muscles at Vic Tanney's gym and holds himself in, firm. All the firmness, as of my being a film maker as distinct from a poet, has to do with centered weakness. He must be strong, he must be composed, he must be almost statuesque at times to contain this fire that moves thru him. He expressed it in one statement he gave me in the 60's — as we used to call to each other in desperation across the yawning void — 'Be a solid moving thru an Inferno.' That has to do with the flickering side of him" (ibid. 227).

10. Regarding McClure's appearance, Sitney adds, "the following staccato pixilation of McClure putting on a beast's head were originally shot and edited in 16mm and reduced, to be included in *15 Song Traits* as well as released in 16mm as *Two: Creeley/McClure*. The solarization of the Creeley portrait would be impossible in 8mm, where there is neither negative film nor laboratory superimposition" (ibid. 217).

11. In a letter to Ronald Johnson, Brakhage wrote, "There are some who would caution us about our use of language, who would say that there's no point in saying things like 'primordial,' that it's ridiculous to talk about a camera that's invented in the late nineteenth century and a projection mode and so on, and then to talk about how it's touching the primordial mind — they'd tell us it's absurd" (*Stan Brakhage: Correspondences* 31).

12. Keat's "negative capability" and Blake's "Marriage of Heaven and Hell" come to mind most immediately regarding the Romantic effort to reconcile, eliminate, or synthesize binaries, out of which a new productive relationship emerges.

13. I am indebted to Peter Womack, Matthew Woodcock, and Sarah Salih at the University of East Anglia for suggesting various possible interpretations of "Ælfscýne." Womack also reminds us that Falstaff calls Prince Hal an "elf-skin" in Shakespeare's *Henry IV* Part 1: "Sblood, you starveling, you elf-skin" (2.4.240).

THE CONVERSATION BETWEEN FRANK O'HARA AND ALFRED LESLIE

1. This and all subsequent quotations of O'Hara's poetry and poetics are from *The Collected Poems of Frank O'Hara*.

2. Gooch 416. Gooch describes *The General* as "a satire on the return of a General MacArthur type to the scene of his battles during World War II in the South Pacific. . . . [The play] ran only four performances over two weekends, [and] starred Taylor Mead, who went on to become an Andy Warhol 'superstar' in *Lonesome Cowboys*" (ibid. 416). Gooch adds that O'Hara loved Mead's "campy delivery of such broad lines as the General's order to his aides, upon arriving in Manila, to have 'every square inch of marble in this palace shining like snow in the Arctic.' So he amended

his dedication of the play 'to Vincent Warren and to Warner Brothers and Taylor Mead'" (ibid. 417).

3. Goble's thesis argues that, far from merely "loving" the movies, O'Hara in fact "argues incessantly with the movies and in so doing makes a series of points about the relationships between language and the visual, poetry and pop culture, memory and history, subject and nation" (59).

4. See Hoberman, *On Jack Smith's Flaming Creatures*, 32–37, for a discussion of when and how *Flaming Creatures* was distributed beginning mid-April 1963.

5. Particularly in terms of sexuality, Frank O'Hara's poetics are again not so far in terms of their use of popular sources from Anger's own sensibility. "Frank O'Hara's poetry about the movies suggests . . . that the 'homosexuality' of going to the movies is not confined to particular places and particular films; that any movie can be made to reveal its sexuality as much more up for grabs than it might want to admit; and that the homosexual as viewer need not concentrate on the representation of sexuality at all" (Goble 85).

6. "The lavishly costumed magic masquerade party [in Anger's *Inauguration of the Pleasure Dome*] derived from the dramatic neo-pagan rituals of Aleister Crowley, featuring various characters from classical mythology and a pantheon that is distinctively Anger's: the Great Beast and the Scarlet Woman, Shiva, Osiris, Astarte and Pan, and Cesare the Somnambulist, from *The Cabinet of Dr. Caligari*. . . . As the celebration becomes more orgiastic, the characters become high on an hallucinogenic brew and transform with costume, make-up, and personality changes. The film itself enters a hallucinated crescendo of editing and superimposition, amplified with a progressive use of color, with tints multiplying and deepening as the tension mounts to the climax of the destruction of the god Pan by his worshippers. The film experimented with psychometric qualities, pulling a viewer out of the regular space-time continuum into another level of consciousness. With *Inauguration*, Anger's works begin to assume the form of religious rituals, here, centering on the consumption of the Eucharist" (Hutchison 90).

7. "Smith's transvestite recreation of the Arabian fantasy world of Maria Montez was . . . only a highly idiosyncratic version of the burlesques of Hollywood films that had been a staple of amateur filmmaking since the 1930s, and Smith had in fact made his initial sketches in this mode when living in Los Angeles in the early 1950s in *Buzzards over Bagdad*, an uncompleted domestic remake of a scene from Universal's *Arabian Nights*" (James, "Amateurs" 87).

8. Susan Sontag's analysis of *Flaming Creatures*, particularly her definition of the film as being "about joy and innocence," can usefully be applied to O'Hara's work: "To be sure, this joyousness, this innocence is composed out of themes which are — by ordinary standards — perverse, decadent, at the least highly theatrical and artificial. But this, I think, is precisely how the film comes by its beauty and modernity" (208).

9. See Gooch, 368–71, for a more detailed discussion of O'Hara's friendship with di Prima.

10. In his memoir, "Frank O'Hara," Brainard wrote, "I remember Frank O'Hara

putting down Andy Warhol and then a week or so later defending him with his life" (167).

11. Leslie's connection to the New American Cinema scene was further established in 1961, when Jonas Mekas invited him, along with filmmakers Lionel Rogosin, Peter Bogdanovich, Robert Frank, Shirley Clarke, Gregory Markopoulos, and Edward Bland, actors Ben Carruthers and Argus Speare Juilliard, and distributors and producers Émile de Antonio, Lewis Allen, Daniel Talbot, Walter Gutman, and David Stone, to be part of the cineaste collective known as "The Group" (James, *To Free the Cinema* 9).

12. "The interest in the ideogram of [Eisenstein and Pound] clearly has to do with what both conceived to be a certain manner of signifying, a more direct connection between signifier and signified than they thought existed in the art of the previous century, or even in language itself. And this conviction that there existed a somehow more direct relation of signification than with conventional language was shared by many of the Moderns. In fact, the notion of a more direct touch with the external world than is possible in words has survived Modernism into contemporary film and photographic theory" (Fleming 88).

13. The Lowell poem, however, is not credited as such at the end of the film. Rather, the only attribution we have is for the hymn music, which was written by nineteenth-century Welsh composer Thomas John Williams. Credits read " 'Ton-y-Botel' sung by Blair Resika at Splash Productions."

14. "Our history, after 1910, may be read in our annual reports, and in the numbers of THE CRISIS. We opened two offices in the Evening Post Building. With Dr. Du Bois came Frank M. Turner, a Wilberforce graduate, who has shown great efficiency in handling our books. In November 1910 appeared the first number of THE CRISIS, with Dr. Du Bois as editor, and Mary Dunlop MacLean, whose death has been the greatest loss the Association has known, as managing editor. Our propaganda work was put on a national footing, our legal work was well under way and we were in truth, a National Association, pledged to a nation-wide work for justice to the Negro race.

"I remember the afternoon that THE CRISIS received its name. We were sitting around the conventional table that seems a necessary adjunct to every Board, and were having an informal talk regarding the new magazine. We touched the subject of poetry.

" 'There is a poem of Lowell's,' I said, 'that means more to me today than any other poem in the world — "The Present Crisis." ' "

"Mr. Walling looked up. 'The Crisis,' he said. 'There is the name for your magazine, *The Crisis*' " (Ovington).

15. Credits at the end of the film include "effects of sound Tony Schwartz," suggesting that many of the sounds heard throughout the film — simultaneous honking, rumbling thunder, what sounds like gunshots, and so on — were in fact electronically manipulated, as opposed to wholly diegetic.

16. In the summer of 1962, the Five Spot officially closed and reopened near St. Mark's Place, at 69 Second Avenue.

17. While O'Hara chose the order in which the subtitles appeared, Leslie edited the ways the subtitles were broken up on the screen. Leslie explains, "My way of working with Frank O'Hara was that I played him the film and he would write his text. What he gave me was simply his text. What I did was cut the text against the picture that I had. When you do or do not calculate on how you cut lines in a poem is one thing. How you cut line breaks on screen . . . time is an important element . . . since you're not in some instances going to control the whole scene with words, people . . . you are controlling their reading of time. Someone might say 'I want to go to the bathroom,' so you can break it up into multiple levels of meaning. Someone says 'I want to go to the bathroom' and I'll put 'I want to go' on the screen by itself" (personal interview).

18. Concluding lines in the "intermission" extend the theme of responsibility, community, and personal freedom: "I have the other / idea about guilt," "It's not in us, it's / in the situation," "It's a rotten life," and, finally, "It's just that things get too much," a line that is repeated a number of times using a kind of flicker effect.

19. As Brossard points out, the word "zoo" mentioned in the subtitles can be found several times in the poem "Second Avenue" (139). The numerous references to a "kangaroo" featured near the end of the film echo O'Hara's "Today," where he writes "Oh kangaroos, sequins, chocolate sodas!" (15). Repeated references to India, Allen, and Peter surely point readers back to the poem, "Vincent and I Inaugurate a Movie Theatre," where O'Hara writes, "Allen and Peter, why are you going away / our country's black and white past spread out / before us is no time to spread over India" (399). Entire lines from poems that are used as subtitles include "is that me who accepts betrayal / in the abstract as if it were insight?" ("Death" 187); "I know so much / about things, I accept / so much, it's like / vomiting" ("Spleen" 187); "I am assuming that everything is all right and difficult" ("Ode to Michael Goldberg ['s Birth and Other Births])" 297); "the rock is least living of the forms man has fucked" ("Ode on Causality" 302); "I am ashamed of my century / for being so entertaining / but I have to smile" ("Naphtha" 338); "NEVERTHELESS (thank you, Aristotle)" ("Biotherm [for Bill Berkson]" 437); and "1. If only more people looked like Jerry Lieber we would all be a lot happier, I think"; "3. There is a man going by with his arm in a sling. I wish men could take care of themselves better"; and "7. There are certainly enough finks in the world without going to a German restaurant" (all from O'Hara's poem, "The Sentimental Units," 467).

20. The subtitle adaptation reads, "You get what D. H. Lawrence is driving at," followed by "when he writes of lust springing from the bowels?"

21. See Ginsberg's *Indian Journals*.

22. Ginsberg would ultimately go to Cuba and Czechoslovakia in the early months of 1965, though he was deported from Cuba for speaking out against the Castro regime's persecution of homosexuals. He was crowned "King of May" in Czechoslovakia, where he also encountered trouble from the authorities and was subsequently deported.

23. Patrice Lumumba was the first prime minister of the Republic of the Congo (now the Democratic Republic of the Congo). Lumumba was known as an intellec-

tual and a charismatic speaker and was a role model for many young black people around the world. He became president of the multiethnic National Congolese Movement, and when the Congo attained independence in 1960, he became prime minister. Soon dismissed by President Joseph Kasavubu, Lumumba was later arrested and then assassinated.

24. The subtitles are, after all, purportedly representing the gibberish of the female protagonist in the film.

25. Gooch helpfully documents a number of instances that show O'Hara's commitment to progressive politics: "O'Hara's appearance with Ginsberg [in the spring of 1964] in a reading protesting the freedom of speech issue lurking behind trying to tax Le Metro for a cabaret license was typical of the political impetus of many of his public readings in the sixties. He was more naturally and temperamentally engaged than most of the other New York School poets. 'Frank at least had a political sense,' says Baraka. 'Kenneth Koch and Kenward Elmslie and all those people were always highly antipolitical, which is why I couldn't get along with them longer than two minutes. Frank was not haughty about it. He had a real feeling for the human element in it.' Politics was a hot vent for O'Hara's spleenish anger. 'I remember on a street near Grace Church having a big argument with him about Vietnam because he was seeing it correctly and I wasn't,' says Berkson of the issue that was heating up in 1964 with Lyndon Johnson's bombing of North Vietnam" (425).

26. Before those of us who resist reading O'Hara as in any way politicized begin sputtering, let us remember that, as Bill Berkson states, "O'Hara thought of himself as a Communist in his youth" ("O'Hara"). Additionally, Brad Gooch writes, "While O'Hara later wrote of politics that 'the only truth is face to face,' he seemed to have gained a keen sense in Grafton that politics is also a way in which social schisms are played out, where richer Protestants tended to be Republican, and Irish Catholics Democratic. . . . As the thirties wore on, Francis became more sympathetic with the Communist movement and economic cooperatives, whereas his father's liberalism stopped at Roosevelt's White House" (28).

27. O'Hara's early poem, "Oranges: 12 Pastorals," was written to accompany his friend Grace Hartigan's oil paintings on paper (see Gooch 236). In "Why I Am Not a Painter," O'Hara writes, "One day I am thinking of / a color: orange. I write a line / about orange. Pretty soon it is a / whole page of words, not lines. / Then another page. There should be / so much more, not of orange, of / words, of how terrible orange is / and life" (262).

28. As Stein rascally put down her protégé Ernest Hemingway's taste for relatively conventional prose in her single line, "A white hunter is nearly crazy" (from her book-length poem *Tender Buttons*), so O'Hara alludes to and extends that critique when he includes the subtitles, "Yes, the only thing I can summon up is a sigh. / Which we all may agree is in the literary sense / a far cry from a hardon / or a bush full of white flags fleeing the hunter," in part 3 of Leslie's film. The disembodied "sigh," not attached syntactically to anything resembling a story, is a "far cry" not just from a hardon but from narrativity itself.

THE CONVERSATIONS BETWEEN ALLEN GINSBERG, CHARLIE CHAPLIN, AND ROBERT FRANK

1. This poem was later republished in different form as "Collaboration: Letter to Charlie Chaplin," in Orlovsky's *Clean Asshole Poems and Smiling Vegetable Songs*, 95–97.

2. See Lawrence Goldstein's chapter, "Hart Crane: Speaking the Mot Juste in the Age of Silents" (Goldstein 39–55), for a fascinating analysis of Crane's poem "Chaplinesque" specifically and a nuanced reading of Crane's cinematic form generally.

3. "Pull my daisy / tip my cup / all my doors are open / Cut my thoughts / for coconuts / all my eggs are broken" (Schumacher 105).

4. I am inspired to use the phrase "swerve away" by Susan McCabe's discussion of the relationship between Stein and Chaplin. McCabe writes, "Chaplin is . . . representative of Stein's circumlocutory comic mode, her swerving from plot, her ability to 'keep centre well half full'" (70).

5. Practically any Chaplin film might serve as an illustration of this, but for now we can refer to the opening scenes of *The Circus*, where Chaplin, the unwitting recipient of a stolen wallet, ends up being chased by the wallet's original owner, then by the original thief who is himself being chased by policemen. Scenes follow rapidly one after the other — a surreal series of exchanges in a hall of mirrors "where, suddenly confronted with multiple images of himself, he has trouble sorting out the true from the false. Reality is fragmented, and the evidence of the eye cannot be trusted. Even the simple action of retrieving his hat exposes him to unlooked-for thumps on the head. However, Charlie derives advantage from the confusion by realizing that he is not the only victim of it. The same fragmentation of reality enables him to boot his pursuer's backside and make his escape. His resourcefulness is carried over to the next episode, when the pursuit leads to a carnival tableau of Noah's Ark dummies. Charlie evades capture by smartly taking the place of a retired automaton, and swiveling on the spot with gestures of paralytic precision. . . . [The] imposture enables him plausibly to improve the occasion by walloping the thief, who has been forced to join in" (Kimber 156).

6. Even the imagined movie in which the two poets have Chaplin starring emphasizes the way Ginsberg and Orlovsky affiliate Chaplin with social and economic outsiders. Chaplin survives the Beat apocalypse not because he was able to wait it out in an expensive bomb shelter, but because he was a janitor going about his "own lost business in the basement / in the midst of great international / air-raid emergencies, sirens, / kremlin riots, flying rockets" ("A Letter to Chaplin").

7. In a famous interview with Tom Clark, Ginsberg described his Blake vision, which occurred to him around 1945: "So anyway — there I was in my bed in Harlem . . . jacking off. With my pants open, lying around on a bed by the windowsill, looking out into the cornices of Harlem and the sky above. And I had just come. And had perhaps hardly even wiped the come off my thighs, my trousers or whatever it was. . . . And just after I came, on this occasion, with a Blake book on my lap — I wasn't

even reading, my eye was idling over the page of 'Ah! Sun-flower,' and it suddenly appeared — the poem I'd read a lot of times before . . . and suddenly I realized that the poem was talking about *me*. . . . Now, I began understanding it, the poem while looking at it, and suddenly, simultaneously with understanding it, heard a very deep earth graven voice in the room, which I immediately assumed, I didn't think twice, was Blake's voice" ("Tom Clark, The Paris Review" 26–27).

8. David Jarraway notes Ginsberg's move away from what he calls the "metaphorical self-effacement" associated with his Blake vision and historicizes Ginsberg's shift by placing it in the context of his trip to India and Ginsberg's return — and subsequent composition of "Wichita" and other poems — to the United States: "Ginsberg's disenchantment with the lure of William Blake's 'Human form divine,' perhaps one of the purest examples of such metaphorical self-effacement, occurs just prior to his return to America from his sojourn in India and the Far East, after which he would undertake his writing of *The Fall of America*" (84).

9. Helen Vendler complains about precisely what I find laudable in Ginsberg's developing poetics, particularly when it comes to Ginsberg's practically cinematographic notations of geographical landscape and his move away from a poetics of prophecy to a more language-centered concentration on the materials of poetry: "The trouble with the present book is that the minute particulars of mankind seem to be vanishing from Ginsberg's latest verse in favor of the minute particulars of geography. In the *Indian Journals* Ginsberg declared that since we now know that visions are 'no longer considerable as objective & external facts, but as plastic projections of the maker & his language,' we must stop being concerned with these 'effects,' eliminate subject matter, and concentrate on language itself" (205). Vendler continues, "In *The Fall of America*, then, we see the disappearance or exhaustion of long-term human relations, an unwillingness to continue the 'old means of humanistic storytelling,' a persistent wish . . . for some 'non-conceptual episodes of experience, and a theory of poetry intending to 'include more simultaneous perceptions and relate previously unrelated (what were thought irrelevant) occurrences'" (206).

10. See Trigilio, *Allen Ginsberg's Buddhist Poetics*, 87–100, for an alternative reading to mine and Jarraway's, one that concentrates fascinatingly on the growing influence of Ginsberg's increasingly rigorous Buddhist practice on the poetics in evidence in "Wichita."

11. While Géfin does not consider the possibility that Ginsberg's early "ideogrammic poetics" progressed into a cinematic poetics, his discussion of surrealism and Ginsberg is nevertheless pertinent to our analysis: "During his 'Howl' period Ginsberg was immersed in surrealist poetry and poetics, and saw Kerouac's advocation of spontaneity reinforced by the basic tenets of this important European literary movement. Spontaneity corresponded to the surrealists' automatic writing, and Ginsberg's juxtapositions of 'hydrogen jukebox,' 'nitroglycerin shrieks,' and 'catatonic piano' are reminiscent of Eluard's '*nuit hermaphrodite*' and Berton's '*coqs de roche*' and '*revolver à cheveux blancs*'" (278). For a more fully considered analysis of the influence of surrealism on Ginsberg, see Tytell.

12. "Wichita Vortex Sutra" originally appeared in the book *Planet News: 1961–1967*, though in Ginsberg's *Collected Poems: 1947–1980*, Ginsberg rearranged the order of his poems and placed "Wichita" in the eighth section of the book, which he titled "The Fall of America (1965–1971)." In the City Lights edition of *The Fall of America*, Ginsberg explained in a "Bibliographical Note" that "'Wichita Vortex Sutra' (in *Planet News*, City Lights Books, 1968) fits in sequence following 'Hiway Poesy LA — Albuquerque — Texas — Wichita' in this book" (189).

13. "Branaman" refers to the painter and filmmaker Bob Branaman, who made a series of short 8 mm films, including a portrait of Ginsberg and a film entitled *Goldmouth* (1965), which Sheldon Renan describes as "around the poet Lawrence Ferlinghetti, doing his first extensive editing outside the camera" (127). For more detailed information on Branaman, see Renan, 127–28.

14. While not strictly a poet or filmmaker, Buchanan was closely tied to the Beat scene of both coasts, was featured in one of Warhol's *Screen Tests*, and was included in Malanga and Warhol's *Screen Tests / A Diary* (7–8). For more information on Buchanan, see Angell, 45.

15. In *Film at Wit's End*, Stan Brakhage writes, "Bruce Conner was born in the early 1930s in Wichita, Kansas, and was brought up there through high-school, in the same area as I lived in my early childhood, just a few miles from Wichita. He came from the same area as Bob Branaman . . . and Michael McClure, the poet. I could go on and on naming filmmakers and poets who were born within a radius of twenty miles in Kansas in the early 1930s — such diverse poets as Ronald Johnson and Ken Irby — all reared in this flat farmland and airplane-building community in and around Wichita; hardly the garden spot of America. . . . Most of them went to San Francisco in their late teens, including myself, and met or re-met each other, mainly through the influence of Robert Duncan" (129).

16. See Bob Rosenthal's "Ginsberg at Home," in *Captured*, 131–36, for more information on Ginsberg's participation in film projects.

17. My use of the term "mythopoeisis" is informed by Sitney, who ascribes it to filmmakers including Anger and Smith. As Sitney writes of Smith's *Heaven and Earth Magic*, "The Romantic myth of a divided and reunited Selfhood is the subject of Harry Smith's *Heaven and Earth Magic*. There, a female figure is injected by a magician with a substance that simultaneously makes her ascend to heaven and divides her body. The mental landscape of heaven is envisioned in a series of cyclic attempts to reconstitute her, ending with both her and the magician being swallowed by a titanic figure. After they descend through his body in an elevator they are defecated by him, whole again, on earth. Smith's film is the major instance of an animated mythopoeic film" (*Visionary Film* xxx–xxxi).

18. Regarding Ginsberg's difficulty in writing a coherent script, Michael Schumacher writes, "One of Allen's pet projects was a film adaptation of 'Kaddish.' Robert Frank, who had filmed *Pull My Daisy* a few years earlier, was in town, and he and Allen worked out a treatment for a script, Allen writing the dialogue himself. Ironically, he found it very difficult to adapt the extremely personal aspects of his youth to the screen" (398–99).

19. Ginsberg makes manifold references to Looney Tunes cartoons throughout his poetry. My personal favorite comes at the end of his poem "This Form of Life Needs Sex." After acknowledging his desire to reproduce, even if that means he will have to "kiss breasts accept / strange hairy lips behind / buttocks," Ginsberg concludes with "and that's my situation, Folks" (*Collected Poems* 284–86).

20. This document was a financial prospectus developed to secure the $80,000 Frank thought he needed to make the film.

21. The film photographer Roscoe Lee Browne (who, in cinema verité fashion, plays the part of the film photographer Roscoe Browne in *Me and My Brother*) was well-known in the Underground film scene for his role as film photographer in Shirley Clarke's film *The Connection*. Frank is clearly inviting intertextual dialogue between the two films by casting Browne in a role similar to the one he played earlier in Clarke's film.

22. Other cast members included Maria Tucci, Jack Greenbaum, Beth Porter, Fred Aimsworth, Richard Orzel, Philippe La Prelle, Otis Young, Sally Boyar, Joel Press, and Lou Waldon.

23. The two cited headlines were on the cover of the *Daily News*. Another scene in the film shows Ginsberg reading the *Wichita Eagle*.

24. Given that Julius is watching his brother and Ginsberg having sex, I would add that a vaguely incestuous undercurrent runs throughout the film. One scene in particular, showing Peter Orlovsky peppering Julius with what he calls "kissy-wissys," is almost unsettlingly intimate and suggests the affection between Peter and Julius is touched by eros. The scene is accompanied by Peter's explanatory voiceover: "When Julius goes to bed at night I give him a kiss . . . a kissy-wissy goodbye and goodnight and . . . sometimes he gives me a big kiss back and sometimes he gives me a little kiss back . . . but he never says 'goodnight Peter' he just says 'goodnight.' I tell him it's not fair he has to say 'Goodnight Peter' because I say 'goodnight Julius.'"

25. A subsequent scene that takes place in a movie theater finds Christopher Walken — playing the part of Robert Frank — interviewing Joseph Chaikin for the part of Julius Orlovsky as they watch Ginsberg and the Orlovskys on the screen. Walken (speaking in a Swedish accent) says to Chaikin, "I can't get Julius to do what I want. I want to use you to replace him. It's very difficult working with him. So you play Julius, and I'll give you your lines."

26. This text was included in an advertisement in the January 12, 1969 issue of the *New York Times* for a series of avant-garde films showing at the New Yorker theater.

27. Jane Kramer reports on Ginsberg's and Orlovsky's trip through Kansas and describes students' general expectations: "The students . . . knew of [Ginsberg] more as a legendary beatnik from the fifties than as the philosopher-king of a seminal hippiedom, and at first they came to his readings primarily to get a look at him — and in the slim hope that Ginsberg, if provoked, would take off his clothes" (95).

28. In the published version of "Wichita Vortex Sutra," the line "crime prevention show sponsored by Wrigley's spearmint" was altered to "Crime Prevention Show, sponsor Wrigley's Spearmint," and it appears several lines after the "Much delight

in weeping" passage. The line "revolving my head to my heart like my mad mother" was altered to "revolving my head to my heart like my mother" and appeared two stanzas after the "Truth breaks through" section. Finally, "What kind of hanging flesh have they, hidden behind their Images" was revised to "What kind of flesh hangs, hidden behind their Images?"

THE CONVERSATIONS BETWEEN ANDY WARHOL, GERARD MALANGA, ALLEN GINSBERG, JOHN ASHBERY, AND FRANK O'HARA

1. "In November 1964, Malanga took Warhol to one of the Monday night readings at the popular Café Le Metro. There, Warhol met Ronald Tavel, who participated in the reading and who soon after began to produce screenplays for Warhol's films. The stories of these meetings have been told often enough in the literature on Warhol. Yet no attention has been paid to the significance of the poetry reading as a specific venue, not to mention to Warhol's interest in the reading as a performance — as art" (Wolf, *Andy Warhol* 64).

2. Regarding the Summer 1967 issue of *Film Culture*, devoted to Warhol's film work, Suárez elaborates on what the differences between Brakhage and Warhol are in terms of the aesthetic and cultural values they believed could represent the Underground. "The Warhol issue clearly tried to imitate the look and tone of a fan magazine. The differences between this issue and a previous one devoted to a compilation of Brakhage's writings, subsequently published as *Metaphors on Vision*, suggests, I believe, the gap between Warhol and the more transcendent sector of the underground. Brakhage's issue is printed on dark sepia paper and sparsely illustrated with abstract stills from his films. It includes numerous pages of scratched, heavily edited typescript and facsimiles of handwritten notes and sketches. Overall, the issue breathes seriousness and emphasizes Brakhage's subjective inscription in his work, an attitude that appears the photographic negative of Warhol's self-erasure and seemingly frivolous plunge into Hollywood glitz" (226).

3. "Tally Brown, theater actress and Factory visitor during the high years of underground production, described in the following terms the dominant conception of stardom at Warhol's studio: 'The Factory was about creating a Hollywood outside Hollywood, where you don't have to bother with learning to act, making the rounds, going to agents, getting your 8X10 glossy, doing small parts being an extra, and gradually working up to becoming a star. You just got on camera and were a Superstar!' The superstar-effect of Warhol's films then confirmed Walter Benjamin's notion that, while reproduction, or reproducibility, eroded the exclusivity and specialness of the objects reproduced, it paradoxically created, when applied to the human figure, an aura of the personality whose most blatant example was the Hollywood star system" (Suárez 228–29).

4. For a plot description and analysis of *Tarzan and Jane* in light of the Los Angeles star system of which Warhol was a part, see David E. James's "'Amateurs in the Industry Town.'"

5. For a good historical overview of Warhol's *Screen Tests*, see Callie Angell's

"Introduction" to *Andy Warhol Screen Tests*, 12–19. I would add here that Warhol's relationship to Los Angeles and Hollywood was significant, particularly as his early shows were held at Irving Blum's gallery in Los Angeles. David E. James writes that "in 1963, at the height of his success as a Pop art painter, [Warhol] had bought a 16-mm camera and photographed Jack Smith in the process of shooting his *Normal Love*; he also shot several hours of the poet John Giorno sleeping. Before the latter footage was developed, he drove cross-country to Los Angeles, where Irving Blum had promised him a second show for his 'Jackie' and 'Elvis' paintings. Accompanying him was Taylor Mead, who had already been featured in two important Underground films directed by Ron Rice, *The Flower Thief* and *The Queen of Sheba Meets the Atom Man*, as well as in Adolfas Mekas's *Hallelujah the Hills* — works that were bringing the New American Cinema to public attention" ("Amateurs" 84–85).

6. See Angell, pp. 24–216, for a list and brief description of all of Warhol's *Screen Tests*.

7. I would add that, as I've argued in my essay "Reading John Ashbery's *The Tennis Court Oath* through Man Ray's Eye," *The Tennis Court Oath* was influenced to a great extent by a variety of cinematic practices.

8. Malanga's poem suggests Ashbery's work because of its general air of sophisticated languor, its run-on syntax, and its slippery subject. The last twelve lines recall Ashbery's poem "Clepsydra" as it uses the poetic line to stretch, turn, and twist in an at-times frustratingly elusive manner: "The friends had not expected that / the headlights would be like / this to discover the road / markings not to cross on the sharp / turns, and dreams might occur into something / for lie, the fear dismantled / to be the deception which surrounds us / for the white rose / growing restlessly as the sun / light reappears after night / fall, exalting the impossibility of the peace / formula in our time we may never achieve" (*Screen Tests/A Diary* 19).

9. The poems in *Screen Tests/A Diary* that refer by name to their subject are the Ted Berrigan poem (6); the Daniel Patrick Cassidy poem (9); the Denis Deegan poem (12); the Giangiacomo Feltrinelli poem (16); the "International Velvet" poem, which uses the superstar's birth name "Susan" (24); the René Ricard poem, which interestingly links the subject to Jack Smith's *The Flower Thief*, as we see in the lines "If the friends had turned / René into the flower / thief's death the cult of the dropout" (45); and the John Wieners poem (53).

10. For example, Malanga, in a letter, kept Ginsberg up to date on his work making a film with the poet John Wieners. "For the past two weeks I have been at work on parts one and two of the John Wieners trilogy in Eastman Color. I have completed shooting of John in Boston and Cambridge, and hopefully will finish Part 2 this coming weekend. Then, John and I go off to Buffalo for Part 3. John mentioned to me that he always wanted someone to do a film of him and I am deeply honored that he has allowed me his time in letting me record him on film" (April 15, 1968).

THE CONVERSATION BETWEEN JOHN ASHBERY AND RUDY BURCKHARDT

1. Recalling his collaborations with Cornell, Burckhardt said, "He called me one day and said, 'Do you want to make a film with me?' I knew his work, his boxes. Somebody told him I was making films, I guess, though he was never interested in my films. It was strictly on his own terms. He picked the place where we should start, Union Square on a cold, cloudy December afternoon. I brought the camera and he brought some rolls of film. Pretty soon I seemed to get it the way he wanted it. We looked at the film together. Most of the time he was very disappointed. 'Oh no that's nothing.' He could look so sad. But once in a while something pleased him and he had this wonderful, slow smile. He liked to film birds; starlings, sparrows, swarms of pigeons, a lonely seagull in the sky. 'I'm a sucker for birds,' he confided" (*Talking Pictures* 128). See Scott MacDonald's "Nathaniel Dorksy and Larry Jordan" in his *A Critical Cinema* for personal recollections on the making of these films.

2. Burckhardt says of this period, "I photographed art for Leo Castelli and other galleries, museums, and *Art News*. I collaborated on films with: Larry Rivers, Kenneth Koch, Joseph Cornell, Red Grooms, Taylor Mead, Nell Welliver, Charles Simonds, Ron Padgett. Alex Katz. In 1974, I grew a beard, and now as a senior citizen, I am admitted free to the Whitney and at half-price to the Guggenheim Museum" (*Mobile Homes* 36).

3. Padgett and Burckhardt interviewed this particular subject for the film.

4. Philip Lopate's discussion of Burckhardt's film, *The Nude Pond*, is pertinent here. He describes the film as "a grand synthesis of the poetic free-association films Rudy Burckhardt has been perfecting for the past ten years. Democratic in its celebration of all contemporary art forms (dance, painting, performance art, music, poetry, and, of course, film), encyclopedic in its images (from New York City interiors to Maine brooks to a Caribbean carnival), it is finally most unique by virtue of its emotional range. The filmmaker has achieved a style which enables him to encompass everything, from the whimsical, even silly, to the deeply philosophical and grave, with all shades of curiosity and neutral observation" (41).

5. See *Mounting Tension* and *Money*, featuring Ashbery, Red and Mimi Grooms, George and Kate Schneeman, and Alex Katz.

6. See *Tarzam*, starring a hilarious Taylor Mead.

7. Regarding *Lurk*, Burckhardt remembers, "In the spring of 1964 a great deal happened: I turned 50, was divorced, married Yvonne Jacquette from Pittsburgh, PA, our son Thomas was born — all in one month! That summer we rented a small house near a pond in Maine. Edwin, Red Grooms, Mimi Gross, Jacob, Thomas (three months), Yvonne and I. We made *Lurk*, the movie, starring Edwin as the mad professor and Red as his creature, based on the original Frankenstein story by Mary Shelley. We all got along easily until the middle of August when the well ran dry and it felt crowded for a while. It was a great summer" (*Talking Pictures* 164).

8. We can refer to Dante's "Sestina" beginning "I have come, alas, to the great circle of shadow," Swinburne's "Sestina" beginning "I saw my soul at rest upon a day,"

Auden's "Paysage Moralisé," Pound's "Sestina: Altaforte," Elizabeth Bishop's "Sestina" beginning "September rain falls on the house," and any number of other sestinas for example of the ways in which the sestina has centered generally on solemn subject matter.

9. Regarding Burckhardt's dissident — if gentle — politics, we should note Scott MacDonald's comment that "despite their lack of any overt polemical edge, Burckhardt's films do provide an implicit politics. In the early trilogy of New York City symphonies and in his many depictions of New York in more recent years — most impressively, perhaps, in *Doldrums* and *Zipper* — Burckhardt's love of New York seems a function of its size and of the diversity of people this size accommodates. As a Swiss émigré who had seen the devastation brought on by the ideology of nationalism and by the German, Italian, and Japanese obsessions with ethnic purity and superiority, Burckhardt's sensibility was a particularly democratic form of live and let live. . . . Burckhardt's filming stance toward those he records is one of equality, and if a contemporary documentary sensibility might complain about his intrusiveness and exploitation — some of those he films seem less than thrilled to be on camera — Burckhardt joins his subjects, filming them in situations in which he must feel, if not in danger, perfectly capable of being confronted if he goes too far: in working-class bars, for example, and at neighborhood events where his ethnicity must stand out" (*Garden* 158–59).

10. In a conversation with Simon Pettet, Burckhardt answered the question "Rudy, how do you edit your movies?" in a way that echoes Ashbery's own "launching pad for free associations" comment: "Sometimes the way things come together by accident is just as good as when you think it out. So I try not to impose any preconceived plan on the editing. I sort of let it take its own course. And I find that if you have a really lively scene, it'll fit in, it'll always fit in, like if a composer finds a melody, he can get it in" (Pettet, *Conversations* n.p.). Yvonne Jacquette's comments on the subject of Burckhardt's editing technique are also revealing regarding our focus on "free association" as a compositional device: "Rudy was sort of literal . . . what he shot followed where he was going. . . . We got this house in Maine in 1965, but we went to Maine in 1964, and he would always bring his camera. . . . He often would shoot with his movie camera the same thing that he was painting. . . . He'd go out to the woods with his camera, still camera, paint, easel. . . . Instead of making a city film, or a Maine film only . . . I think the idea of this was informed by his understanding of poetic juxtaposition. . . . Poetry showed him you could do both. So what if the viewer has to jump around with you from Disneyland to Maine . . . most of the films are that . . . the place he happened to be. . . . He knew how John [Ashbery] worked . . . he knew that John might take something from a telephone conversation and put that into the poem."

11. Belgrad argues that the twentieth-century American avant-garde — including the New York School and Beat scenes — promoted ideals of communal spontaneity and "nowness" as part of a dissident stance directed against a loathed academic scene and related conservative rationalism. As Belgrad writes, "The culture of

spontaneity developed an oppositional version of humanism, rooted in an alternative metaphysics embodied in artistic forms. The basic attributes of this alternative metaphysics can be summarized as intersubjectivity and body-mind holism. . . . Spontaneity posed intersubjectivity, in which 'reality' was understood to emerge through a conversational dynamic" (5). Belgrad adds that "by 1960, the culture of spontaneity was poised to have a powerful impact on American society. It embodied a cohesive set of values distinctly divergent from the culture of corporate liberalism. Its tenets and practices offered a template for expressions of social dissent" (247).

12. In "The System," Ashbery tackles Frost's mournful binary by turning the two paths into an Escher-like circuit: "That's the way it goes. For many weeks you have been exploring what seemed to be a profitable way of doing. You discovered that there was a fork in the road, so first you followed what seemed to be the less promising, or at any rate the more obvious, of the two branches until you felt you had a good idea of where it led. Then you returned to investigate the more tangled way, and for a time its intricacies seemed to promise a more complex and therefore a more practical goal for you, one that could be picked up in any number of ways so that all its faces or applications could be thoroughly scrutinized. And in so doing you began to realize that the two branches were joined together again, farther ahead; that this place of joining was indeed the end, and that it was the very place you set out from, whose intolerable mixture of reality and fantasy had started you on the road which has now come full circle" (365).

13. Burckhardt rarely credited the composers whose works he included in his films. I'm indebted to Alvin Curran for letting me know which of his pieces were featured in *Ostensibly*. Curran wrote, "the pieces are both from an LP/Cassette, put out by New Albion records in the late 80's for solo piano 'For Cornelius' played by Ursula Oppens, and 'Era Ora' for two pianos played by Oppens and Frederic Rzewski."

14. One might want to explore further the potential connections between Burckhardt's and Warhol's cinematic practices. Like Warhol, for example, Burckhardt used Taylor Mead to play the role of Tarzan in his film, *Tarzam*. Warhol had used Mead earlier for his film *Tarzan and Jane Regained. . . . Sort of.*

FILMOGRAPHY

Author's Note: This filmography is by no means comprehensive. Rather, it should be understood primarily as a starting point for people relatively new to the work of the New American Cinema. This filmography does not include references to earlier dada and surrealist film and, with some exceptions, to later work affiliated with the structural film movement. In the name of encouraging access to these films, I have listed titles available as DVDs to the best of my ability and knowledge. That said, the ideal way to appreciate these films is to experience them projected onto a screen in a dark theater. Unless otherwise noted, work that has yet to be released on DVD is listed here according to where it is archived at the Film-Makers Cooperative in New York (hereafter FMC) and/or Canyon Cinema in San Francisco (hereafter CC). The Kenneth Anger, Stan Brakhage, James Broughton, John Cassavetes, and Maya Deren DVDs listed below include films discussed in this book unless otherwise noted.

Some films listed here are not in circulation, though they may be viewed at the film library of the Museum of Modern Art (hereafter MOMA) by advance arrangement (minimum of two weeks' notice). To arrange viewings, contact Charles Silver, Associate Curator, Department of Film and Video at The Museum of Modern Art, 11 West 53rd Street, New York, NY 10019. E-mail: Charles_Silver@moma.org.

The Film-Makers Cooperative is located at the Clocktower Gallery, 108 Leonard Street, 13th floor, New York, NY 10013. To order films see www.film-makerscoop .com.

Canyon Cinema is located at 145 Ninth Street, Suite 260, San Francisco, California 94103. To order films see www.canyoncinema.com.

Readers may also want to consult the online catalog of LUX Films at http://catalogue.lux.org.uk/ for these and related works. LUX is located at 18 Shacklewell Lane, London E8 2EZ, United Kingdom.

A number of films referenced here and in the book proper are available to view online on Kenneth Goldsmith's incomparable Web site, Ubuweb (www.ubu.com).

Adam, Helen, and William McNeill. *Daydream of Darkness* (1963). DVD. In *A Helen Adam Reader*. Ed. Kristin Prevallet. Orono, ME: National Poetry Foundation, 2008.

Anger, Kenneth. *The Films of Kenneth Anger Volume 1*. DVD. Fantoma Films, 2007.

———. *The Films of Kenneth Anger Volume 2*. DVD. Fantoma Films, 2007.

Baillie, Bruce. *Castro Street* (1966). 16mm, black and white, color, sound, 10 min. (CC, FMC).

———. *Mass of the Dakota Sioux* (1963–1964). 16mm, black and white, sound, 20.5 min. (CC, FMC).

———. *Quick Billy* (1967–1970). 16mm, black and white, color, sound, 60 min. (CC).

Balch, Anthony, with William Burroughs, Bryon Gysin, and Ian Sommerville. *Three Films*. DVD. Cherry Red UK, 2007.

Belson, Jordan. *Five Essential Films*. DVD. Center for Visual Music, 2007.

Boultenhouse, Charles. *Dionysius* (1963). 16mm, color, sound, 26 min. (FMC).

———. *Handwritten* (1959). 16mm, color, sound, 9 min. (FMC).

Brakhage, Stan. *Anticipation of the Night* (1958). 16mm, color, silent, 40 min. (CC, FMC).

———. *By Brakhage: An Anthology*. DVD. Criterion, 2003.

———. *15 Song Traits* (1965–1981). 16mm, color, silent, 38.5 min. (CC, FMC).

———. *Flesh of Morning* (1956). 16mm, black and white, sound, 22 min. (CC, FMC).

———. *In Between* (1955). 16mm, color, sound, 10.5 min. (CC, FMC).

———. *Thigh Line Lyre Triangular* (1961). 16mm, color, silent, 6 min. (CC, FMC).

———. *Tho't Fal'n* (1978). 16mm, color, silent, 9 min. (CC, FMC).

———. *Two: Creeley/McClure* (1965). 16mm, color, silent, 3 min. (CC, FMC).

Broughton, James. *The Films of James Broughton*. DVD. Facets, 2006.

Burckhardt, Rudy. *City Pasture* (1975). 16mm, color, sound, 41.5 min. (CC, FMC).

———. *The Climate of New York* (1948). 16mm, black and white, sound, 21 min. (FMC).

———. *Doldrums* (1972). 16mm, color, sound, 18 min. (FMC).

———. *Lurk* (1964). 16mm, black and white, sound, 36.5 min. (CC, FMC).

———. *Money* (1968). 16mm, black and white, sound, 45 min. (CC, FMC).

———. *Mounting Tension* (1950). 16mm, black and white, sound, 20 min. (FMC).

———. *The Nude Pond* (1985). 16mm, color, sound, 29.75 min. (FMC).

———. *Ostensibly* (1989). 16mm, color, sound, 16 min. (FMC).

———. *Tarzam* (1969). 16mm, color, sound, 35 min. (FMC).

———. *Wayward Glimpses* (1992). 16mm, color, sound, 20 min. (FMC).

———. *Zipper* (1987). 16mm, color, sound, 25 min. (CC, FMC).

———, and Joseph Cornell. *The Aviary* (1955). 16mm, black and white, silent, 5 min. (FMC).

———, and ———. *Nymphlight* (1957). 16mm, color and black and white, sound, 18.75 min. (FMC).

———, and ———. *What Mozart Saw on Mulberry Street* (1956). 16mm, black and white, sound, 6 min. (FMC).

———, and Red Grooms. *Shoot the Moon* (1962). 16mm, black and white, sound, 24 min. (FMC).

Cassavetes, John. *Five Films*. DVD. Criterion, 2004.

Clarke, Shirley. *The Connection*. (1961). DVD. Jazz Movie Classics, 2004.

———. *Portrait of Jason* (1967). DVD. Second Run, 2005.

Conner, Bruce. *A Movie* (1958). 16mm, black and white, sound, 12 min. (MOMA).

———. *Cosmic Ray* (1962). 16mm, black and white, sound, 5 min. (MOMA).
———. *Looking for Mushrooms* (1967). 16mm, color, sound, 14 min. (MOMA).
———. *Marilyn Times Five* (1973). 16mm, black and white, sound, 13 min. (MOMA).
———. *Report* (1967). 16mm, black and white, sound, 13 min. (MOMA).
Conrad, Tony. *The Flicker* (1966). 16mm, black and white, sound, 30 min. (CC, FMC).
De Hirsch, Storm. *Charlotte Moorman's Avant-Garde Festival #9* (1965). Super 8, color, silent, 10 min. (FMC).
———. *Divinations* (1964). 16mm, color, sound, 5.5 min. (FMC).
———. *Goodbye in the Mirror* (1964). 16mm, black and white, sound, 80 min. (FMC).
———. *Newsreel: Jonas in the Brig* (1964). 16mm, black and white, silent, 5 min. (FMC).
———. *Peyote Queen* (1965). 16mm, color, sound, 9 min. (CC, FMC).
———. *Shaman, a Tapestry for Sorcerers* (1967). 16mm, color, sound, 12 min. (FMC).
———. *The Tattooed Man* (1969). 16mm, color, sound, 35 min. (CC, FMC).
———. *Third Eye Butterfly* (1968). 16mm, color, sound, 10 min. (FMC).
Deren, Maya. *Experimental Films*. DVD. Mystic Fire Video, 2007.
Dorsky, Nathaniel. *A Fall Trip Home* (1964). 16mm, color, sound, 11 min. (CC).
———. *Hours for Jerome* (1980–1982). 16mm, color, silent, 45 min. (CC).
———. *Ingreen* (1964). 16mm, color, sound, 12 min. (CC).
———. *Summerwind* (1965). 16mm, color, sound, 14 min. (CC).
Emshwiller, Ed. *Dance Chromatic* (1959). 16mm, color, sound, 7 min. (FMC).
———. *George Dumpson's Place* (1965). 16mm, color, sound, 8 min. (CC, FMC).
———. *Image, Flesh & Voice* (1969). 16mm, black and white, sound, 77 min. (CC, FMC).
———. *Lifelines* (1960). 16mm, color, sound, 7 min. (CC, FMC).
———. *Relativity* (1966). 16mm, color, sound, 38 min. (CC, FMC).
Frampton, Hollis. *Zorns Lemma* (1970). 16mm, color, sound, 60 min. (LUX).
———. *The Complete Film Works Volume 1: "Pull My Daisy"* (1959, with Alfred Leslie), *"The Sin of Jesus"* (1961), *"Me and My Brother"* (1968). DVD. Steidl, 2007.
Gehr, Ernie. *Serene Velocity* (1970). 16mm, color, silent, 23 min. (CC).
Genet, Jean. *Un Chant d'Amour* (1950). DVD. Cult Epics, 2007.
Harrington, Curtis. *Fragment of Seeking* (1946). 16mm, black and white, sound, 13.75 min. (FMC).
———. *On the Edge* (1949). 16mm, black and white, sound, 6 min. (FMC).
———. *The Wormwood Star* (1956). 16mm, color, sound, 10 min. (FMC).
Heliczer, Piero. *The Autumn Feast* (1967). 16mm, color, sound, 14 min. (FMC, LUX).
———. *Dirt* (1966). 16mm, color, sound, 12 min. (FMC, LUX).
Jacobs, Ken. *Blonde Cobra* (1963). 16mm, color and black and white, sound, 33 min. (FMC).

———. *Little Stabs at Happiness* (1963). 16mm, color, sound, 15 min. (CC, FMC).

———. *Soft Rain* (1968). 16mm, color, silent, 12 min. (FMC).

———. *Star-Spangled to Death* (1956–1960). DVD. Electronic Arts Intermix, 2004.

———. *Tom, Tom the Piper's Son* (1969). 16mm, color and black and white, silent, 115 min. (FMC).

Jordan, Larry. *Duo Concertantes* (1964). 16mm, black and white, sound, 9 min. (CC, FMC).

———. *Gymnopedies* (1965). 16mm, color, sound, 5.75 min. (CC, FMC).

———. *Hamfat Asar* (1965). 16mm, black and white, sound, 13 min. (CC, FMC).

———. *Hildur and the Magician* (1969). 16mm, black and white, sound, 70 min. (CC).

———. *Visions of a City* (1978). 16mm, black and white, sound, 6.25 min. (CC, FMC).

Kubelka, Peter. *Adebar: 5X* (1957). 16mm, black and white, sound, 7.5 min. (FMC).

———. *Arnulf Rainer* (1960). 16mm, 35mm, black and white, sound, 6.5 min. (CC, FMC).

———. *Schwechater* (1958). 16mm, black and white, sound, 2 min. (CC, FMC).

———. *Unsere Afrikareise* (1966). 16mm, color, sound, 12.5 min. (CC, FMC).

Kuchar, George. *Color Me Shameless* (1967). 16mm, black and white, sound, 30 min. (CC, FMC).

———. *Eclipse of the Sun Virgin* (1967). 16mm, color, sound, 15 min. (CC, FMC).

———. *Encyclopedia of the Blessed* (1968). 16mm, color and black and white, sound, 43 min. (CC, FMC).

———. *Hold Me While I'm Naked* (1966). 16mm, color, sound, 15 min. (CC, FMC).

Land, Owen (formerly George Landow). *Diploteratology* (1967). 16mm, black and white, silent, 7 min. (CC, FMC).

———. *The Film That Rises to the Surface of Clarified Butter* (1968). 16mm, black and white, sound, 8.75 min. (FMC).

———. *Film in Which There Appear Sprocket Holes, Edge Lettering, Dirt Particals, etc.* (1966). 16mm, color, silent, 4.5 min. (FMC).

———. *Remedial Reading Comprehension* (1970). 16mm, color, sound, 5 min. (CC, FMC).

Leslie, Alfred. *The Last Clean Shirt* (1964). 16mm, black and white, sound, 39 min. (LUX).

Maas, Willard. *Geography of the Body* (1943). DVD. In *Avant-Garde 2: Experimental Cinema 1928–1954.* Kino International, 2007.

———. *Mechanics of Love* (1955). 16mm, black and white, sound, 7 min. (CC, FMC).

———. *Orgia* (1967). 16mm, color, sound, 12 min. (CC, FMC).

Maclaine, Christopher. *Beat* (1958). 16mm, color, sound, 6 min. (FMC).

———. *The End* (1953). 16mm, color and black and white, sound, 34.75 min. (FMC).

———. *The Man Who Invented Gold* (1957). 16mm, color, sound, 14 min. (FMC).

———. *Scotch Hop* (1959). 16mm, color, sound, 5.5 min. (FMC).

Malanga, Gerard. *In Search of the Miraculous* (1967). 16mm, color and black and white, sound, 30 min. (FMC).

Markopoulos, Gregory. *Galaxie* (1966). 16mm, color and black and white, sound, 96 min. (MOMA).

Mekas, Adolfas. *Hallelujah the Hills* (1965). 16mm, black and white, sound, 82 min. (FMC).

Mekas, Jonas. *The Brig* (1964). 16mm, black and white, sound, 68 min. (FMC).

———. *Guns of the Trees* (1962). 16mm, black and white, sound, 75 min. (FMC).

———. *Walden* (1969). 16mm, color, sound, 180 min. (FMC).

Menken, Marie. *Andy Warhol* (1965). 16mm, color, silent, 22 min. (FMC).

———. *Arabesque for Kenneth Anger* (1961). 16mm, color, sound, 4 min. (FMC).

———. *Hurry! Hurry!* (1957). 16mm, color, sound, 3 min. (CC, FMC).

———. *Mood Mondrian* (1965). 16mm, color, silent, 5.5 min. (FMC).

———. *Visual Variations on Noguchi* (1945). DVD. In *Avant-Garde 2: Experimental Cinema 1928–1954*. Kino International, 2007.

Nelson, Robert. *Bleu Shut* (1970). 16mm, color, sound, 30 min. (CC).

———. *Confessions of a Black Mother-Succuba* (1965). 16mm, black and white, sound, 16 min. (CC).

———. *The Great Blondino* (1967). 16mm, color, sound, 43 min. (MOMA).

———. *Oh Dem Watermelons* (1965). 16mm, color, sound, 11 min. (CC).

Peterson, Sidney. *The Cage* (1947). DVD. In *Avant-Garde 2: Experimental Cinema 1928–1954*. Kino International, 2007.

———, and James Broughton. *The Potted Psalm* (1946). DVD. In *Avant-Garde 2: Experimental Cinema 1928–1954*. Kino International, 2007.

Reeves, Jennifer. *Chronic* (1996). 16mm, color, sound, 40 min. (FMC).

———. *Shadows Choose Their Horrors* (2005). 16mm, color, sound, 40 min. (FMC).

———. *The Time We Killed* (2004). 16mm, sound, 94 min. (CC, FMC).

Rice, Ron. *Chumlum* (1964). 16mm, color, sound, 26 min. (FMC).

———. *The Flower Thief* (1960). 16mm, black and white, sound, 75 min. (FMC).

———. *The Queen of Sheba Meets the Atom Man* (1982). 16mm, black and white, sound, 109 min. (FMC).

———. *Senseless* (1962). 16mm, black and white, sound, 28 min. (FMC).

Rubin, Barbara. *Christmas on Earth* (1963). 16mm, black and white, silent, 29 min. (FMC).

Sharits, Paul. *N:O:T:H:I:N:G* (1968). 16mm, color, sound, 35 min. (CC, FMC).

———. *Piece Mandala/End War* (1966). 16mm, color and black and white, sound, 5 min. (CC, FMC).

———. *Ray Gun Virus* (1966). 16mm, color, sound, 14 min. (CC, FMC).

———. *T,O,U,C,H,I,N,G* (1968). 16mm, color, sound, 12 min. (CC, FMC).

Smith, Harry. *Heaven and Earth Magic Feature* (1961). 16mm, black and white, sound, 66 min. (FMC).

Smith, Jack. *Scotch Tape* (1962). 16mm, color, sound, 3 min. (CC, FMC).

Snow, Michael. *Back and Forth* (1969). 16mm, color, sound, 52 min. (CC, FMC).

———. *New York Eye and Ear Control* (1964). 16mm, black and white, sound, 34 min. (CC, FMC).

———. *Wavelength* (1967). 16mm, color, sound, 45 min. (CC, FMC).

Sonbert, Warren. *Carriage Trade* (1972). 16mm, color, silent, 75 min. (CC, FMC).

———, and Wendy Appel. *Amphetamine* (1966). 16mm, black and white, sound, 10 min. (CC).

Vanderbeek, Stan. *Poem Field No. 1* (1965). 16 mm, color, sound, 4 min. (FMC).

———. *Poem Field No. 2* (1967). 16mm, color, sound, 6 min. (CC, FMC).

———. *Poem Field No. 5* (1967). 16mm, color, silent, 7 min. (CC, FMC).

———. *Poem Field No. 7* (1967). 16mm, color, sound, 4 min. (FMC).

Warhol, Andy. *Blow Job* (1964). 16mm, black and white, silent, 30 min. (MOMA).

———. *Empire* (1964). 16mm, black and white, silent, 8 hr. (MOMA).

———. *Chelsea Girls* (1966). 16mm, black and white, color, sound, 210 min. (MOMA).

———. *Couch* (1964). 16mm, black and white, silent, 58 min. (MOMA).

———. *Kiss* (1964). 16mm, black and white, silent, 54 min. (MOMA).

———. *Tarzan and Jane, Regained . . . Sort of* (1963). 16mm, black and white, silent, 66 min. (MOMA).

———. *Sleep* (1963). 16mm, black and white, silent, 6 hr. (MOMA).

Whitehead, Peter. *Peter Whitehead and the Sixties*. DVD. BFI Video, 2007.

Wieland, Joyce. *Barbara's Blindness* (1967). 16mm, black and white, sound, 17 min. (FMC).

———. *Pierre Vallières* (1972). 16mm, color, sound, 33 min. (CC, FMC).

———. *Rat Life and Diet in North America* (1968). 16mm, color, sound, 16 min. (FMC).

———. *Solidarity* (1973). 16mm, color, sound, 11 min. (CC).

BIBLIOGRAPHY

Abel, Richard. "American Film and the French Literary Avant-Garde (1914–1924)." *Contemporary Literature* 17.1 (Winter 1976): 84–109.

———. "Contribution of the French Literary Avant-Garde to Film Theory and Criticism (1907–1924)." *Cinema Journal* 14.3 (Spring 1975): 18–40.

Aiken, Edward A. " 'Emak Bakia' Reconsidered." *Art Journal* 43.3 (Autumn 1983): 240–46.

———. "Reflections on Dada and the Cinema." *Post Script: Essays in Film and the Humanities* 3.2 (Winter 1984): 5–19.

Aldrich, Michael, Edward Kissam, and Nancy Blecker. "Improvised Poetics: An Interview with Allen Ginsberg." *Spontaneous Mind: Selected Interviews, 1958–1996.* Ed. David Carter. New York: Harper Collins, 2001. 124–58.

Alexandre, Maxime, Louis Aragon, Hans Arp et al. "Hands Off Love." *History of Surrealism.* Ed. Maurice Nadeau. Trans. Richard Howard. New York: Macmillan, 1966. 262–71.

Allan, Blaine. "The Making (and Unmaking) of *Pull My Daisy*." *Film History* 2 (1988): 185–205.

———. *The New American Cinema, 1956–1960.* Toronto: Funnel Experimental Film Theatre, 1984. n.p.

Allen, Donald. *The New American Poetry, 1945–1960.* New York: Grove Press, 1960.

Angell, Callie. *Andy Warhol Screen Tests: The Films of Andy Warhol Catalogue Raisonné.* New York: Abrams, in association with Whitney Museum of American Art, 2006.

Anger, Kenneth. *Kenneth Anger's Hollywood Babylon.* New York: Straight Arrow Press, 1975.

———. Letter to Robert Duncan. December 3, 1954. State University of New York, Buffalo. Poetry/Rare Book Collection. Robert Duncan Papers. © The Jess Collins Trust and reproduced with permission.

———. Letter to Robert Duncan. August 24, 1968. State University of New York, Buffalo. Poetry/Rare Book Collection. Robert Duncan Papers. © The Jess Collins Trust and reproduced with permission.

———. "Program Notes for Kenneth Anger's Magick Lantern Cycle." *Film-Maker's Cooperative Catalogue.* New York: Film-Maker's Cooperative, 1966. n.p.

Angerame, Dominic. "Welcome to Canyon Cinema." *Canyon Cinema.* 2007. http://www.canyoncinema.com/contents.html (accessed May 15, 2007).

Arthur, Paul. "Qualities of Light: Stan Brakhage and the Continuing Pursuit of Vision." *Film Comment* 31.5 (1995): 67–75.

———. "Routines of Emancipation: Alternative Cinema in the Ideology and Politics of the Sixties." *To Free the Cinema: Jonas Mekas and the New York Underground*. Ed. David E. James. Princeton, NJ: Princeton University Press, 1992. 17–48.

Ashbery, John. "Farm Implements and Rutabagas in a Landscape." *The Mooring of Starting Out: The First Five Books of Poetry*. By John Ashbery. New York: Ecco, 1998.

———. "The Impossible: Gertrude Stein." *Selected Prose*. Ed. Eugene Ritchie. Ann Arbor: University of Michigan Press, 2004. 11–15.

———. "Interview with Daniel Kane." *What Is Poetry: Conversations with the American Avant-Garde*. By Daniel Kane. New York: Teachers & Writers, 2003. 27–36.

———. Letter to Frank O'Hara. September 6 [n.y.]. New York Public Library. New York, NY. Berg Collection.

———. "Ostensibly." April Galleons. New York: Farrar, Strauss, and Giroux, 1999. 55–56.

———. Personal interview. September 18, 2005.

———. *Reported Sightings: Art Chronicles, 1957–1987*. Ed. David Bergman. New York: Knopf, 1989.

———. *Selected Prose*. Ed. Eugene Richie. Ann Arbor: University of Michigan Press, 2005.

———. "The System." *The Mooring of Starting Out: The First Five Books of Poetry*. By John Ashbery. New York: Ecco, 1998.

———. "The Tennis Court Oath." *The Mooring of Starting Out: The First Five Books of Poetry*. By John Ashbery. New York: Ecco, 1998.

———. "Three Poems." *The Mooring of Starting Out: The First Five Books of Poetry*. By John Ashbery. New York: Ecco, 1998.

Auriol, Jean-George. "Whither the French Cinema." *transition* 15 (February 1929): 257–63.

Bakaitis, Vyt. "Notes on Displacement: The Poems and Diary Films of Jonas Mekas." *To Free the Cinema: Jonas Mekas and the New York Underground*. Ed. David E. James. Princeton, NJ: Princeton University Press, 1992. 121–37.

Baker, R. C. "The Octopussarian Drugstore Cowboy: Alfred Leslie Has Not Left the Building." *Village Voice* (New York), November 24–30, 2004.

Baraka, Amiri. *The Autobiography of LeRoi Jones/Amiri Baraka*. New York: Freundlich Books, 1984.

———. *The Baptism* and *The Toilet*. New York: Grove Press, 1967.

Belasco, Daniel. "The Vanished Prodigy." *Art in America*, no. 11 (December 2005): 61–67.

Belgrad, Daniel. *The Culture of Spontaneity: Improvisation and the Arts in Postwar America*. Chicago: University of Chicago Press, 1998.

Berkson, Bill. " 'The Arctic Honey Blabbed over the Report Causing Darkness': An

Interview with John Ashbery." 1970. New York Public Library. New York, NY.
Berg Collection, Ms. John Ashbery Papers.

———. "O'Hara." E-mail to the author. August 18, 2006.

Berrigan, Ted. *The Sonnets*. New York: Grove Press, 1964.

Bertholf, Robert. "Afterword." *Medieval Scenes, 1950 and 1959*. By Robert Duncan.
Kent, OH: Kent State University Libraries, 1978. n.p.

Birmingham, James. E-mail to the author. August 30, 2007.

Bissette, Stephen R. "Curtis Harrington and the Underground Roots of the Mod-
ern Horror Film." *Underground U.S.A.: Filmmaking beyond the Hollywood
Canon*. Ed. Xavier Mendik and Steven Jay Schneider. London: Wallflower
Press, 2002. 40–50.

Blaetz, Robin, ed. *Women's Experimental Cinema: Critical Frameworks*. Durham,
NC: Duke University Press, 2007.

Blake, William. *Blake's Poetry and Designs*. Ed. Mary Lynn Johnson and John E.
Grant. New York: Norton, 1979.

Bloom, Harold. "The Charity of the Hard Moments." *John Ashbery: Modern Critical Views*. Ed. Harold Bloom. New York: Chelsea House, 1985. 44–72.

Brainard, Joe. "Frank O'Hara." *Homage to Frank O'Hara*. Ed. Bill Berkson and
Joe LeSueur. Bolinas, CA: Big Sky, 1988. 167–69.

Brakhage, Marilyn. "Rhythms of Vision in Stan Brakhage's *City Streaming*."
Canadian Journal of Film Studies 14.1 (Spring 2005): 5–11.

Brakhage, Stan. "The Camera Eye — My Eye." *The New American Cinema*. Ed.
Gregory Battcock. New York: Dutton, 1967. 211–26.

———. "The Dark Tower." Interview with Bruce Kawin. *By Brakhage: An Anthology*. 2002. DVD. Criterion, 2003.

———. *Essential Brakhage: Selected Writings on Filmmaking*. New York: McPherson, 2001.

———. *Film at Wit's End*. Kingston, NY: McPherson, 1989.

———. Letter to James Broughton. April 25, 1962. Kent State University. Kent, OH.
Department of Special Collections and Archives. James Broughton Papers.
Series 1, Box 10, Folder 45.

———. Letter to James Broughton. May 5, 1962. Kent State University. Kent, OH.
Department of Special Collections and Archives. James Broughton Papers.
Series 1, Box 10, Folder 58.

———. Letter to Robert Creeley. May 25, 1962. Stanford University Libraries. Stanford, CA. Department of Special Collections. Creeley Papers. Series 1, Box 14,
Folder 21.

———. Letter to Robert Creeley. May 27, 1962. Stanford University Libraries. Stanford, CA. Department of Special Collections. Creeley Papers. Series 1, Box 14,
Folder 21.

———. Letter to Robert Creeley. June 1, 1962. Stanford University Libraries. Stanford, CA. Department of Special Collections. Creeley Papers. Series 1, Box 14,
Folder 21.

———. Letter to Robert Creeley. March 1964. Stanford University Libraries. Stanford, CA. Department of Special Collections. Creeley Papers. Series 1, Box 14, Folder 22.

———. Letter to Robert Creeley. December 1, 1977. Stanford University Libraries. Stanford, CA. Department of Special Collections. Creeley Papers. Series 1, Box 14, Folder 28.

———. Letter to Robert Creeley. July 2, 1978. Stanford University Libraries. Stanford, CA. Department of Special Collections. Creeley Papers. Series 1, Box 14, Folder 28.

———. Letter to Robert Kelly. June 19, 1963. University of Buffalo. Buffalo, NY. Poetry/Rare Book Collection. Robert Kelly Papers.

———. Letter to Robert Kelly. March 12, 1967. University of Buffalo. Buffalo, NY. Poetry/Rare Book Collection. Robert Kelly Papers.

———. Letter to Shirley B. Wendell. February 20, 1981. Museum of Modern Art Film Library. New York, NY.

———. "Letters: San Francisco Film Scene." *Film Culture* 29 (1963): 76–81.

———. *Metaphors on Vision*. Ed. P. Adams Sitney. New York: Film Culture, 1963.

———. "Poetry and Film." *Brakhage Scrapbook: Collected Writings, 1964–1980.* Ed. Robert Haller. New Paltz, NY: Documentext, 1982. 218–31.

———. "Stan Brakhage: Correspondences." *Chicago Review* 47.4 (2001), 48:1 (2002).

———. "Stan and Jane Brakhage (and Hollis Frampton) Talking." *Brakhage Scrapbook: Collected Writings, 1964–1980.* Ed. Robert Haller. New Paltz, NY: Documentext, 1982. 169–89.

———. *Two: Creeley/McClure*. New York: Film-Maker's Cooperative, 1965.

Briggs, K. M. *The Anatomy of Puck: An Examination of Fairy Beliefs among Shakespeare's Contemporaries and Successors*. London: Routledge and Kegan Paul, 1959.

Brossard, Olivier. "The Last Clean Shirt." *Jacket Magazine*. August 23, 2003. http://jacketmagazine.com/23/bross-ohara.html (accessed August 12, 2007).

Broughton, James. *Making Light of It*. San Francisco: City Lights Books, 1977.

Burckhardt, Rudy. "The Cinema of Looking: Rudy Burckhardt and Edwin Denby in Conversation with Joe Giordano." *Jacket Magazine*. February 2003. http://jacketmagazine.com/21/denb-giord.html (accessed April 21, 2006).

———. *Mobile Homes*. Calais, VT : Z Press, 1979.

———. "Program Notes for *City Pasture*." *Film-Maker's Cooperative On Line Catalog*. April 21, 2006. http://www.filmmakerscoop.com/catalog/b.html#top (accessed April 21, 2006).

———, and Simon Pettet. *Talking Pictures*. Cambridge, MA: Zoland Books, 1994.

Calende, John. "Kenneth Anger Rising." *Oui* 60 (October 1976): 113–17.

Camper, Fred. "Stan Brakhage Filmography." *This Is Fred Camper's Website*. June 12, 2007. http://www.fredcamper.com/Brakhage/Filmography.html (accessed July 27, 2007).

Carr, C. "The Art and Artifacts of the World According to Jack Smith." *Village Voice* (New York), December 2, 1997.

Cendrars, Blaise. *Modernities and Other Writings*. Ed. Monique Chefdor. Trans. Esther Allen and Monique Chefdor. Lincoln: University of Nebraska Press, 1992.

Child, Abigail. *This Is Called Moving: A Critical Poetics of Film*. Tuscaloosa: University of Alabama Press, 2005.

Clearfield, Andrew M. *These Fragments I Have Shored: Collage and Montage in Early Modernist Poetry*. Ann Arbor, MI: UMI Research Press, 1984.

Cocteau, Jean. *Two Screenplays: The Blood of a Poet and the Testament of Orpheus*. Trans. Carol Martin-Sperry. London: Marion-Boyars, 1993.

Corn, Alfred. "The Gay Artist as Critic." *Gay and Lesbian Review* 12.2 (March–April 2005): 10–15.

Costello, Bonnie. "John Ashbery and the Idea of the Reader." *Contemporary Literature* 23.4 (Autumn 1982): 493–514.

Creeley, Robert. "Conversation with Charles Bernstein." *Just in Time: Poems 1984–1994*. By Robert Creeley. New York: New Directions, 2001. 1–32.

———. *For Love: Poems 1950–1960*. New York: Scribners, 1962.

———. "H.D." *The Collected Essays of Robert Creeley*. Berkeley: University of California Press, 1989. 81–82.

———. "Here." *The Collected Essays of Robert Creeley*. Berkeley: University of California Press, 1989. 83–86.

———. "Mehr Licht . . ." *Film Culture* 47 (Summer 1969): 22, 24.

———. *Pieces*. New York: Charles Scribner's Sons, 1969.

———. "Three Films." *Was That a Real Poem and Other Essays*. Ed. Donald Allen. Bolinas, CA: Four Seasons Foundation. 1979. 120–31.

———. *Words*. New York: Charles Scribner's Sons, 1967.

Culler, Jonathan. *Structuralist Poetics: Structuralism, Linguistics, and the Study of Literature*. London: Routledge and Kegan Paul, 1975.

Curran, Alvin. "Burckhardt's 'Ostensibly?'" E-mail to the author. August 1, 2006.

Curtis, David. "A Tale of Two Co-ops." *To Free the Cinema: Jonas Mekas and the New York Underground*. Ed. David E. James. Princeton, NJ: Princeton University Press, 1992. 255–65.

Damon, Maria. "Triangulated Desires and Tactical Silences in the Beat Hipscape: Bob Kaufman and Others." *College Literature* 27.1 (Winter 2000): 139–57.

Dargis, Manohla. "Me and My Brother." *New York Times*, November 10, 2006.

Davenport, Guy. "Two Essays on Brakhage and His Songs." *Film Culture* 40 (1966): 8–12.

Davidson, Michael. *Guys Like Us: Citing Masculinity in Cold War Poetics*. Chicago: University of Chicago Press, 2004.

———. *The San Francisco Renaissance: Poetics and Community at Mid-Century*. New York: Cambridge University Press, 1989

———. "'Skewed by Design': From Act to Speech Act in Language Writing." *Artifice and Indeterminacy: An Anthology of New Poetics*. Ed. Christopher Beach. Tuscaloosa: University of Alabama Press, 1999. 70–76.

Deleuze, Gilles. *Cinema 1: The Movement-Image*. St. Paul: University of Minnesota Press, 1986.

Deren, Maya, with Arthur Miller, Parker Tyler, Dylan Thomas, and Willard Maas. "Poetry and Film: A Symposium." *Film Culture* 29 (Summer 1963): 55–63.

Dixon, Wheeler Winston. *The Exploding Eye: A Re-Visionary History of the 1960s American Experimental Cinema.* Albany: State University of New York Press, 1997.

Doolitle, Hilda (H.D.). *Tribute to Freud.* Boston: David R. Godine, 1974.

Duncan, Robert. *Bending the Bow.* New York: New Directions, 1968.

———. *Fictive Certainties.* New York: New Directions, 1985.

———. *The H.D. Book.* Ed. Victor Coleman et al. Centre for Contemporary Canadian Art. Canadian Art Database. http://www.ccca.ca/history/ozz/ english/books/hd_book/HD_Book_by_Robert_Duncan.pdf (accessed May 17, 2007).

———. Letter to James Broughton. Fall 1952. Kent State University. Kent, OH. Department of Special Collections and Archives. James Broughton Papers. Series 1, Box 6, Folder 108. Printed with the permission of the Literary Estate of Robert Duncan. © The Literary Estate of Robert Duncan.

———. Letter to James Broughton. February 24, 1965. Kent State University. Kent, OH. Department of Special Collections and Archives. James Broughton Papers. Series 1, Box 6, Folder 68. Printed with the Permission of the Literary Estate of Robert Duncan. © The Literary Estate of Robert Duncan.

———. Letter to Robert Creeley. January 2, 1960. Stanford University. Stanford, CA. Department of Special Collections. Robert Creeley Papers. Series 1, Box 40, Folder 29. © The Jess Collins Trust and reproduced with permission.

———. Letter to Stan Brakhage. June 14, 1962. State University of New York, Buffalo. Poetry/Rare Book Collection. Robert Duncan Papers. © The Jess Collins Trust and reproduced with permission.

———. "Notebooks" (unpublished diaries). State University of New York, Buffalo. Poetry/Rare Book Collection. Robert Duncan Papers. © The Jess Collins Trust and reproduced with permission.

———. *Writing Writing: A Composition Book, for Madison 1953, Stein Imitations.* Albuquerque, NM: Sumbooks, 1964.

DuPlessis, Rachel. *H.D.: The Career of That Struggle.* Sussex, UK: Harvester Press, 1986.

Edelberg, Cynthia. *Robert Creeley's Poetry: A Critical Introduction.* Albuquerque: University of New Mexico Press, 1978.

Eder, Richard. "Film: The Oddments of 'City Pastures.'" *New York Times*, December 12, 1975.

Ehrenstein, David. "Ron Rice: The Joker of the Anarchy-Garde." *Reader*, April 16, 1982.

Eisenstein, Sergei. *Film Form: Essays in Film Theory.* Trans. Jay Leyda. New York: Harcourt, 1977.

Elder, R. Bruce. *The Films of Stan Brakhage in the American Tradition of Ezra Pound, Gertrude Stein, and Charles Olson.* Waterloo, ON, Canada: Wilfrid Laurier University Press, 1998.

Elledge, Jim. "'Never Argue with the Movies': Love and the Cinema in the Poetry of Frank O'Hara." *Frank O'Hara: To Be True to a City*. Ed. Jim Elledge. Ann Arbor: University of Michigan Press, 1990. 350–58.

Ellingham, Lewis, and Kevin Killian. *Poet Be Like God: Jack Spicer and the San Francisco Renaissance*. Hanover, NH: Wesleyan University Press, 1998.

Epstein, Andrew. "'I Want to Be at Least as Alive as the Vulgar': Frank O'Hara's Poetry and the Cinema." *The Scene of My Selves: New Work on New York School Poets*. Eds. Terence Diggory and Stephen Paul Miller. Orono, ME: National Poetry Foundation, 2001. 93–122.

Faas, Ekbert. *Young Robert Duncan: Portrait of the Poet as Homosexual in Society*. Santa Barbara, CA: Black Sparrow Books, 1983.

Ferlinghetti, Lawrence. *A Coney Island of the Mind*. New York: New Directions, 1968.

Fleming, Bruce E. "The Ideogram in Pound and Eisenstein: Sketch for a Theory of Modernism." *Southwest Review* 74.1 (Winter 1989): 87–98.

Foster, Stephen, ed. *Hans Richter: Activism, Modernism, and the Avant-Garde*. Cambridge, MA: MIT Press, 1998.

Frank, Robert. Letter to Allen Ginsberg. October 15, 1963. Stanford University Libraries. Stanford, CA. Department of Special Collections. Ginsberg Papers. Series 1, Box 24, Folder 31. © Robert Frank, reproduced with permission.

———. Letter to Allen Ginsberg. October 23, 1963. Stanford University Libraries. Stanford, CA. Department of Special Collections. Ginsberg Papers. Series 1, Box 24, Folder 31. © Robert Frank, reproduced with permission.

———. Letter to Allen Ginsberg. November 1, 1963. Stanford University Libraries. Stanford, CA. Department of Special Collections. Ginsberg Papers. Series 1, Box 24, Folder 31. © Robert Frank, reproduced with permission.

———. Letter to Allen Ginsberg. November 18, 1963. Stanford University Libraries. Stanford, CA. Department of Special Collections. Ginsberg Papers, Series 1, Box 24, Folder 31. © Robert Frank, reproduced with permission.

———. Letter to Allen Ginsberg. November 4, 1965. Stanford University Libraries. Stanford, CA. Department of Special Collections. Ginsberg Papers. Series 1, Box 24, Folder 31. © Robert Frank, reproduced with permission.

———. "Prospectus." December 20, 1965. Stanford University Libraries. Stanford, CA. Department of Special Collections. Ginsberg Papers. Series 1, Box 24, Folder 32.

Franklin, Paul. "The Terpsichorean Tramp: Unmanly Movement in the Early Films of Charlie Chaplin." *Dancing Desires: Choreographing Sexualities on and off the Stage*. Ed. Jane C. Desmond. Madison: University of Wisconsin Press, 2001. 35–73.

Frazer, James George. *The Golden Bough: A Study in Magic and Religion*. New York: Macmillan, 1922.

Freidberg, Anne. "Approaching Borderline." *Millenium Film Journal*, nos. 7–9 (Fall, Winter 1980–1981): 130–39.

Frost, Robert. *The Road Not Taken and Other Poems*. New York: Dover, 1993.

Galm, Ruth. "The Millennium Film Workshop in Love." *Captured: A Film/Video History of the Lower East Side.* Ed. Clayton Patterson. New York: Seven Stories Press, 2005. 101–4.

Géfin, Laszlo. "Ellipsis: The Ideograms of Ginsberg." *On the Poetry of Allen Ginsberg.* Ed. Lewis Hyde. Ann Arbor: University of Michigan Press, 1984.

Ginsberg, Allen. "Allen Ginsberg Lecture on Expansive Poetics, Sons of Whitman, June, 1981." Internet Archives. March 10, 2001. Naropa University Internet Archives. http://www.archive.org/details/Allen_Ginsberg_lecture_on_expansive_poet_81P117 (accessed December 7, 2006).

———. "Back to the Wall." *Deliberate Prose: Selected Essays, 1952–1995.* Ed. Bill Morgan. New York: Harper Collins, 2000. 6–9.

———. *Collected Poems: 1947–1980.* New York: Harper & Row, 1984.

———. *The Fall of America: Poems of These States 1965–1971.* San Francisco: City Lights, 1972.

———. "Howl (for Carl Solomon)." *Holy Soul Jelly Roll: Poems and Songs, 1949–1993.* 1956. Recorded March 18, 1956. Rhino, 1994.

———. *Indian Journals.* San Francisco: City Lights Books, 1970.

———. "Interview with Barry Farrell." *Spontaneous Mind: Selected Interviews, 1958–1996.* Ed. David Carter. New York: Harper Collins, 2001. 54–66.

———. "Interview with 'Helen.'" *Spontaneous Mind: Selected Interviews, 1958–1996.* Ed. David Carter. New York: Harper Collins, 2001. 433.

———. "Notes Written on Finally Recording *Howl.*" *Deliberate Prose: Selected Essays 1952–1995.* Ed. Bill Morgan. New York: Harper Collins, 2000. 229–32.

———. *Planet News: 1961–1967.* San Francisco: City Lights, 1971.

———. "Robert Frank: Robert Frank to 1985 — A Man." *Deliberate Prose: Selected Essays 1952–1995.* Ed. Bill Morgan. New York: Harper Collins, 2000. 465–70.

———. "Tom Clark, the Paris Review." *Spontaneous Mind: Selected Interviews, 1958–1996.* Ed. David Carter. New York: Harper Collins, 2001. 17–53.

———, and Peter Orlovsky. "A Letter to Chaplin from Allen Ginsberg and Peter Orlovsky." *Film Culture* 40 (Spring 1966): 7.

Gizzi, Peter, ed. *The House That Jack Built: The Collected Lectures of Jack Spicer.* Hanover, NH: University Press of New England, 1998.

Goble, Mark. "'Our Country's Black and White Past': Film and the Figures of History in Frank O'Hara." *American Literature* 71.1 (March 1999): 57–92.

Goldensohn, Barry. "Memoir of Hollis Frampton." *October* 32 (Spring 1985): 7–16.

Golding, Alan. *From Outlaw to Classic: Canons in American Poetry.* Madison: University of Wisconsin Press, 1995.

———. "The 'New American Poetry' Revisited, Again." *Contemporary Literature* 39.2 (Summer 1998): 180–211.

Goldstein, Laurence. *The American Poet at the Movies: A Critical History.* Ann Arbor: University of Michigan Press, 1994.

Gooch, Brad. *City Poet: The Life and Times of Frank O'Hara.* New York: Knopf, 1993.

Guest, Barbara. *Herself Defined: The Poet H.D. and Her World*. New York: Double-day, 1984.

Gunning, Tom. "The Cinema of Attractions: Early Film, Its Spectator, and the Avant-Garde." *Early Cinema: Space, Frame, Narrative*. Ed. Thomas Elsaesser; with Adam Barker. London: BFI Publishing, 1990. 56–62.

———. "Love at the Movies: The Desire and Pursuit of the Hole." *Tableau: The Newsletter for the Division of the Humanities at the University of Chicago*, no. 4 (Fall 2001).

Hall, Alaric. *Elves in Anglo-Saxon England: Matters of Belief, Health, Gender, and Identity*. Rochester, NY: Boydell & Brewer, 2007.

Haller, Robert. *Kenneth Anger: A Filmmaker's Filming Monograph*. Minneapolis-St. Paul, MN: Film in the Cities/Walker Art Center, 1980.

———, ed. *Perspectives on Jerome Hill & Anthology Film Archives*. New York: Anthology Film Archives, 2005.

Hardy, Robin. "Master in Hell." *Body Politic: A Magazine for Gay Liberation*, April 1982.

Harrington, Stephanie Gervis. "City Sleuths Douse 'Flaming Creatures.'" *Village Voice* (New York), March 12, 1964.

Hartley, George. *Textual Politics and the Language Poets*. Bloomington: Indiana University Press, 1989.

Hegel, George Wilhelm Friedrich. *Lectures on the History of Philosophy*. Trans. E. S. Haldane. London: K. Paul, Trench, Trübner, 1833–1836. Also in Hegel-by-HyperText. Ed. Andy Blunden. 1996. Marxists.org. http://www.marxists.org/reference/archive/hegel/works/hp/hpboehme.htm (accessed August 19, 2005).

Henderson, David. Personal interview. April 8, 1998.

Hesiod. *Works and Days*. Trans. David W. Tandy and Walter C. Neale. Berkeley, CA: University of California Press, 1996.

Hewett, Greg. "Revealing 'The Torso': Robert Duncan and the Process of Signify-ing Male Homosexuality." *Contemporary Literature* 35.3 (Fall 1994): 522–46.

Hoberman, J. "Duplicitously Ours: Brakhage in New York." *Village Voice* (New York), April 8–14, 1981.

———. "Explorations: The Short Happy Life of the Charles." *American Film: Journal of the Film and Television Arts* 7 (March 1982): 22+.

———. "The Forest and *The Trees*." *To Free the Cinema: Jonas Mekas and the New York Underground*. Ed. David E. James. Princeton, NJ: Princeton University Press, 1992. 100–120.

———. *On Jack Smith's Flaming Creatures and Other Secret-Flix of Cinemaroc*. New York: Granary Books, 2001.

———, and Edward Leffingwell, eds. *Wait for Me at the Bottom of the Pool: The Writings of Jack Smith*. London: Serpent's Tail, 1997.

Homer. *The Odyssey of Homer*. Translated by Richmond Lattimore. New York: HarperPerennial, 1991.

Horak, Jan-Christopher. "The First American Film Avant-garde, 1919–1945." *Experimental Cinema: The Film Reader*. Ed. Wheeler Winston Dixon and Gwendolyn Audrey Foster. New York: Routledge, 2002. 19–52.

Hutchison, Alice L. *Kenneth Anger*. London: Black Dog, 2004.

Imbriglio, Catherine. "'Our Days Put on Such Reticence': The Rhetoric of the Closet in John Ashbery's *Some Trees*." *Contemporary Literature* 36.2 (Summer 1995): 249–89.

Jacquette, Yvonne. Personal interview. September 5, 2006.

James, David E. *Allegories of Cinema: American Film in the Sixties*. Princeton, NJ: Princeton University Press, 1989.

———. "'Amateurs in the Industry Town': Stan Brakhage and Andy Warhol in Los Angeles." *Grey Room* (Summer 2003): 80–93.

———. *To Free the Cinema: Jonas Mekas and the New York Underground*. Princeton, NJ: Princeton University Press, 1992.

Jarnot, Lisa. "Duncan Essay." E-mail to the author. August 23, 2005.

———. *Some Other Kind of Mission*. Providence, RI: Burning Deck Press, 1996.

Jarraway, David. "'Standing by His Word': The Politics of Allen Ginsberg's Vietnam Vortex." *Journal of American Culture* 16 (Fall 1993): 81–88.

Johnson, Jerry. "Film at Wit's End: An Interview with Stan Brakhage." *Austin Chronicle*, September 12, 1997.

Jonas, Gerald. "The Story of Grove." *New York Times*, January 21, 1968.

Kadlec, David. "Early Soviet Cinema and American Poetry." *Modernism/modernity* 11.2 (2004): 299–331.

Kane, Daniel. *All Poets Welcome: The Lower East Side Poetry Scene in the 1960s*. Berkeley: University of California Press, 2003.

———. "Reading John Ashbery's *The Tennis Court Oath* through Man Ray's Eye." *Textual Practice* 21.3 (2007): 551–75.

Katz, Vincent. "Mobile Homes: The Art of Rudy Burckhardt." *Rudy Burckhardt*. Ed. Vincent Katz and Phillip Lopate. New York: Abrams, 2004. 183–93.

———. "Rudy Burckhardt: Art's Friendship." *Rudy Burkhardt*. Ed. Vincent Katz and Phillip Lopate. New York: Abrams, 2004. 47–51.

Kelman, Ken. "Film as Poetry." *Film Culture* 29 (1963): 22–27.

———. "Perspective Reperceived: Brakhage's 'Anticipation of the Night.'" *The Essential Cinema: Essays on the Films in the Collection of Anthology Film Archives*. Ed. P. Adams Sitney. New York: Anthology Film Archives, 1975. 234–39.

Kerouac, Jack. *The Beat Generation: The Lost Work*. New York: Da Capo Press, 2006.

———. "Essentials of Spontaneous Prose." *Modern and Contemporary American Poetry*. Ed. Al Filreis. July 18 2007. University of Pennsylvania. http://www.writing.upenn.edu/~afilreis/88/kerouac-spontaneous.html (accessed September 14, 2008).

———. *On the Road: The Original Scroll*. Ed. Howard Cunnell. New York: Penguin, 2008.

Kimber, John. *The Art of Charlie Chaplin*. Sheffield, UK: Sheffield Academic Press, 2000.

Kipling, Rudyard. *Rewards and Fairies*. New York: Doubleday, 1910.

Kirby, Lynne. *Parallel Tracks: The Railroad and Silent Cinema*. Durham, NC: Duke University Press, 1996.

Knapp, James F. "Discontinuous Form in Modern Poetry: Myth and Counter-Myth." *boundary 2* 12.1 (1983): 149–66.

Koch, Kenneth. "Interview with Daniel Kane." *What Is Poetry: Conversations with the American Avant-Garde*. By Daniel Kane. New York: Teachers & Writers, 2003. 86–99.

Koponen, Sandra. "The 60s: Notes on the Underground." *Captured: A Film/Video History of the Lower East Side*. Ed. Clayton Patterson. New York: Seven Stories Press, 2005. 113–20.

Kostelanetz, Richard. "How to Be a Difficult Poet." *New York Times Magazine*, May 23, 1976.

Kramer, Jane. *Allen Ginsberg in America*. New York: Random House, 1968.

Kuenstler, Frank. *Lens*. New York: Film Culture, 1964.

Kuenzli, Rudolf E., ed. *Dada and Surrealist Film*. Cambridge, MA: MIT Press, 1996.

Leslie, Alfred. "Letter to Peter." *Moving Picture Poetics: Sampling 50 Years of Poets and Cinema*. San Francisco: Hugo Ball Room Press, 2004. 8.

———. Personal interview. February 27, 2006.

Longenbach, James. "Ashbery and the Individual Talent." *American Literary History* 9.1 (Spring 1997): 103–27.

Lopate, Phillip. "Rudy Burckhardt's Life and Work: How Wide is 6th Avenue?" *Rudy Burckhardt*. Ed. Vincent Katz and Phillip Lopate. New York: Abrams, 2004. 7–45.

Lucie-Smith, Edward. "Edward Lucie Smith: An Interview with Frank O'Hara." *Standing Still and Walking in New York*. By Frank O'Hara. Ed. Donald Allen. San Francisco: Grey Fox, 1983. 3–9.

Maas, Willard. Letter to James Broughton. May 27, 1956. Kent State University. Kent, OH. Department of Special Collections and Archives. James Broughton Papers. Series 1, Box 7, Folder 176.

———. Letter to James Broughton. January 20, 1957. Kent State University. Kent, OH. Department of Special Collections and Archives. James Broughton Papers. Series 1, Box 8, Folder 18.

MacDonald, Scott. *Avant-Garde Film: Motion Studies*. New York: Cambridge University Press, 1993.

———. *Canyon Cinema: The Life and Times of an Independent Film Distributor*. Berkeley: University of California Press, 2008.

———. "Cinema 16: Documents toward a History of the Film Society." *Wide Angle* 19.1 (January 1997): 3–48.

———. "Cinema 16: An Interview with Amos Vogel." *Film Quarterly* 37.3 (Spring 1984): 19–29.

———. *A Critical Cinema: Interviews with Independent Filmmakers*. Berkeley: University of California Press, 1988.

———. *The Garden in the Machine: A Field Guide to Independent Films about Place*. Berkeley: University of California Press, 2001.

———. "Poetry and Avant-Garde Film: Three Recent Contributions." *Poetics Today* 28.1 (January 2007): 1–41.

MacNeill, Máire. *The Festival of Lughnasa: A Study of the Survival of the Celtic Festival of the Beginning of Harvest*. Dublin: Oxford University Press, 1962.

Maeterlinck, Maurice. *The Blue Bird: A Fairy Play in Six Acts*. Trans. Alexander Teixeira De Mattos. New York: Dodd, Mead, 1919.

Magee, Michael. *Emancipating Pragmatism: Emerson, Jazz, and Experimental Writing*. Tuscaloosa: University of Alabama Press, 2004.

Malanga, Gerard. E-mail to the author. January 10, 2008. Used with permission.

———. Letter to Allen Ginsberg. October 6, 1966. Stanford University Libraries. Stanford, CA. Department of Special Collections. Ginsberg Papers. Series 1, Box 41, Folder 27. Copyright © Gerard Malanga. Used with permission.

———. Letter to Allen Ginsberg. November 29, 1967. Stanford University Libraries. Stanford, CA. Department of Special Collections. Ginsberg Papers. Series 1, Box 24, Folder 31. Copyright © Gerard Malanga. Used with permission.

———. Letter to Allen Ginsberg. January 8, 1968. Stanford University Libraries. Stanford, CA. Department of Special Collections. Ginsberg Papers. Series 1, Box 24, Folder 31. Copyright © Gerard Malanga. Used with permission.

———. Letter to Allen Ginsberg. April 15, 1968. Stanford University Libraries. Stanford, CA. Department of Special Collections. Ginsberg Papers. Series 1, Box 41, Folder 27. Copyright © Gerard Malanga. Used with permission.

———. Letter to James Broughton. November 24, 1963. Kent State University. Kent, OH. Department of Special Collections and Archives. James Broughton Papers. Series 1, Box 11, Folder 24. Copyright © Gerard Malanga. Used with permission.

———, and Andy Warhol. *Screen Tests/A Diary*. New York: Kulchur Press, 1967.

Markopoulos, Gregory. *Poems*. New York: Film Culture, 1964.

Matthews, J. H. *Surrealism and Film*. Ann Arbor: University of Michigan Press, 1971.

McCabe, Susan. *Cinematic Modernism: Modernist Poetry and Film*. Cambridge: Cambridge University Press, 2005.

McClure, Michael. "Note in a Depression Early '58." In *The New American Poetry*. Ed. Donald Allen. 422–23.

———, and Steve Anker. "Realm Buster: Stan Brakhage." *Chicago Review* 47.4, 48:1 (Winter, Spring 2001–2002): 171–80.

McDonald, Gerald, Michael Conway, and Mark Ricci, eds. *The Films of Charlie Chaplin*. New York: Citadel Press, 1965.

Mekas, Jonas. "A Few Notes on My Life on the Lower East Side and Cinema." *Captured: A Film/Video History of he Lower East Side*. Ed. Clayton Patterson. New York: Seven Stories Press, 2005. 97–100.

————. "Movie Journal." *Village Voice* (New York), June 29, 1961.

————. "Movie Journal." *Village Voice* (New York), May 2, 1963.

————. "Movie Journal." *Village Voice* (New York), May 17, 1973.

————. "Press Release." *Film Culture* 29 (1963): 7–8.

Meskil, Paul. "Police Cold to 'Flaming' Film." *New York World Telegram*, March 4, 1964.

Michelson, Annette. "From Magician to Epistemologist: Vertov's *The Man with a Movie Camera*." *The Essential Cinema: Essays on the Films in the Collection of Anthology Film Archives*. Ed. P. Adams Sitney. New York: Anthology Film Archives, 1975. 95–111.

Miles, Barry. *Ginsberg: A Biography*. New York: Simon & Schuster, 1989.

Milton, John. *Paradise Lost and Other Poems*. Ed. Edward Le Comte. New York: Signet Classic, 2003.

Milton, Joyce. *Tramp: The Life of Charlie Chaplin*. New York: Harper Collins, 1996.

Moen, Kristian. E-mail to the author. November 15, 2006.

Monaghan, Patricia. *The Encyclopedia of Celtic Mythology and Folklore*. New York: Facts on File, 2004.

Morgan, Bill. "Film, Radio, and Television Appearances by Allen Ginsberg." *The Works of Allen Ginsberg, 1941–1994: A Descriptive Bibliography*. Westport, CT: Greenwood Press, 1995. 375–83.

Morris, Adalaide. "The Concept of Projection: H.D.'s Visionary Powers." *Contemporary Literature* 25.4 (Winter 1984): 411–36.

Murphy, J. J. "Chris MacLaine: 'The Man Who Invented Gold.'" *Film Quarterly* 33.2 (Winter 1979–1980): 44–47.

Nelson, Cary. *Our Last First Poets: Vision and History in Contemporary American Poetry*. Urbana: University of Illinois Press, 1981.

Nesthus, Mary. "The 'Document' Correspondence of Stan Brakhage." *Chicago Review* 47.4, 48:1 (Winter, Spring 2001–2002): 133–56.

Nichols, Bill, ed. *Maya Deren and the American Avant-Garde*. Berkeley: University of California Press, 2001.

Nichols, Maria Pramaggiore. "Performance and Persona in the US Avant-Garde: The Case of Maya Deren." *Cinema Journal* 36.2 (Winter 1997): 17–40.

North, Michael. "Words in Motion: The Movies, the Readies, and the 'Revolution of the Word.'" *Modernism/modernity* 9.2 (April 2002): 205–23.

O'Hara, Frank. *Amorous Nightmares of Delay: Selected Plays*. Ed. Joe LeSueur. Baltimore: Johns Hopkins University Press, 1997.

————. *Awake in Spain*. New York: American Theatre for Poets, 1960.

————. *The Collected Poems of Frank O'Hara*. Berkeley: University of California Press, 1995.

————. "The General Returns from One Place to Another." *Amorous Nightmares of Delay: Selected Plays*. Ed. Joe LeSueur. Baltimore: Johns Hopkins University Press, 1997. 187–217.

————. Letter to James Broughton. July 15, 1957. Kent State University. Kent, Ohio. Department of Special Collections and Archives. Series 1, Box 8, Folder 37.

———, and Frank Lima. "Love on the Hoof." *Amorous Nightmares of Delay: Selected Plays.* Ed. Joe LeSueur. Baltimore: Johns Hopkins University Press, 1997. 173–76.

Olson, Charles. "Projective Verse." *Selected Writings.* Ed. Robert Creeley. New York: New Directions, 1966. 15–26.

Orlovsky, Peter. *Clean Asshole Poems and Smiling Vegetable Songs.* San Francisco: City Lights Books, 1978.

Osterweil, Ara. "Absently Enchanted: The Apocryphal, Ecstatic Cinema of Barbara Rubin." *Women's Experimental Cinema: Critical Frameworks.* Durham, NC: Duke University Press, 2007. 127–51.

Ovington, Mary White. "How the National Association for the Advancement of Colored People Began." *The Crisis Online.* http://www.thecrisismagazine.com/excerpt1914.htm (accessed September 13, 2006).

Perloff, Marjorie. *Frank O'Hara: Poet among Painters.* Chicago: University of Chicago Press, 1998.

———. *The Futurist Moment: Avant-Garde, Avant Guerre, and the Language of Rupture.* Chicago: University of Chicago Press, 1986.

———. "Normalizing John Ashbery." *Jacket Magazine,* January 1998. http://jacketmagazine.com/02/perloff02.html (accessed April 30, 2007).

Pettet, Simon. *Conversations with Rudy Burckhardt about Everything.* New York: Vehicle Editions, 1987.

Pike, Robert. "A Letter from the West Coast." *Film Culture* 11.4 (November 14, 1957): 9–10.

Pound, Ezra. *The Cantos of Ezra Pound.* New York: New Directions, 1950.

———. *Ezra Pound and the Visual Arts.* Ed. Harriet Zinnes. New York: New Directions, 1980.

———. *Pound/Zukofsky: Selected Letters of Ezra Pound and Louis Zukofsky.* Ed. Barry Ahearn. New York: New Directions Press, 1987.

———. "Pound's 'A Retrospect' — Including 'A Few Don'ts.'" *Modern American Poetry.* Department of English, University of Illinois at Urbana. http://www.english.uiuc.edu/maps/poets/m_r/pound/retrospect.htm (accessed September 14, 2008).

———. "'A Retrospect' — Including 'A Few Don'ts.'" *Modern American Poetry.* Department of English, University of Illinois at Urbana. http://www.english.uiuc.edu/maps/poets/m_r/pound/retrospect.htm (accessed September 14, 2008).

Powell, Anna. "A Torch for Lucifer: Occult Symbolism in the Films of Kenneth Anger." *Moonchild: The Films of Kenneth Anger.* Vol. 1. Ed. Jack Hunter. New York: Creation Books, 2002. 56–67.

Prevallet, Kristin. "Jack Spicer's Hell in 'Homage to Creeley.'" *Jacket Magazine,* April 1999. http://jacketmagazine.com/07/spicer-prevallet.html (accessed October 31, 2006).

———. "Notes on *Daydream of Darkness.*" *Moving Picture Poetics: Sampling 50 Years of Poets and Cinema.* San Francisco: Hugo Ball Room Press, 2004. 5.

"Pure Film." *Newsweek*, December 21, 1970.

Ragona, Melissa. "Swing and Sway: Marie Menken's Filmic Events." *Women's Experimental Cinema: Critical Frameworks*. Durham, NC: Duke University Press, 2007. 20–39.

Rasula, Jed. "Spicer's *Orpheus* and the Emancipation of Pronouns." *boundary 2* 6.1 (Autumn 1977): 51–102.

Ray, Man. *Self-Portrait*. New York: Little, Brown, 1998.

Renan, Sheldon. *An Introduction to the American Underground Film*. New York: Dutton, 1967.

Rice, Ron. "Diaries, Notebooks, Scripts, Letters, Documents." *Film Culture* 39 (1965): 87–126.

Robinson, David. *Chaplin: His Life and Art*. London: Penguin Books, 2001.

Rosenthal, Bob. "Ginsberg at Home." *Captured: A Film / Video History of the Lower East Side*. Ed. Clayton Patterson. New York: Seven Stories Press, 2005. 131–36.

Ross, Andrew. "Taking the Tennis-Court Oath." *The Tribe of John Ashbery and Contemporary Poetry*. Ed. Susan Schultz. Tuscaloosa: University of Alabama Press, 1995. 193–210.

Rowe, Carel. "Illuminating Lucifer." *Film Quarterly* 4.26 (1974): 24–34.

Sanders, Ed. *Fuck You/a magazine of the arts* 4.1 (August 1962): n.p.

Sargeant, Jack. *Naked Lens: Beat Cinema*. New York: Creation Books, 1997.

———. "Voyeurism, Sadism, and Transgression: Screen Notes and Observations on Warhol's 'Blow Job' and 'I, a Man.'" *Underground U.S.A.: Filmmaking beyond the Hollywood Canon*. Ed. Xavier Mendik and Steven Jay Schneider. London: Wallflower Press, 2002. 86–95.

Scharnhorst, Gary. "Moodie, My Dad, Allen Ginsberg, and Me: Reflections on Wichita and 'Wichita Vortex Sutra.'" *Midwest Quarterly* 45 (2004): 369–80.

Schumacher, Michael. *Dharma Lion: A Critical Biography of Allen Ginsberg*. New York: St. Martin's Press, 1992.

Schüpbach, Hannes. "The Shifting Measure of People, Buildings, and Nature: Films by Rudy Burckhardt." *Rudy Burckhardt — New York Moments: Photographs and Films*. By Anita Haldemann and Hannes Schüpbach. Basel, Switzerland: Kunstmuseum, 2005. 119–36.

Sellin, Eric. "Simultaneity: Driving Force of the Surrealist Aesthetic." *Twentieth Century Literature* 21.1 (February 1975): 10–23.

Shadow. "Biography for Marjorie Cameron." Internet Movie Database. 2005. http://www.imdb.com/name/nm0131669/bio (accessed August 24, 2005).

Sharits, Paul. "Notes on Films." *Film Culture* 47 (Summer 1969): 13–16.

Shaw, Lytle. *Frank O'Hara: The Poetics of Coterie*. Iowa City: University of Iowa Press, 2006.

Shoptaw, John. *On the Outside Looking Out: John Ashbery's Poetry*. Cambridge, MA: Harvard University Press, 1995.

Sitney, P. Adams. "'Anticipation of the Night' and 'Prelude.'" *Film Culture* 26 (Winter 1962): 54–57.

———. *Modernist Montage: The Obscurity of Vision in Cinema and Literature.* New York: Columbia University Press, 1990.

———. "Tone Poems." *Artforum* 46.3 (November 2007): 341+.

———. "A Tour with Brakhage: Underground Movies Are Alive along the Pacific." *Village Voice* (New York), December 5, 1968.

———. *Visionary Film: The American Avant-Garde, 1942–2000.* 3rd ed. New York: Oxford University Press, 2002.

———, ed. *The Avant-Garde Film: A Reader of Theory and Criticism.* New York: Anthology Film Archives, 1987.

Sitney, Sky. "The Search for the Invisible Cinema." *Grey Room* 19 (Spring 2005): 102–13.

Snyder, Phillip V. *The Christmas Tree Book: The History of the Christmas Tree and Antique Christmas Tree Ornaments.* New York: Penguin, 1977.

Sontag, Susan. "Jack Smith's *Flaming Creatures.*" *The New American Cinema.* Ed. Gregory Battcock. New York: Dutton, 1967. 204–10.

Stein, Gertrude. "Portraits and Repetitions." *Lectures in America.* New York: Random House, 1935. 165–206.

———. *Tender Buttons: Objects, Food, Rooms.* New York: Courier Dover Publications, 1997.

Steiner, Konrad. "A Real Sample." *Moving Picture Poetics: Sampling 50 Years of Poets and Cinema.* San Francisco: Hugo Ball Room Press, 2004. 1.

Sterritt, David. *Mad to Be Saved: The Beats, the '50s, and Film.* Carbondale and Edwardsville, IL: Southern Illinois University Press, 1998.

———. "Recognizing the Poetic Value of Film." *Christian Science Monitor,* October 4–10, 1996.

———. *Screening the Beats: Media Culture and the Beat Sensibility.* Carbondale: Southern Illinois University Press, 2004.

Suárez, Juan. *Bike Boys, Drag Queens, & Superstars: Avant-Garde, Mass Culture, and Gay Identities in the 1960s Underground Cinema.* Bloomington: Indiana University Press, 1996.

Suárez-Toste, Ernesto. "'The Tension Is in the Concept': John Ashbery's Surrealism." *Style* 38.1 (Spring 2004): 1–16.

Tambellini, Aldo. "A Syracuse Rebel in New York." *Captured: A Film/Video History of the Lower East Side.* Ed. Clayton Patterson. New York: Seven Stories Press, 2005. 41–56.

Taubin, Amy. "Packaging Brakhage." *Soho Weekly News* (New York), April 15, 1981.

Trigilio, Tony. *Allen Ginsberg's Buddhist Poetics.* Carbondale: Southern Illinois University Press, 2007.

———. "'Strange Prophecies Anew': Rethinking the Politics of Matter and Spirit in Ginsberg's *Kaddish.*" *American Literature* 71.4 (December 1999): 773–95.

Trotter, David. Review of *Cinematic Modernism: Modernist Poetry and Film,* by Susan McCabe. *Modernism/modernity* 13.2 (2006): 394–96.

Turim, Maureen. "Sounds, Intervals, and Startling Images in the Films of Abigail Child." *Women's Experimental Cinema: Critical Frameworks*. Durham, NC: Duke University Press, 2007. 263–89.

Turquety, Benoît. "'Our St. Matthew Passion': Louis Zukofsky & Film." *Jacket*. Ed. John Tranter. 2006. http://jacketmagazine.com/30/z-turquety.html (accessed April 12, 2007).

Tyler, Parker. "Harrington, Markopoulos, and Boultenhouse: Two Down and One to Go?" *Film Culture* 21 (Summer 1960): 33–38.

———. "A Preface to the Problems of the Experimental Film." *Film Culture* 17 (February 1958): 5–8.

———. *Underground Film, a Critical History*. New York: Grove Press, 1969.

———. "Willard Maas." *Film Culture* 20 (1959): 53–58.

Tytell, John. "The Legacy of Surrealism." *On the Poetry of Allen Ginsberg*. Ed. Lewis Hyde. Ann Arbor: University of Michigan Press, 1984. 171–82.

Varela, Willie. "Excerpts from a Conversation with Stan Brakhage." *Canyon Cinemanews* 1 (1977): 4–8.

Vendler, Helen. "Review of *Fall of America*." *On the Poetry of Allen Ginsberg*. Ed. Lewis Hyde. Ann Arbor: University of Michigan Press, 1984. 203–9.

Vincent, John. *Queer Lyrics: Difficulty and Closure in American Poetry*. New York: Palgrave, Macmillan, 2002.

Waldrop, Keith. "A Reason for Images: One Key to Modernism." *Modern Language Studies* 15.3 (Summer 1985): 72–84.

Warhol, Andy, and Pat Hackett. *Popism: The Warhol Sixties*. New York: Harcourt, 1980.

Weiler, A. H. "'Me and My Brother' Opens: Film by Robert Frank Is at New Yorker: The Real-Unreal World of a Catatonic Seen." *New York Times*, February 3, 1969. http://movies2.nytimes.com/mem/movies/review.html?_r=1&res=9D0CE6D8153DE134BC4B53DFB4668382679EDE&oref=slogin (accessed December 1, 2006).

Welles, Orson, and Herman J. Mankiewicz. *Citizen Kane: The Daily Script*. http://www.dailyscript.com/scripts/citizenkane.html (accessed July 26, 2007).

Williams, Michaela. "Be Aware of a Greek Bearing a Camera." *Daily News* (Chicago), December 17, 1966.

Wolf, Reva. *Andy Warhol, Poetry, and Gossip in the 1960s*. Chicago: University of Chicago Press, 1997.

———. "Collaboration as Social Exchange." *Art Journal* 52.4 (Winter 1993): 59–66.

Young, Allen. "From the Book *Allen Ginsberg: Gay Sunshine Interview*." *Spontaneous Mind: Selected Interviews 1958–1996*. Ed. David Carter. New York: Harper Collins, 2001. 303–42.

Youngblood, Gene. *Expanded Cinema*. Introduction by R. Buckminster Fuller. New York: Dutton, 1970.

INDEX

Industrial Poetics:
Demo Tracks for a Mobile Culture
By Joe Amato

Jorie Graham:
Essays on the Poetry
Edited by Thomas Gardner
University of Wisconsin Press, 2005

Gary Snyder and the Pacific Rim:
Creating Countercultural Community
By Timothy Gray

We Saw the Light:
Conversations between the New
American Cinema and Poetry
By Daniel Kane

History, Memory, and the Literary Left:
Modern American Poetry, 1935–1968
By John Lowney

Paracritical Hinge:
Essays, Talks, Notes, Interviews
By Nathaniel Mackey
University of Wisconsin Press, 2004

Frank O'Hara:
The Poetics of Coterie
By Lytle Shaw

Radical Vernacular:
Lorine Niedecker and
the Poetics of Place
Edited by Elizabeth Willis